Pope John Paul II's

THEOLOGICAL JOURNEY

—— to the ——

PRAYER MEETING

OF RELIGIONS IN ASSISI

Part II, Volume I

The "Trinitarian Trilogy":
Redemptor Hominis, Dives in Misericordia,
Dominum et Vivificantem

Fr. Johannes Dörmann

ANGELUS PRESS
2918 TRACY AVENUE, KANSAS CITY, MISSOURI 64109

Pope John Paul II's Theological Journey to the Prayer Meeting of Religions at Assisi

Part II, Volume I

First Encyclical: *Redemptor Hominis*

Fr. Johannes Dörmann

Translated from the German for Angelus Press with permission from the author by Rev. Fr. Christopher Brandler, with reference research by Peter Chojnowski, Ph.D.

ANGELUS PRESS

2918 TRACY AVENUE
KANSAS CITY, MISSOURI 64109
PHONE (816) 753-3150
FAX (816) 753-3557
ORDER LINE (800) 966-7337

ISBN 0-935952-58-6 Part II, Volume I
ISBN 0-935952-57-8 Set
FIRST PRINTING—March 1996

Printed in the United States of America

Library of Congress Cataloging-in-Publication Data

Dörmann, Johannes, 1922-
[Theologische Weg Johannes Pauls II zum Weltgebetstag der Religionen in Assisi. English]
Pope John Paul II's Theological Journey to the Prayer Meeting of Religions at Assisi / Johannes Dörmann.
p. cm.
Translation of: *Der theologische Weg Johannes Pauls II zum Weltgebetstag der Religionen in Assisi.*
Contents: pt. 2. Volume 1.
Includes bibliographical references.
ISBN 0-935952-52-7 (v. 1 : pbk.)
1. John Paul II, Pope, 1920-   . 2. Catholic Church–Doctrines–History–20th century.
3. Swiatowy Dzień Modlitwy o Pokój (1986 : Assisi, Italy) 4. Swiatowy Dzień Modlitwy o Pokój (1986 : Assisi, Italy) I. Title.
BX1378.4.D6713   1994   261.2–dc20   94-25185   CIP
                            10 9 8 7 6 5 4 3 2

CONTENTS

FOREWORD

The Second Part appears in three sections: (1) *Redemptor Hominis* [= *RH*], (2) *Dives in Misericordia* [= *DiM*], (3) *Dominum et Vivificantem* [= *DeV*] [i.e., the three major dogmatic Encyclicals of John Paul II]. In the present work, which is the first section, we will analyze the Pope's inaugural Encyclical *Redemptor Hominis*. The main purpose of this comprehensive analysis is, as in the First Part, an accurate understanding of the Pope's thinking. But that means we must trace his line of thought from his own theological principles.

Part I has already given us the key to understanding the Pope's theology, and will serve as a basis for Part II, the "trinitarian trilogy."

The theme "Assisi" has not lost its relevance. The Pope himself vividly expressed the thought behind the world prayer meeting of October 27, 1986 in numerous speeches. In his message for World Peace Day on January 1, 1992 under the motto:

> "Believers of all religions: A united effort for world peace!,"

the Pope took up the theme once again. The secretariat of the German Episcopal Conference put out a pamphlet under the same title, with a foreword by Bishop Karl Lehmann of Mainz.* The alleged purpose of the publication is to help "the parish communities and all interested parties to put the Pope's intentions into practice." After the "model" of Assisi was reproduced on an international scale

---

* *"Glaubende aller Religionen: Vereint für den Aufbau des Friedens,"* World Peace Day, January 1, 1992, Arbeitshilfe Nr. 92, Sekretariat der Deutschen Bischofskonferenz, Bonn.

in numerous subsequent prayer meetings, it should henceforth be incorporated into parish life. The time has arrived, because: "Even in our society we find a growing number of believers of non-Christian religions, travelers or residents who are foreign workers, refugees or students. Towards these, especially the Moslems, each has a responsibility, in his own way, to promote a peaceful coexistence among persons of different beliefs" (Lehmann). Faced with this situation it will daily become more urgent to clarify the papal "theology of Assisi."

INTRODUCTION

TO JOHN PAUL II'S
"TRINITARIAN TRILOGY"

T he First Part ends with the question: "Is the New
Theology of Cardinal Wojtyla also the theology of
Pope John Paul II?"[1]
The answer is: The philosophical-theological principles
of the professor and archbishop Karol Wojtyla have fully
entered into the words and actions of Pope John Paul II.
Through the diligent exercise of the office of Peter he developed them and finally presented their main element before the eyes of all mankind through the public manifestation of the world religions' prayer for peace at Assisi.[2]
Therefore Part I forms also the basis for understanding and
interpreting the Pope's theology. The most important mile-
stones on John Paul II's theological journey to the prayer
meeting at Assisi are the three dogmatic Encyclicals *Redemptor Hominis* (1979), *Dives in Misericordia* (1980) and
Dominum et Vivificantem (1986), which the Pope himself
has referred to as the "trinitarian trilogy."[3]

---

1 Johannes Dörmann, *Pope John Paul II's Theological Journey to the
Prayer Meeting of Religions in Assisi, Part I–From the Second Vatican
Council to the Papal Elections* (Angelus Press, 1994), p. 123.

2 *Ibid.*, pp. 6-9; 21-46. See also my detailed presentation and analysis
of the prayer meeting, "One Truth and Many Religions–Assisi: Beginning of a New Age," *Respondeo* 8 (Abensberg 1988).

3 John Paul II, at the announcement of *Dominum et Vivificantem* on
Pentecost Sunday 1986 in the noon address at St. Peter's (*L'Osserva-
tore Romano*, English ed. [= *OR*, Eng.], May 26, 1986, p. 1).

1.   From learned professor to reigning Pontiff.

How many were familiar with the efforts of the scholar Karol Wojtyla towards a major synthesis of scholastic tradition, modern philosophy and theology, of mysticism and a conciliar world view? How many were familiar with the essays, mostly in Polish, written by the founder of the "Lublin-Krakow ethical school" or with the philosophical "struggle for man" which was carried out there?[4]

Through Cardinal Wojtyla's election to the Papacy, *the personal philosophy and theology of a professor and bishop attains the status of general relevance for the Church as a whole.*

Even as bishop, Karol Wojtyla continued to exercise his teaching career as a professor. While archbishop he remained professor, and as professor he was archbishop. This synthesis characterizes the personality of Karol Wojtyla. The philosophical-theological interest is not accidental in his case, but essential. Despite the exhausting and time-consuming exercise of his office as bishop, his philosophical-theological interests remained the intellectual and spiritual mainspring of his activity.

Through Cardinal Wojtyla's election to the Papacy, *the pontificate of John Paul II is formed by the philosophical-theological-spiritual nucleus of this powerful personality.*

As Bishop Karol Wojtyla so Pope John Paul II understands his office and duties in the light of the Council. The main source for his papal writings are the Council documents. Their interpretation depends on the understanding of the Council, as expressed already by the bishop of Krakow.[5]

---

4 Cf. Karol Wojtyla, Andrzej Szostek, Tadeusz Styczén, *The Struggle for Man* (Kevelaer 1979).–Representative of the personalism of the "Wojtyla school."

5 E.g. *Von der Königswurde des Menschen* [*On the Kingly Dignity of Men*] (Stuttgart 1980).–Cf. Vol. I, pp. 9-19; 21-46.

Then, too, the pastoral efforts of John Paul II follow in the footsteps of Paul VI and are directed towards the implementation of the decisions of the Second Vatican Council, as the Pope himself strongly emphasizes (see below *Redemptor Hominis*).

Like Cardinal Wojtyla so Pope John Paul II is a man of Vatican II: He is a Pope of the Conciliar Church.

It makes a *big difference* whether a learned professor or the reigning Pontiff proclaims his personal philosophy and theology, whether a bishop or the successor of Peter makes his own understanding of the Council the norm of his apostolate, whether a bishop or the Vicar of Christ organizes an interfaith prayer meeting, whether a diocese or the universal Church takes part in the journey towards Assisi.

2. Assisi: John Paul II's grand vision of universal religious peace.

The interfaith worship of Assisi was no chance event in the pastoral order; it was *a major event of dogmatic significance*, emanating from the heart of the theology and personality of Karol Wojtyla, and presented before the entire world by Pope John Paul II as the visible expression of the intentions of Vatican II with the authority of the office of Peter. As a programmatic demonstration of the conciliar pan-ecumenism by the Pope himself, the "Assisi event" carries dogmatic weight, which marks the course of the Church into the third millennium.[6]

At the same time, the prayer meeting was *a major event of pastoral importance*. Assisi is the "model" which must be faithfully imitated, and according to which the pan-ecumenical objectives of Vatican II should be gradually real-

---

6   From the Vatican's standpoint: Assisi means "a breakthrough in the history of mankind," which "penetrates deep into man's consciousness" and which should "usher in the beginning of a new age" (*OR*, German ed. [= *OR*, dt.], Nov. 28, 1986, p. 2).

ized in the Church and in the world. The Pope wished and
still wishes the prayer service for peace, as practiced there,
to be understood as "an anticipation of what God would
very much like to see realized through the historical development of mankind."[7] Assisi was therefore not only the
initial thrust, the "beginning of a new age," but also by the
very fact the "anticipation" of the main objective: the "con-
vergence of all religions."[8] Assisi is *the starting point for a
pastoral process, which if faithfully imitated should guide and
transform the entire faith and practice of Christianity as well
as the religious awareness of all mankind.* That is the pastoral
dimension of the international series of prayer meetings in
Kyoto (1987), Rome (1988), Warsaw (1989), Bari (1990),
and Malta (1991), as well as numerous imitations on a
lower scale. The pastoral success is remarkable: The "spirit
of Assisi" has advanced since then to the tiniest country
parishes.

In Assisi, the Pope presented before all mankind his
grand vision of universal religious peace as the intention
behind Vatican II.[9]

3. Public manifestation of the new religion under the auspices of the Pope.

To understand the "Assisi event" is to understand the
"historical turning-point," officially introduced into the
Church since the Council, and likewise to understand the
reigning Pontiff. The reverse is also true.[10] There is public
talk of a "new religion,"[11] and not only of manifest innova-

---

7 John Paul II, Closing address in Assisi (*OR*, dt., Nov. 7, 1986, p. 10, 5).

8 See *OR*, dt., Nov. 28, 1986.

9 John Paul II, Christmas address to the Cardinals and members of the Roman Curia on Dec. 22, 1986 (*OR*, Eng., Jan. 5, 1987, p. 7.–See Part I, pp. 9-19).

10 Eugen Biser, *Die glaubensgeschichtliche Wende* (Graz 1986).

11 Eugen Biser, *Glaubenswende* [*Conversion*] (Freiburg i. Br. 1987).

tions in theology and liturgy. This "historical turning-point" was in the making among theologians long before Vatican II, and was nowhere given more official status, as the "new religion" of the Conciliar Church, than in Assisi under the Pope's leadership. A primary task of present-day theology is to shed light on this dramatic incident of the "new religion" inaugurated by the Pope himself.

The pontificate of John Paul II plays a key role in the "new religion," but not as though the Pope's theology and administration present something entirely new. His theology is eclectic, only a special version in the broad spectrum of "new theologies"; and his administration, as he understands it, is merely a continuation of the path marked out by Pope Paul VI and Vatican II.[12] Since John Paul II is personally convinced of the *New Theology*, founded on the pan-ecumenical ideas of Vatican II, since he places himself as Pope at the head of the liberal-religious movements for unity, and leads them to the unforeseen summit of their endeavors, to the prayer meeting of religions in Assisi, he has in effect, with the authority of the office of Peter, aided and abetted the various ecumenical groups in the Church and the world towards a spectacular breakthrough.[13] *Thus Assisi became the visible manifestation of the Conciliar Church's new religion under the auspices of the Pope.*

4. The "trinitarian trilogy"—heart of John Paul II's theology.

Considering the large quantity of papal writings and speeches, of more or less important addresses of the Holy See, drawn up by various collaborators on different occasions, all of which is by no means a homogeneous, coherent body, the question arises: Where and how, amidst the bulk of apostolic pronouncements, can we come to know

[12] John Paul II, *Redemptor Hominis* 2; 3; 7.
[13] For a more detailed analysis, see my essay in note 2, pp. 126ff.

the Pope's personal theology? Is it a theologically coherent body? If so, how can we pick it out from the heterogeneous bulk of material?

By the very nature of the matter, the Pope's theology does not appear in professorial essays, but in official pronouncements, dogmatic Encyclicals and pontifical acts. Consequently, it does not claim to be a rigid, scientific demonstration, but gradually comes more into focus in the course of exercise of the apostolic office.

Furthermore, the theology of John Paul II is not easy to recognize in its structure and entirety, because of the particularity of the language, the meditative character of the statements, the associative-circular mode of thought, the different purposes of the pronouncements, the heterogeneous bulk of material and subjects discussed, but especially on account of the use of traditional language and concepts, which, however, in the context of the *New Theology* undergoes a total change in meaning.

From the beginning of John Paul II's administration, we can clearly see that he is determined to dedicate his pontificate to a grand theological vision. It is equally clear that the Pope intended from the beginning to present his theology as a coherent body. This holds especially for the three major dogmatic Encyclicals, which he has referred to as the "trinitarian trilogy," and therefore which he understands as a *theological whole*. At the announcement of his Encyclical on the Holy Ghost *Dominum et Vivificantem* (May 30, 1986), John Paul II himself declared that it forms a kind of "trinitarian trilogy" along with the two other Encyclicals *Dives in Misericordia* (Nov. 30, 1980) and *Redemptor Hominis* (Mar. 4, 1979), which deal with the Father and the Son.[14]

This "trinitarian trilogy" should be considered therefore as a theological whole. It forms the very core of John Paul

---

14 See above, Note 3.

II's theology. From this core we can understand the Pope's entire pontificate.

Moreover, the promulgation of the "trinitarian trilogy" encompasses the entire period from the beginning of the pontificate (*Redemptor Hominis*, Mar. 4, 1979) down to the year of the prayer meeting at Assisi (*Dominum et Vivificantem*, May 30, 1986). The "trinitarian trilogy" presents *the theological basis for the dogmatic preparation and realization of that event.*

In Assisi, the first commandment is at stake: The one true God in three divine persons stands alongside the gods of various religions.[15] The confrontation (or reconciliation of all the gods?) takes place in the midst of all religions, including the Christian faith and Catholic theology.

By associating the three Encyclicals *Redemptor Hominis*, *Dives in Misericordia* and *Dominum et Vivificantem* with the Son, the Father and the Holy Ghost, and by designating them as the "trinitarian trilogy," the Pope *connects these Encyclicals directly with the trinitarian controversy, which is the dogmatic crystallization point in the present theological upheaval.*

The "trinitarian trilogy" is, however, not a "trilogy of the Trinity," hence not a treatise on God's unity of nature and trinity of persons, but it is the main part of John Paul II's theology, which according to the Pope, has its ultimate foundation in the three divine persons. The Pope's teaching on the Trinity as such must be extracted specifically from the three Encyclicals, and can be fully grasped only after a complete analysis of them.

5. The "trinitarian trilogy" as the Pope's *New Theology* and the problem of its interpretation.

John Paul II considers the realization of Vatican II in the

---

15 Cf. Part I, pp. 15ff.–For more detail, see my essay in note 2, p. 126-181.

life of the Church as the main task of his pontificate. In this "new phase of the self-realization of the Church, in keeping with the epoch in which it has been our destiny to live" (*DiM* 15,3), and because of the importance of the office of Peter, the "trinitarian trilogy" takes on a crucial role as the Pope's personal theology. However, there lies a considerable problem, as we can show by a short sketch and summary of the Pope's theology:

– The "trinitarian trilogy" is a genuine fruit from the tree of the knowledge of Vatican II: *it belongs to the genus of "New Theology."*[16]

The Council's decision to discard traditional "scholastic terminology" in favor of a "pastoral Council language" was apparently rather harmless at first sight, but has visibly taken its toll:

This discarding of traditional terminology has meant the disappearance of the *philosophia perennis* and the silent rupture with the "Catholic system" of classical theology (John Henry Newman) and with the conceptual expression of Church dogmas.[17]

But the break with tradition was the first step necessary for the Council's theological innovations, *which marked the official birth of a pluralism of "new theologies," which from then on would be "legitimate."*[18]

Thus we are looking at an absolute novelty in the history of the Church's teaching: a special version of the "New Theology" has assumed its place on the Chair of Peter and characterizes the teaching and pontificate of John Paul II.

– The very idea of the *"New Theology"* means rejecting the "Catholic system" of the "outdated theology," while retaining its own novelties which have a particular individual structure and framework. It is *per se* pluralistic because

---

16 Cf. Part I, pp. 38-45.

17 *Ibid.*

18 *Ibid.*

of the wide variety of modern philosophies and ways of thinking. It attempts to re-define the Christian faith in the mental framework of modern thinking. All this implies two things for the accurate interpretation of the *"New Theology"*: –1. The basic requirement for an adequate understanding of the truth is the intellectual renunciation of the "Catholic system." Since this new thinking does not spring from the "Catholic system," it cannot be understood by means of that system either. –2. Since each version of the *New Theology* has its special philosophical and theological principles, its particular emphasis, its own individual terminology and language, it must also be understood and interpreted based on the underlying principle of the respective author. Traditional notions, which have their fixed place and clear meaning in the "Catholic system," suddenly take on another meaning in the context of a new theology. Yet there is an additional factor: Karol Wojtyla was not only a scientist, philosopher and theologian, but also a writer and poet, which he remained even as pope. Thus, while reading the texts formulated by the Pope, we must take careful notice of his literary devices and expressive, poetic language.

Such then is the problem of interpreting papal documents by means of the personal theology and language of the author.

Obviously, the substance of the Catholic faith remains intact only if the content of the dogmatic notions as defined by the Church is also kept intact in the respective version of the *New Theology*.

– John Paul II's intention is to convey the message of Vatican II not only to the Church, but to all mankind. That was also the intention of Vatican II (*Lumen Gentium* 1,1). To achieve this end effectively, the Pope summarizes the pastoral and theological content of the Council documents in the "trinitarian trilogy"; he formulates, in his version of the *New Theology*, the new insights of the conciliar message which will mark the Church's future course of action. He traces the essential program in his inaugural Encyclical right at the beginning of his pontificate. That means:

The theological message of Vatican II is substantially identical with the Pope's New Theology expressed in the Encyclicals. For John Paul II, Vatican II is quite simply the voice of the Holy Ghost.[19] By ascribing to the self-styled pastoral Council the highest conceivable teaching authority, which he directly links up to that of his apostolic office, the Pope accordingly raises his *New Theology*, which sets forth the doctrine of the Council, to an absolute status.

– The post-conciliar era is marked by the controversy over the "spirit of the Council" and the "correct understanding of the Council."[20] Amidst this clash of opinions, the "trinitarian trilogy" is in a sense the official interpretation of what the Council really taught, desired, and of what it understood by the "*accommodata renovatio Ecclesiae.*" That means:

The "trinitarian trilogy" is an authentic interpretation of the Second Vatican Council by the Pope. It should put a stop to the theological dispute over the "spirit of the Council" and the "correct understanding of the Council": With the authority of the Holy Ghost, the Council and the office of Peter, the Pope indicates the general orientation for theological thought and for the life of the Church into the third millennium. And this orientation leads to Assisi!

– In our day, the fruits of the post-conciliar pluralism of numerous "new theologies" are plain for all to see: The abandonment of the "Catholic system" and the unleashing of countless–even inculturated–new theologies have led to a breakdown in the unity of the Catholic faith handed down for centuries. In the era of pan-ecumenism and interfaith dialogue, the traditional ideas of heresy and paganism

---

[19] John Paul II, *Redemptor Hominis* 3, and *op. cit.*
[20] Cf. Part I, p. 43-46.

were simply eliminated from theological vocabulary. The clear identity of the Catholic faith disappeared in the haze of a theological, ecumenical, multicultural and interfaith pluralism.

Rome and the episcopal conferences are concerned about "spreading the faith."[21] The survival of the Church is in question. But how can the faith be handed down and remain stable, unless that faith be clearly defined?

*Now if the Pope himself presents the substance of the last ecumenical Council in his version of the **New Theology**, and if in his Encyclicals he proposes to plot the course for the "Church of the future" at the threshold of the third millennium while at the same time claiming to uphold the entire deposit of faith, then the problem of theological pluralism and the transmission of the faith suddenly appears in a new light.*

– The authors of the "new theology" were fully convinced that the traditional "Catholic system," by reason of its association with an antiquated metaphysics, with a static frame of mind, and with an entirely outdated view of the world and of history, was totally out of touch with reality and hence was incapable of getting through to 20th century man.[22] The "full-scale reduction of all facets of reality to mere history" in modern thought requires similar modifications for theology.[23] The rise of the "new theology" represents an "unprecedented radical change."[24]

Each major version of the *"New Theology"* comes across as a philosophical-theological new invention, which how-

---

21 E.g., the study session from Nov. 16-18, 1988 for members of the German Bishops' Conference and the Central Committee of German Catholics in Bonn, whose theme was: "The future of the faith in our country–on the situation and the transmission of the faith."

22 Cf. Part I, pp. 37ff.

23 Cf. Walter Kasper, *Einführung in den Glauben* [*Introduction to the Faith*] (Mainz 1972), p. 134. A brief sketch of the problem of the "historicity of the faith" pp. 134-151.

24 Cf. Bernhard Welte, Vol. I, p. 38 and note 26.

ever purports to maintain the entire Christian faith in the
setting of modern thought. It fully replaces the traditional
"Catholic system."[25] The scope of such an enterprise is
reminiscent of St. Thomas Aquinas and would surely require the academic prowess of the Angel of the Schools in
order to succeed.

*The "trinitarian trilogy": Redemptor Hominis (1979),
Dives in Misericordia (1980) and Dominum et Vivificantem (1986), can be considered as the core of a lively presentation of the Pope's "New Theology," which is based on Vatican
II, and which gives a new explanation of the entire Christian
faith for the Church and for all mankind at the threshold of
the third millennium, thereby displacing the "Catholic system"
of the pre-conciliar Church.*

As we have just shown, the task of interpreting the Encyclicals is by no means easy. Therefore, we will first give
the reader a condensed summary of the author's theological
principles (6 & 7), which will serve as the key to an adequate understanding of his thought.

6. A new type of man-centered theology.

The key text for Karol Wojtyla's *New Theology* is one
from which he draws his idea of revelation (see below 7.),
namely the following passage from the Pastoral Constitution *Gaudium et Spes* (22,1-2):

> In reality it is only in the mystery of the Word made
> flesh that the mystery of man truly becomes clear. For
> Adam, the first man, was a type of him who was to come,
> Christ the Lord, Christ the new Adam, in the very revela-
> tion of the mystery of the Father and of his love, fully

---

[25] E.g. the monumental work compiled by Johannes Feiner, Magnus
Löhrer and numerous collaborators: *Mysterium Salutis. Grundriß
heilsgeschichtlicher Dogmatik* [*Outline of Dogmatic Salvation History*]
(Einsiedeln–Zürich–Cologne 1965ff.). The whole work is "built on
the principal ideas of salvation history" (Vol. I, p. XIX).

reveals man to himself and brings to light his most high calling...

He who is the "image of the invisible God" (Col.1:15), is himself the perfect man who has restored in the children of Adam that likeness to God which had been disfigured ever since the first sin. Human nature, by the very fact that it was assumed, not absorbed, in him has been raised in us also to a dignity beyond compare. For, by his incarnation, he, the son of God, has in a certain way united himself with each man. He worked with human hands, he thought with a human mind. He acted with a human will and with a human heart he loved. Born of the Virgin Mary, he has truly been made one of us, like to us in all things except sin.[26]

Later on in the text, the Council Fathers present the work of the Redemption and the Paschal mystery, which God renews in the Christian believer. The text then concludes with the following observation (*Gaudium et Spes* 22,5):

All this holds true not for Christians only but also for all men of good will in whose hearts grace is active invisibly. For since Christ died for all, and since all men are in fact called to one and the same destiny, which is divine, we must hold that the Holy Spirit offers to all the possibility of being made partners, in a way known to God, in the paschal mystery.

In his commentary on Article 22 of *Gaudium et Spes* Joseph Ratzinger says: "One is indeed allowed to say that here, for the first time in a magisterial text, a new type of entirely Christocentric theology appears, which, in relation to Christ, ventures theology as anthropology, which thereby becomes for the first time radically theological, Christ as man in the talk of God, disclosing the deepest

---

26 On this Council text cf. Cardinal Wojtyla's commentary in *Zeichen des Widerspruchs* [*Sign of Contradiction*] (Freiburg i. Br. 1979), pp. 119-121.

unity of theology."[27]

The Council's assertion regarding the work of the Redemption and the Paschal mystery: "All this holds true not for Christians only, but also for all men of good will," insinuates that the universality of the work of the Redemption is extended automatically from the objective (i.e. Christ made salvation possible for all men) to the subjective sphere (i.e. all men go to heaven). But this is precisely the question which Joseph Ratzinger raises with regard to the Council's assertion cited above: If, according to the Vatican II Constitution on the Church and despite the Church's generally accepted teaching, the possibility of salvation need not be dependent upon the explicit recognition of God (*Lumen Gentium* 16), are we, then, still authorized in drawing a distinction between Christians and non-Christians in the question of salvation? Does not the division of mankind into the saved and the damned come across as an arrogant, inadmissible form of particularism?[28]

But *Gaudium et Spes* 22 means nothing less for the Council Father Karol Wojtyla than it does for Joseph Ratzinger.[29] One might say that Karol Wojtyla's *New Theology* adequately expresses this "new type of entirely Christocentric theology,...which...ventures theology as anthropology." One might even say that the Council Father Karol Wojtyla takes up the Council's assertion: the work of the Redemption and the Paschal mystery hold true "not for Christians only, but also for all men of good will," and proceeds to

---

[27] *Lexikon für Theologie und Kirche* (= *LThK*) (Freiburg i. Br. 1968), Vol. XIV, p. 350.

[28] *Ibid.*, p. 351.–Another text from *Gaudium et Spes*, which points in the same direction, runs (78,3): "Christ, the Word made flesh, the prince of peace, reconciled all men to God by the Cross, and, restoring the unity of all in one people and one body, he abolished hatred in his own flesh, having been lifted up through his resurrection he poured forth the Spirit of love into the hearts of men."

[29] Cf. Cardinal Wojtyla, [*Sign of Contradiction*], pp. 119-121.

formulate his thesis of universal salvation, which in turn eliminates the "distinction between Christians and non-Christians in the question of salvation." But it was not long before this "new type of entirely Christocentric theology" would develop into a new type of entirely man-centered theology.

From the foregoing we may infer *the main principle for interpretation*, which gives us direct access towards the understanding of the "trinitarian trilogy." It is the maxim derived from *Gaudium et Spes* 22,5: What holds for the Christian holds also in principle for all men. That means: *The reader of the Encyclicals goes right to the heart of the matter, if he understands the text in reference to the thesis of universal salvation.*

7.   The principles behind man-centered theology.

"As a revealed religion, Christianity has its final objective foundation in God's own message to mankind and in mankind's acceptance of that message."[30] Revelation and faith are the principles of knowledge also in classical theology.[31] Of course it is only public, biblical revelation (i.e. as opposed to private revelations, whether approved by the Church or not) which we are discussing here.[32]

Karol Wojtyla's *New Theology* has its final foundation in a new idea of revelation and faith which greatly differs from the traditional idea. As Cardinal, he derived this new

---

[30] Josef Neuner and Heinrich Roos, *Der Glaube der Kirche in den Urkunden der Lehrverkündigung* [*The Faith of the Church in the Dogmatic Pronouncements*] (Regensburg 1965, 7th Ed.), p. 29.

[31] Cf. Matthias Joseph Scheeben, Theologische Erkenntnislehre. *Handbuch der katholischen Dogmatik* III [*Handbook of Catholic Dogma*] (Freiburg i. Br. 1948, 2nd Ed.).

[32] *Ibid.*–Wolfhart Pannenberg, *Wissenschaftstheorie und Theologie* [*Scientific Theory and Theology*] (Frankfurt a. M. 1973), founds theology on all religions as witnesses to the divine reality, therefore on comparative religions (pp. 315ff.).

idea (*Sign of Contradiction*, pp. 119-121) from the above quoted Council text (*Gaudium et Spes* 22,1-2); as Pope, he has preserved it intact in his "trinitarian trilogy."[33] A comprehensive study and analysis of this new idea of revelation and faith was presented in Part I (pp. 78-123). Hence a brief restatement of the conclusions will suffice here.

7.1 Universal salvation as revelation *a priori*.

There are mainly two definitions of revelation, which Cardinal Wojtyla derives from *Gaudium et Spes* 22,1-2, and then interprets. The first definition runs:

> Revelation consists in a fact, the fact that by his Incarnation the Son of God united himself with every man, became man himself, one of us.[34]

This definition is the focal point of that self-styled "entirely new Christocentric theology, which, in relation to Christ, ventures theology as anthropology." The success of the venture will depend largely on precisely how one understands the union of the Son of God with each person. Cardinal Wojtyla does not understand it the same way as the Church has traditionally exposed it, namely as a material union; he understands it in the context of his thesis of universal salvation, namely as a formal, supernatural union.[35] The same holds for the Pope's *New Theology*, thus also for his "trinitarian trilogy." Although the thesis of universal salvation easily goes unnoticed for the average reader of the Encyclicals, there are nonetheless prominent passages where clear and blatant assertions can be found. For instance, we hear in *Redemptor Hominis* (11,4) that each

---

33 The thought behind *Sign of Contradiction* entered fully into the inaugural Encyclical.

34 Cardinal Wojtyla, [*Sign of Contradiction*], p. 121.

35 For the proof that not only the material, but also the formal union is meant here, see Part I, Chapters III and IV.

human being has reached in Christ "the dignity of both the grace of divine adoption and the inner truth of humanity." With equal clarity the Encyclical says elsewhere (*RH* 13,3) that each human being, from the first moment of his existence, "keeps intact the image and likeness of God Himself," and further, that "with each one Christ has united Himself forever."[36]

But if the Son of God, through his Incarnation, has formally united Himself with each human being, then the Christ-centered perspective has become entirely man-centered, whereupon theology can only dissolve into transcendental anthropology.[37]

Karol Wojtyla maintains that, fundamentally, the Redemption was already accomplished through the Incarnation. Such a thesis is by no means new, since it arose at the very outset of theological speculation, which endeavored to penetrate the mystery of the Redemption. St. Irenaeus of Lyons (+c. 202) is a well-known proponent of this teaching, with his so-called recapitulation theory or his mystic theory of Redemption, which for all that never became a Church doctrine:

Commenting on Eph 1:10 (*recapitulare*), St. Irenaeus asserts that "Christ as the second Adam saved and united with God the whole human race. In this view, salvation of man had already taken place in principle through the Incarnation of the Son of God. Side by side with this theory which gave to the Passion and Death of Christ a subordinate significance only, St. Irenaeus also expounds the Pauline teaching of the ransoming and reconciling through Christ's death on the Cross. Cf. *Adv. haer.* III 16,9; IV 5,4; V 1,1f; 14,2-5; 16,3; 17,1."[38]

---

36 Cf. Part I, pp. 80ff.

37 *Ibid.*, p. 122.

38 Ludwig Ott, *Fundamentals of Catholic Dogma* (St. Louis: Herder Book Company, 1954), p. 186.

The subjective reality of universal salvation through the Incarnation is referred to as *revelation*, and thus Cardinal Wojtyla shifts *revelation* to *the subjective consciousness of mankind*. In classical theology, public revelation (*stricte dicta revelatio seu locutio Dei ad homines*) is an objective fact and principle of knowledge. But in Karol Wojtyla's *New Theology*, revelation is also a subjective fact and principle of knowledge, more exactly an *internal, subjective, ontological, "supernatural" reality of human existence and of the person a priori* (i.e. prior to experience).

The fact of universal salvation as revelation *a priori* in the subjective consciousness of each person is the primary, transcendental principle of knowledge in Karol Wojtyla's theology. Like the fact of universal salvation, so also revelation *a priori* is universal. It is present in everyone and in all religions.

At first glance the thesis of universal salvation seems like a mere broadening of horizons with respect to the Church's traditional teaching, like a deliverance, so long overdue, from a narrow-minded particularism, or "division of mankind into the saved and the damned."[39] The work of Redemption accomplished by God appears more universal, more considerate, more worthy of God. This improvement upon the traditional teaching comes across as such a "slight modification": It eliminates the traditional distinction of subjective and objective Redemption. It isolates the Redemption from any subjective requirements on the part of mankind, and makes it consist merely in the work of divine grace, the work of the overflowing love and mercy of God, which is not limited even by man's response. In God's sight, the categories of time and space are almost entirely insignificant.[40]

---

[39] Cf. for this question, Joseph Ratzinger, Commentary on *Gaudium et Spes*, *LThK, op. cit.*, XIV, p. 351.

[40] Cardinal Wojtyla, [*Sign of Contradiction*], p. 103.

Since the substance of the faith (*fides quae creditur*) may not be touched, universal salvation becomes a pure question of interpretation and of consciousness. But does this thesis really preserve the substance of the faith? Just one example to show what we mean: One of the Pope's constantly recurring axioms runs thus: The truth about man "is revealed to us in its fullness and depth in Christ" (*DiM* 1,2).[41]

Of course this Council statement is not wrong, but it can receive various interpretations, depending on whether it is seen in the light of the Church's traditional teaching or of the Pope's *New Theology*:

In the Church's traditional teaching, the "truth about man" is primarily his being universally subject to sin, as well as his absolute need of Redemption (Rom 3:9-31). The Church has always taught the objective, but not the subjective universality of the Redemption. The objectively universal Redemption came about through the sacrifice of Jesus Christ on the Cross; the subjective Redemption takes place through the application of the fruits of the Redemption to each individual in the process whereby the sinner is justified under certain conditions required on his part, above all "by virtue of faith in Jesus Christ" (Rom 3:22).

Justification presupposes man's condition as a sinner in absolute need of Redemption. Through justification, man is delivered from the state of original sin and raised to the dignity of a redeemed, adopted child of God (D 793-796). Justification therefore includes a real passage from death to life (D 795). Faith, baptism, and the Church are necessary for salvation (*necessitas medii*).

Besides the ordinary means, the Church has always acknowledged the extraordinary means of salvation, "which are known to God alone" (*Gaudium et Spes* 22,5), but she never based her theology on hidden and subjective factors

---

[41] Cf. also below *Redemptor Hominis*, 2.

known only to God, but on what God has objectively revealed, namely on public revelation.

On the contrary, the Council Father Karol Wojtyla, through his thesis of universal salvation, founds his theology on the hidden subjective factors which are known to God alone. Therefore he would sooner base his theology on love and on the Holy Ghost than on Christ.[42] With the help of the thesis which says that the Son of God, through his Incarnation, formally united himself with each human being, Karol Wojtyla brings to light what was hidden in the dark caverns of man's consciousness and known to God alone: the "anonymous Christian"! Thus universal salvation and revelation *a priori* become synonymous, and this equation serves as a first axiom of his *New Theology*.

Thus when we hear this principle in the Pope's theology: The truth about man "is revealed to us in its fullness and depth in Christ," we must interpret it in the context of universal salvation. The "slight modification" of the Church's traditional teaching turns out to be a "serious modification" in the substance of the key doctrine of the Redemption.

7.2 Salvation history as revelation *a posteriori.*

For the second definition of revelation Cardinal Wojtyla appeals to the same Council text (*Gaudium et Spes* 22,1-2). Accordingly the Council taught:

> the anthropological, even anthropocentric character of the revelation offered to mankind in Christ. This revelation is centered on man: Christ "fully reveals man to man himself." But he does so by revealing the Father and the Father's love (cf. John 17:6).[43]

---

42 Cf. Part I, p. 117 and note 19.

43 Cardinal Wojtyla, [*Sign of Contradiction*], p. 120.–On the problem of "being in Christ" as the man's innermost nature, see Part I, p. 97.

The "revelation offered to mankind in Christ" is of course historical revelation as reflected in the life and teachings of Jesus. We may thus speak of a "double revelation" (Karl Rahner).[44]

The relationship between revelation *a priori* and *a posteriori* is more clearly laid out and summarized: "Christ reveals man to himself." That means: the "mystery of man," made clear by revelation *a posteriori* offered in Christ, consists in the fact that every man, from the first moment of his existence, possesses *a priori* "being in Christ," *which belongs to his innermost nature as man.* Hence man's innermost nature and "being in Christ"are identical.

If that be the case, then the "new type of entirely Christocentric theology ... , which, in relation to Christ, ventures theology as anthropology" becomes a new type of entirely man-centered theology. Then "double revelation" acquires a double man-centered character; then man or "the truth about man" becomes the actual object of double revelation. Then the assertion holds: "This revelation is centered on man"!–Therefore not on Christ, nor on God!

If man, from the first moment of his conception, keeps intact not only the *imago*, as *Redemptor Hominis* (13,3) asserts, but even the *similitudo Dei* (= revelation *a priori*), then the "revelation offered to mankind in Christ" (= revelation *a posteriori*) consists merely in "proclaiming" to all mankind their Redemption in Christ which is already accomplished, and hence their paramount dignity as participants of God's grace, as children of God. Revelation which comes to us through salvation history becomes the mirror of man's innermost nature. This kind of revelation is *per se* "man-centered."

Consequently, salvation history itself, in which revelation has occurred, loses its genuinely *historical* character; this holds for the historical work of salvation accomplished by

---

44 Cf. Part I, pp. 112ff.

Jesus Christ, and equally for human actions on which sal-vation depends. If each person is radically saved and justi-fied *a priori*, then the Redemption is ultimately not an event which was realized in history, but something which belongs to human nature as such; then, too, the gift of "being in Christ" is no longer a question of application and decision on the part of man in history, but merely a matter of human consciousness. The "offer" of self-awareness, which Christ makes to mankind "by revealing the Father and the Father's love," is directed towards an *exercise of consciousness* in order to bring to light man's innermost nature as well as the "truth about man and his dignity."

We may conclude: To the fact of universal salvation as revelation *a priori* corresponds the historical revelation *a posteriori* embodied in the life and teachings of Jesus, which "reveals" to man, or "makes him aware" of the dignity of his innermost nature. In the process of man's "self-aware-ness," consciousness plays the decisive role. Like revelation *a priori*, so also revelation *a posteriori* is essentially "man-centered."

To the "double revelation" corresponds the "double faith."[45]

7.3 The "double revelation": Foundation for a covenant theology of salvation history.

The main thread of the Cardinal's theology, which we can extract from *Sign of Contradiction*, may be referred to as a *covenant theology of salvation history*. It is no theological novelty, but as such holds a place in the general spectrum of modern "dogmatic salvation history," and is reminiscent of the debates of the 16th century Reformers in that do-main.[46] But what is particular about the theologian Karol

---

[45] *Ibid.*, pp. 117ff.

[46] Cf. Paul Jacobs, Article Föderaltheologie in: *Religion in Geschichte und Gegewart* (Tübingen 1957), I, col. 1518-1520.–As for Coccejus,

Wojtyla's covenant theology is the fact that his idea of salvation history is determined by the principle of "double revelation."

Karol Wojtyla's covenant theology of salvation history, in turn based on the principle of "double revelation," has its biblical foundation in Genesis 1-3. In order to understand the basic structure of the world and history (pp. 30-36),[47] one must "go back to the fundamental reality of the creation of the world and mankind, especially the first covenant, which is the basis for the final covenant" (p. 35).

The starting point is the covenant which God made with Adam, that is with all mankind (p. 29). From this Adam-covenant, or "original covenant," the whole history of salvation springs forth, which then gradually unfolds as covenant history. In this respect, Karol Wojtyla's *New Theology* attains a remarkable unity.

The Cardinal distinguishes in general between the "God of infinite majesty" (pp. 18-28) and the "God of the Covenant" (pp. 29-37).

The "God of infinite majesty" is the God of Isaias, who is three times Holy (Is. 6:3), the Creator of the world, the Absolute (p. 27; 30). Men of all religions turn to this God "in His absolute transcendence" (p. 27), to the God, "who transcends absolutely the whole of creation, all that is visible and comprehensible."[48] We could say: *For the Pope, the God of infinite majesty, the God and Creator of all mankind, is the God common to all religions.*[49]

Because of the "transcendence of the human person," "the living union between God and the human soul" is

---

so also for Cardinal Wojtyla, the "tree of the knowledge of good and evil" is a symbol of human nature ([*Sign of Contradiction*], pp. 33f.).–Cf. on this whole paragraph, the Pope's Redemption doctrine contained in *Redemptor Hominis* (7-12) in this volume.

[47] All page references in the text are from [*Sign of Contradiction*].

[48] Cf. Part I, pp. 50ff.

[49] *Ibid.*

both possible and real. It is realized "especially in silence" (p. 28). Since all men participate somehow in this "marvelous transcendence of the human spirit," the "Church of the living God" (pp. 27ff) includes all humanity. This "Church" appeared for the first time in history on the occasion of the prayer meeting in Assisi for peace.[50]

The deepest mystery of the "marvelous transcendence of the human spirit" and "the Church of the living God" is, however, not yet clearly expressed by all this, but only suggested: For we can only speak of the "Church" in relation to Christ. Thus the following maxim is discreetly hinted at: "The Church of the living God" is the Church of "anonymous Christianity." For the first time in history, *it was manifested in Assisi before the eyes of all mankind: the common worship of all religions to the God of all religions.*[51]

The thesis of universal salvation, of "anonymous Christianity" is clearly expressed in the special version of Cardinal Wojtyla's covenant theology as follows:

The "God of infinite majesty" is at the same time the "God of the Covenant." At the moment when man was created, God's covenant with Adam, that is, with all mankind, was made (p. 29; 36).

Creation and covenant are "the revelation of God the Father, who gives to creation its true meaning, by the covenant which is the purpose of the creation of man in the image of God" (p. 33). The creation of man and the making of the covenant with Adam take place in one and the same act.

Just as creation and covenant take place in one and the same act, so too "the motive for creation and the motive for the covenant" are one and the same: God's love (p. 30). "God the Creator becomes the God of the Covenant"–out

---

50 Cf. my essay "Assisi: Beginning of a New Age," *Respondeo* 8, pp. 144-181.

51 *Ibid.*

of divine love (p. 30).

That means: "Love is the motive for creation and consequently love is also the motive for the covenant. One could say that in this motive, the eternal plan for man's salvation as embodiment of God's love for man, and personal transcendence of man's rising above the rest of creation come together, both springing from the same root" (p. 31).

Concerning the "original covenant" of the Creator with Adam we learn in addition that it is "on God's side a gift of grace and on man's side ... a state of original justice (*stato della primitiva giustizia*) and happiness" (p. 34). Adam, the covenantor with God, was accordingly created as the "image and likeness of God" in a state of original justice (pp. 31ff; 34). Now does redeemed "being in Christ" also belong to this "original justice"? Obviously yes, because the Cardinal says: "Man exists 'in Christ,' according to God's eternal plan for man's salvation, from the very beginning" (p. 108). Now existing-in-Christ (in St. Paul's sense) means possessing "being in Christ" (p. 108), and so it means being redeemed and justified through Christ's saving deed. The Cardinal says it quite openly: "All men from the beginning to the end of the world have been redeemed and justified by Christ through his Cross" (p. 103).

Accordingly Adam is in the very first moment of his creation an "anonymous Christian."

Because the God of infinite majesty is the God of the Covenant (p. 37); because the motive for man's creation and for the covenant with Adam is one and the same, namely God's love; because creation and covenanting take place in one and the same act; then both being in the image of God and being-in-Christ belong *to man's nature*.[52]

The covenant with Adam as also the covenants with Abraham and Moses lie "on the level of man's being as man." They are pointed towards the "conclusive covenant

---

[52] Cf. Part I, pp. 97f., 114.

with man, i.e. the covenant with mankind in the Son of God" (p. 36).

In this second covenant is revealed "the covenant's final dimension." It is revealed in Jesus Christ's having called God his *Father*. This is explained as follows: "In the full revelation of God's fatherhood is contained the full and conclusive confirmation of that covenant which has been made at the moment of man's creation. After this original covenant was destroyed by original sin, it had to be restored through the Redemption on a still deeper basis and in still fuller measure. 'O happy fault, which gained us so great a Redeemer'" (pp. 36ff).

In the redemption takes place the full revelation of the fatherhood of the covenanting God: the Father so loved the world that he sent his only-begotten Son into the world. The Son became man through the Holy Ghost, was born of the Virgin Mary, and he performed the work of Redemption. In the same way the Father sent the Holy Ghost who carries on the Son's work and fulfills all holiness (p. 37).

In this way "the covenant's full and final dimension," already contained in the first basic covenant (p. 36), was fully revealed and confirmed in the second, conclusive covenant. What had already with man's creation and the simultaneous covenant with Adam been immersed in human history, found its full confirmation and revelation in the second covenant. In the idea of the Adam-covenant was embodied God's historical work of salvation from the creation of man to the end of the world.

However, the Cardinal also says that the first covenant "which was made at the moment of man's creation," "was also destroyed as a consequence of original sin" and accordingly "had to be restored through the Redemption on a still deeper basis and in still fuller measure" (p. 36).

So, after the nature of the first covenant is made clear, the question remains: what exactly is meant by the "destruction" of the first covenant and its restoration by the Redemption through the second covenant? Or, putting the question another way, within this covenant theology of salvation history, what is the relationship between the first and second covenant, given what was said about the first covenant?

Concerning the "second, final, conclusive covenant," the Cardinal says it is the "completion" (p. 30), the "perfection" (pp. 36ff) and the "full confirmation" (pp. 36ff), of the first, basic covenant.

The use of words is astonishing: one would expect that a destroyed covenant would require the making of a fresh covenant, since a destroyed covenant cannot be completed, perfected, or confirmed. Rather, the destroyed covenantal relation would have to be remade through a new covenant, and restored that way.

There is a fundamental truth of Christianity at stake here: the highly controversial doctrine of original sin.[53] According to Catholic doctrine, on account of Adam's sin, which is here original sin, he lost the supernatural *similitudo Dei*; the natural *imago Dei* was "wounded."[54] Moreover, the Church teaches that man, through the blood of Christ, was objectively redeemed from original sin, from his condition of fallen human nature, and raised to the dignity of a redeemed, adopted child of God through the process of justification (D 793-796). The Redemption is the new and eternal covenant in the blood of Christ, which he shed for us unto the forgiveness of sins, as the Church daily confesses and proclaims through the words of Our

---

[53] Ludwig Ott, *op. cit.*, pp. 94-112.–Matthias Joseph Scheeben, *op. cit.*, VII, pp. 209ff.; 254ff.–Karl-Heinz Weger, *Theologie der Erbsünde.* Quaestiones Disputatae 44 (Freiburg i. Br. 1970).–Christoph Schönborn, Albert Görres, Robert Spaemann, *Zur kirchlichen Erbsündenlehre. Stellungnahme zu einer brennenden Frage* (Freiburg 1991).

[54] Cf. Part I, pp. 80-86.

Lord repeated at every Mass in the Consecration.

But the Cardinal says something quite different: He says that the original covenant "was destroyed as a result of original sin." *But this "destruction" of the first covenant does not mean that the "image and likeness of God" has been also destroyed.*[55] On the contrary, the Pope's thesis runs: Each human being, from the first moment of his existence, "keeps intact the image and likeness of God Himself" (*Redemptor Hominis* 13,3). That means:

God's first basic covenant with mankind may be "destroyed" as a result of original sin, but in the process man has not lost his dignity as "image and likeness of God."

The Cardinal likewise makes clear that the second, final and conclusive covenant which God the Father made with mankind in the Son of God restored, completed, perfected and confirmed "in the Redemption on an even deeper basis" the first, basic, destroyed covenant. The completion, perfection and confirmation of the first by the second covenant consists clearly in the fact that Adam, as image and likeness of God, received in a completing, perfecting and confirming manner also "being in Christ," and that *a priori* in the moment of creation as a dowry attached to the destroyed first covenant.

The question remains: what version of salvation history do we have here?

Cardinal Wojtyla himself provides the answer in a sentence not easy to understand: "Man exists 'in Christ,' and does so according to God's eternal plan of salvation from the very beginning; however, through Christ's death and resurrection this 'being in Christ' has become a historical fact rooted in time and space" (pp. 108ff). That means in terms of salvation history: the covenantal gift of "being in Christ" imparted to mankind *a priori* in the Adam covenant becomes *a posteriori* a fact rooted in salvation history.

---

55 *Ibid.*, cf. pp. 79-86.

Obviously we have here a special version not only of the original covenant between God and Adam, but also of the work of Redemption wrought by Christ. The principle of "double revelation" governs both: not only the covenant with Adam but also salvation history as wrought by Christ. Another distinction of the Cardinal shows the same principle: he distinguishes between "the eternal plan of salvation" or the "divine order, the divine view of man and the world" on the one hand, and on the other hand the historical order and view with its categories of time and space. As opposed to "the divine order, the categories of time and space are almost entirely insignificant" (p. 103;108). Upon this distinction the Cardinal bases his proposition that "all men from beginning to end of the world have been redeemed and justified by Christ through his Cross" (p. 103). That means: according to God's order Adam is redeemed and justified in advance, Adam already exists "in Christ" and possesses "being in Christ," Adam is already an "anonymous Christian." In the order of salvation history, what was given *a priori* becomes *a posteriori* a fact in history, rooted in time and space. From this distinction too it emerges clearly that the principle of double revelation governs the character both of salvation history and of the original covenant. We can conclude:

The second, final and conclusive covenant of the Father with mankind in the Son is the historical backing up, confirmation and revelation of what God had out of love already imparted to his image, Adam, as a covenantal gift **a priori**. *So to every man from beginning to end of the world has been imparted not only the dignity of image of God but also the dignity of supernatural sonship of God, in the Son, the Redeemer, as the true being of man as man* (RH 11,4; 13,3). *Every man is* **a priori** *an "anonymous Christian," from the very moment and in the very act of his creation. Through salvation history what is given in advance becomes in addition,* **a posteriori**, *a historical fact and revelation rooted in* *time and space.*

It may by now have become clear: *"Double revelation" is the principle of the Pope's covenant theology of salvation history. Through it the thesis of universal salvation is anchored on the basis of covenantal theology, and through it the history of salvation and revelation receives its specific supra-historical character. The objective passage of biblical history becomes subjective existential "historicity."*

7.4 A more broad-minded perspective of the faith.

Karol Wojtyla's covenant theology of salvation history, based on the principle of "double revelation," lays the logical foundation for a new, coherent, dogmatic perspective of the faith, for a *more broad-minded theology*:

The Pope's doctrine of a *more broad-minded God* proclaims the God of all religions: the God of Assisi.

This is for the Pope the "God of infinite majesty" and the "God of the Covenant." In the act of creation and of making a covenant, which is irrevocable and unbreakable, he has imparted to Adam the entire measure of his love as man's Creator and Redeemer. From the revelation of the New Testament, every Christian knows:

God the Creator the God of the Covenant is none other than the Holy Trinity: The Father sends the Son and the Holy Spirit into the heart of each human being. So runs the "central truth of the faith": "All (human beings) are created by God the Creator, and all are saved by Christ, the Savior."[56]

---

56 John Paul II, Address to the clergy of Rome, second Roman synod after Vatican II (*OR*, dt., Mar. 8, 1991): "The Second Vatican Council stands as an extensive document, consisting of various single documents of different character, and is therefore a powerful magisterial and pastoral guideline for the Church of the future. I myself am deeply aware and convinced that it was a work of the Holy Spirit, who helped and directed us to follow through with this Council and thus to express our views in that hour....Our synod is

The "central truth of the faith," understood in the sense
of universal salvation, contains all the elements of a new,
more broad-minded dogmatic perspective of the faith. According to the *more broad-minded Christology* [= theology
concerning Christ], "the Son of God, through his Incarnation, formally united himself with each human being."[57]
The Incarnation means accordingly not only the union of
the Son with human nature in Jesus Christ, but the formal
union of the Son with each human being, with all mankind, from the beginning of creation until the end of the
world. The axiom of universal salvation is therefore specifically rooted in the universality of the Incarnation.

The *more broad-minded soteriology* [= theology of Re-
demption] is already contained in the more broad-minded
Christology: The work of the Savior is not only objectively
but also subjectively universal: "All men from the beginning until the end of the world are saved and justified by
Christ through his Cross."[58] The non-Christian world is
"anonymous Christianity." The "distinction between
Christians and non-Christians in the question of salvation"
is eliminated. The traditional distinction between the ob-

---

different, it cannot be exactly like the first. It must be different
because of the Second Vatican Council, which has given us a new
outlook on the Church, an outlook more open for the universality
of the people of God: the Catholic universality, which is realized in
the Catholic Church, and also the human universality, which is
realized in certain sense in all mankind, since all men have the same
Creator and Savior. All are created by God the Creator and all are
saved by Christ the Savior. Thus the ecclesiology of the Second
Vatican Council finds the key for its interpretation ultimately in this
central truth of the faith. All this poses for us many problems in the
area of ecumenism, with regard to dialogue with other religions and
spiritual traditions, with the various living conditions of mankind,
with the entire present-day world in its different dimensions."

57 Cardinal Wojtyla, [*Sign of Contradiction*], p. 121.

58 *Ibid.*, p. 103.–Cf. the Pope's Redemption doctrine in *Redemptor
Hominis* (Ch. 2., 7-12), where still unanswered questions are addressed.

jective universality of the Redemption and subjective justification is therefore unauthorized.

The *more broad-minded pneumatology* [= theology of the
Holy Ghost] is rooted in the more broad-minded Christology and soteriology: For "the full dimension of the mystery
of the Redemption," in which Christ is "united with the
Father and with each human being," consists in the fact
that he constantly communicates the Holy Ghost to everyone.[59] The Holy Ghost is present and working in the hearts
of all human beings.[60]

The *more broad-minded anthropology and doctrine of grace*
flows from the creation of man, with whom God made a
covenant: Each human being keeps intact the "image and
likeness of God," and maintains his imperishable dignity as
a participant of God's grace, as a member of redeemed
humanity.[61] The original covenant overthrows the "dual-
ism"of nature and grace once and for all. For "each man, *in
virtue of his very human nature*, is called upon to partake of
the fruits of the Redemption wrought by Christ and even
to share in Christ's own life."[62]

The *more broad-minded ecclesiology* [= theology of the
Church] follows directly from the "central truth of the
faith." "The Church of the living God unites all mankind."
This awareness has caused the Conciliar Church (= "the
Church of our time"), in the light of this truth, "to re-de-
fine her own essence at the Second Vatican Council."[63]

Two essential distinctions constitute the new understanding of the Church: 1. All men belong to the Church
of the living God: It is all cultures and religions which

59 John Paul II, *Redemptor Hominis* 18,3-4.
60 John Paul II, *Sollicitudo rei socialis* (*OR*, dt., Feb. 26, 1988, p. 17,
40).
61 John Paul II, *Redemptor Hominis* 11,4.
62 Thus John Paul II in the Apostolic Brief *Euntes in Mundum* (*OR*,
dt., Mar. 25, 1988, p. 7, I, 2).
63 Cardinal Wojtyla, [*Sign of Contradiction*], p. 27.

make up the people of God, who are on pilgrimage towards the same transcendental goal, as was symbolically
expressed at Assisi.[64] It is the mystical body of Christ in the
wider sense, which in virtue of the Incarnation includes all
mankind.[65] It is the Church of "anonymous Christianity,"
which has not yet become aware of its nature. 2. Alongside
this comprehensive view, we should also acknowledge a
more restricted understanding of the Church: To the
Church in the narrower sense belong all Christians, who
are conscious of their Christianity. Accordingly "all Christian believers belong to the people of God of the new
covenant."[66] All Christians form "the body of Christ in the
community of the people of God."[67] In a word: This
Church, made up of all churches and church communities,
is the "ecumenical Church." One of these is the Conciliar
Church, which re-defined her own essence at Vatican II in
the following terms: "The Church, in Christ, is in the
nature of sacrament – a sign and instrument, that is, of
communion with God and of unity among all men" (*Lumen Gentium* 1,1).

In the Pope's eyes, this novel idea is the key definition of
the Conciliar Church, and of course in the following sense:
The Church is called a "sign of unity among all men,"
hence: "All men are included in this sacrament of unity."[68]
The Church is also called an "instrument for unity among
all men," hence: It is the Church's mission to "proclaim"to
all mankind, to "make them aware" of their hidden, "ontological" unity in Christ.

The Pope's *more broad-minded theology* establishes a *"new*

---

64 Cf. my essay "Assisi: Beginning of a New Age," *Respondeo* 8, pp.
158ff.

65 Cf. Part I, p. 67-72.

66 John Paul II, Wednesday audience Nov. 6, 1991 (*Deutsche Tagespost*
Nov. 19, 1991, p. 5).

67 John Paul II, *Redemptor Hominis* 21,3.

68 Cardinal Wojtyla, [*Sign of Contradiction*], p. 37.

criterion" for interpreting the world: "The awareness of the common fatherhood of God, of the brotherhood of all in Christ–'children in the Son'–and of the presence and life-giving action of the Holy Spirit will bring to our vision a new criterion for interpreting the world."[69]

The express purpose of the pontificate, which is inspired by this theology, is Church unity, Christian unity, the unity of all religions, the unity of all mankind–in the God of Assisi.[70] For the Pope, the worship offered to this God is "an anticipation of what God would very much like to see realized through the historical development of mankind,"[71] as well as "the foretaste of a more peaceful world."[72]

The crucial problem for today's believing Catholic is: The Pope views this "new, more broad-minded perspective" of the truly "Catholic universality" of the faith, which Vatican II gave to the "Church of the future,"[73] merely as a deeper, more complete grasp of the old faith. A Catholic can choose either to view the new perspective as the Pope does, or to admit that a break with tradition has indeed occurred, and what is more, that a substantially new faith has indeed arisen. The question is whether he should disregard all doctrinal concerns, and simply accompany the Pope on his pilgrimage to the "mystical mountain" in Assisi,[74] or whether he should shudder at the thought of it.

---

69 John Paul II, *Sollicitudo rei socialis* (*OR*, dt., Feb. 26, 1988, p. 17, 40).

70 Cf. John Paul II, *Redemptor Hominis* 6,2.

71 John Paul II, Closing address in Assisi (*OR*, dt., Nov. 7, 1986, p. 10, 5).

72 *Ibid.*

73 See above, Note 58.

74 Thus John Paul II in Assisi. Cf. my essay, "Assisi: Beginning of a New Age," *Respondeo* 8, pp. 172-181.

REDEMPTOR HOMINIS: JOHN PAUL'S INAUGURAL ENCYCLICAL ADDRESSED TO ALL MANKIND AT THE THRESHOLD OF THE THIRD MILLENIUM

1. Outline and arrangement.

The inaugural Encyclical *Redemptor Hominis* (Mar. 4, 1979) is quite literally John Paul II's *administration plan*. It contains not only the Pope's New Theology, but also the practical guidelines for the new pontificate.

Redemptor Hominis is the first and most important milestone on the Pope's theological journey to the prayer meeting of religions in Assisi. The Encyclical is not only a milestone, but also the theological foundation of the whole pontificate, which reaches its climax in the "Assisi event."[1]

The inaugural Encyclical displays a harmonious unity. That does not mean that each point is systematically presented in all of its details. Rather, the author treats the subject matter in such a way that he reiterates the main themes respectively from chapter to chapter, then examines them from another angle in a more circular and meditative thinking pattern, and finally enriches them by means of associations. Thus the central dogmatic content only comes into focus step by step.

---

[1] Cf. Johannes Dörmann, "One Truth and Many Religions–Assisi: Beginning of a New Age," *Respondeo* 8 (Abensberg 1988), pp. 126-181.

The elegance of the language, the style and the composition becomes apparent upon closer examination and despite first impressions, and is the fruit of the Encyclical's skillful arrangement. Frequently, one only grasps the exact sense of a theological statement through full appreciation of the organized unity of composition and language. An extensive stylistic analysis of the Encyclical would go beyond the confines of this essay, but we can give a few classic examples at the outset.[2]

The main purpose of this essay is the presentation of the Pope's theology in *Redemptor Hominis*. For isolated theological statements do not lead to Assisi, but the Pope's theology as a whole leads to the "mystical mountain" of St. Francis.

The Pope's theology is by no means clear. Rather, it must be carefully extracted from the texts. As "*New Theology*," by reason of its special philosophical-theological basis, it takes on a special pattern. Our interpretation will be based on the Pope's theological principles of knowledge, as they were presented in Part I and in the Introduction (see above, Art. 7, pp. 17-36). The conclusions therefrom will be presupposed as a safe working hypothesis, which must also hold good for the text of the Encyclical.

With close attention to the wording of the Encyclical, we will attempt to pick out the theological highlights, and likewise to show how the Pope's theology in *Redemptor Hominis* gradually comes into focus, on the basis of the man-centered "double revelation." Thus our essay will serve as a running commentary on the Encyclical.

The outline and arrangement of our essay will correspond to the outline and arrangement of the inaugural Encyclical:

After discussing the title, addressees, and salutation, there follows the text and analysis of the Encyclical, which is arranged in four chapters:

---

2 See Chapter I, 1.3 Digression, p. 57.

I. Outline of the New Pontificate (1-6).
II. The Mystery of the Redemption (7-12).
III. Redeemed Man and His Situation in the Modern World
(13-17).
IV. The Church's Mission and Man's Destiny (18-22).[3]

The Encyclical texts are quoted in full so that the reader
may examine the theological statements in the Pope's own
words, thoughts, and ideas. Classical theological language
undergoes a change in meaning as a result of the Pope's
particular idea of revelation, and we can only notice this
subtle change of the entire traditional faith in light of the
major texts. The Encyclical texts are also quoted in full to
save the reader the trouble of looking them up.[4]

2. Title–addressees–salutation.

An Encyclical's title, addressees, and salutation normally
require no special attention. But it is different in the case of
an unusual Encyclical.

The *title* is: *Redemptor Hominis*. To whom is the Encyclical dedicated: the Savior or mankind?

The author himself gives conflicting answers as to the
Encyclical's material object: One time he says that *Redemptor Hominis* is dedicated to the Son, and is the first Encyclical of his "trinitarian trilogy"[5]; another time, it is dedicated

---

3 The chapter and article headings correspond for the most part with
those of the official English translation. We will specify any differences.

4 The English translation is no slavish rendition of the Latin original,
but is meant to be easily grasped by the reader. We will quote the
Latin original (AAS 71 [1979], pp. 257-324) only in those places
where we deem it absolutely necessary. It is hard to understand why
the Latin text's solemn form "we" (nos) is rendered in English by the
first person singular.

5 John Paul II, at the announcement of *Dominum et Vivificantem* on
Pentecost Sunday 1986 in the noon address at St. Peter's (*OR*, dt.,
May 30, 1986, p. 1).

to man, as he says at the very beginning of *Dives in Miseri-cordia* (1980). We quote the whole passage from *Dives in Misericordia*, because it resolves the apparent contradiction (*DiM* 1,2):

> Following the teaching of the Second Vatican Council and paying close attention to the special needs of our times, I devoted the Encyclical *Redemptor Hominis* to the truth about man. a truth that is revealed to us in its fullness and depth in Christ. A no less important need in these critical and difficult times impels me to draw attention once again in Christ to the countenance of the "Father of mercies and God of all comfort." We read in the Constitution *Gaudium et Spes*: "Christ the new Adam...fully reveals man to himself and brings to light his lofty calling," and does it "in the very revelation of the mystery of the Father and of his love." The words that I have quoted are clear testimony to the fact that man cannot be manifested in the full dignity of his nature without reference—not only on the level of concepts but also in an integrally existential way—to God. Man and man's lofty calling are revealed in Christ through the revelation of the mystery of the Father and His love.

The reference to *Gaudium et Spes* 22 resolves the "contradiction." This Council text, which recurs in all Encyclicals of the "trinitarian trilogy" in conspicuous passages, is the decisive key text, from which the Pope derives the principle of knowledge in his *New Theology*, namely his man-centered idea of revelation and the faith.

In the light of this idea of revelation, the apparent contradiction vanishes by itself. The main thesis of man-centered "double revelation" runs:

"Revelation consists in a fact, the fact that by his Incarnation the Son of God united himself with every man, became man himself, one of us."[6] This "revelation *a priori*"

---

6 Cardinal Karol Wojtyla, [*Sign of Contradiction*] (Freiburg i. Br. 1979) p. 121.–Cf. for the concept of revelation: Introduction,

is the axiom of universal salvation. The Incarnation is accordingly not only the union of the Son with his human nature which he took from the Virgin Mary, but also the (formal) union with all men. The christological outlook is at the same time also anthropological. Thus the Encyclical is dedicated both to the Son and to man.

To revelation *a priori* corresponds revelation *a posteriori*, that is to say the historical revelation, through which Christ, by revealing the Father and his love, reveals to man the full dignity of his innermost nature. Therefore, by reason of the principle of man-centered "double revelation," the Encyclical's central reference point is *man, who has been redeemed and justified a priori.*[7]

Through this text from *Dives in Misericordia,* the Pope himself has given us the key to a clear understanding of the inaugural Encyclical and of its title:

The key to a clear understanding of the inaugural Encyclical is the Pope's idea of revelation. The title Redemptor Hominis *summarizes most concisely the thesis of universal salvation and places it programmatically at the beginning of the inaugural Encyclical and the new pontificate.*

Consequently, the Encyclical's addressees have a special significance: For the first time in the history of *dogmatic* Encyclicals, a Pope turns not only "to his venerable brothers in the episcopate, to the priests and religious families, to the sons and daughters of the Church," but also "to all men and women of good will." If the *Redemptor Hominis* is the Savior of man who is redeemed and justified *a priori,* then clearly all mankind belongs to the "hidden" Church.

In the list of addressees, the new Pontifex [= literally, a bridge-builder] *is already constructing the bridge to all mankind, in order to proclaim to them the new, more broad-*

---

above, Nr. 7, pp. 17-36.

7   Cf. Introduction, above, Nr. 7.1-2, pp. 18-24.

minded view of the Conciliar Church.[8]

The *Encyclical's salutation* runs: *"Venerabiles Fratres ac dilecti Filii."* Which of the addressees are the "Venerable Brothers and dear sons and daughters"? Of course the bishops and Catholics. But are the other addressees left out? In Assisi, the Pope addressed the representatives of the world religions also as "brothers and friends," exchanged fraternal greetings with them and sat at table with them.[9]

The *Encyclical's title, addressees, and salutation* are no mere humanitarian gesture embracing all mankind, but the expression of the new Pope's theology and conception of his duties: Through the Incarnation, the *Redemptor Hominis* has united himself inseparably with each man forever, and thus all mankind is "entrusted to the solicitude of the Church" (Cf. *RH* 13,3).

---

[8] John Paul II, Address to the clergy of Rome, where the conciliar "new outlook of the Church" is stressed as "an outlook which is more open for the universality of the people of God" (*OR*, dt. Mar. 8, 1991).

[9] See Footnote 1.

CHAPTER I

OUTLINE OF THE NEW PONTIFICATE*

1. Theme and main points of the Encyclical.**

The Encyclical's first two paragraphs (*RH* 1,1; 1,2) make a general statement of the theme and main points. Each paragraph can be considered as an organic whole.

1.1 General statement of the theme and main points.

As in any introduction to an extensive treatise, *Redemptor Hominis* begins the general statement of the theme and main points with some general indications.

The Encyclical begins as follows, give or take a few minor omissions (*RH* 1,1):

> The Redeemer of man, Jesus Christ, is the center of the universe and of history. To Him go my thoughts and my heart in this solemn moment of the world that the Church and the whole family of present-day humanity are now living. In fact, this time, in which God in His hidden design has entrusted to me, after my beloved predecessor John Paul I, the universal service connected with the Chair of St. Peter in Rome, is already very close to the year 2000.
>
> At this moment it is difficult to say what mark that year will leave on the face of human history....For the Church, the People of God spread...to the most distant limits of the earth, it will be the year of a great Jubilee. We

---

* Chapter heading in the English translation="Inheritance."
** Heading in the English translation="At the Close of the Second Millennium."

are already approaching that date, which...will recall and reawaken in us in a special way our awareness of the key truth of faith which St. John expressed at the beginning of his Gospel: "The Word became flesh and dwelt among us," (Jn. 1:14) and elsewhere: "God so loved the world that he gave his only Son, that whoever believes in him should not perish but have eternal life" (Jn. 3:16).

The *theme of the Encyclical* is: The Redeemer of man, Jesus Christ, is "the center of the universe and of history." To Him the Pope wishes to turn his mind and his heart in this unique moment of history which the Church and humanity are living.

The *main points* are: Jesus Christ, the Redeemer of man, and the present era. This general indication is specified as follows:

– The *Redeemer of man* is the center of the universe and of history: That glory is His through the Incarnation of the Logos. Thus the Encyclical's first main point is clearly defined: It is the "key truth of faith," the *Incarnation of the Son of God.* The author proclaims this truth–as climax and conclusion of the first paragraph–through the mouth of the Evangelist himself: "The Word became flesh and dwelt among us" (Jn. 1:14). Further, the author mentions the divine motive of the Incarnation immediately: "God so loved the world that he gave his only Son, that whoever believes in him should not perish but have eternal life" (Jn. 3:16).

– On the *uniqueness of our time*, a parallel statement is made: The year 2000 is near! This thought traverses John Paul II's entire pontificate. The Pope speaks again and again of the approaching year 2000 or beginning of the third millennium. He mentions it so frequently and so intensely, that the present era appears unique, not simply upon the reckoning of the secular calendar, but precisely because of its essentially religious, millenniarist character. The Encyclical's own words: "*haec ipsa aetas anno bis mille-*

simo iam admodum appropinquat," are instinctively reminiscent of Jesus' call to penance, by which he proclaims the beginning of the messianic age of salvation: "The kingdom of God is at hand!" (*appropinquavit regnum Dei,* Mk. 1:15).

This quasi-religious connection between our era and the year 2000 becomes manifestly religious, inasmuch as the Pope establishes the character of this date as the "important memorial anniversary" of the Incarnation of the Word.

Thus both main points of the theme are clearly defined: The Incarnation of the Son and the uniqueness of our era in their relation to the year 2000, the memorial anniversary of the birth of Christ. St. John's testimony on the Incarnation of the Son, whom the Father sent, that whoever believes in him should not perish but have eternal life, is a biblical teaching which in itself is far removed from the thesis of universal salvation. What is more, this passage requires faith for salvation, and thus refutes the thesis of universal salvation. But the Encyclical does not stop there. Rather, the Pope throws in another scriptural passage, this time from Hebrews, and states the main points of the Encyclical a second time, by which the final course of the Encyclical is then charted.

1.2 More specific and definitive statement of the theme and main points.

The second statement of the theme can also be considered as an organic whole. The unabridged text runs (*RH* 1,2):

> We also are in a certain way in a season of a new Advent, a season of expectation: "In many and various ways God spoke of old to our fathers by the prophets; but in these last days he has spoken to us by a Son ..." (Heb. 1:1-2) by the Son, His Word, who became man and was born of the Virgin Mary.
>
> This act of redemption marked the high point of the

history of man within God's loving plan. God entered the
history of humanity and, as a man, became an actor in
that history, one of the thousands of millions of human
beings but at the same time Unique! Through the Incarnation God gave human life the dimension that He intended man to have from his first beginning; he has
granted that dimension definitively–in the way that is
peculiar to Him alone, in keeping with His eternal love
and mercy, with the full freedom of God–and He has
granted it also with the bounty that enables us, in considering the original sin and the whole history of the sins of
humanity, and in considering the errors of the human
intellect, will and heart, to repeat with amazement the
words of the sacred liturgy: "O happy fault...which gained
us so great a Redeemer!"

In the first two sentences, the main points of the Encyclical are slightly modified, and appear as follows:

The Redeemer of man is the Word begotten eternally of
the Father, given a human nature by the Virgin Mary–and
the present era is a time of expectation, the time of a new
Advent.

At first glance, there seems to be no essential difference
with the first statement of the theme. A more exact consideration, however, brings out the new twist.

The first thing we notice: *In the second statement of the
theme, St. John's requirement of the faith for salvation is missing.*

The reason for quoting Hebrews 1:1-2 is obvious: There
is mention of the *Son*, through whom God *"in these last
days ... has spoken to us."* Thus the two starting-points towards the Encyclical's main points are clearly marked:
a) the Incarnation of the Son, and b) the "last times," the
new Advent.

a)   The Incarnation of the Son.

The Encyclical makes the following statements on the
saving deed of the Incarnation: The Son, through whom

God has spoken to us in these last times, is the "Word, who became man and was born of the Virgin Mary." The Encyclical seems to proclaim the central christological dogma of the Incarnation of the Word. But afterwards it says: In this saving deed, according to God's plan for salvation through His love, the history of mankind has reached its high point. For God Himself entered into the history of mankind. He became an actor in that history as a man, one of thousands of millions of human beings but at the same time Unique. Through the Incarnation, God gave human life that dimension which He wished it to have from the beginning. This He has done definitively, in a way peculiar to Him alone. The praise of this saving deed, which is in keeping with His eternal love and mercy, culminates in the *Exsultet* of the Easter Vigil.

On the foregoing, the reader will allow some questions and remarks:

According to the divine plan for salvation, of which surely the *Redemption* is an essential part, does the history of mankind already reach its high point with the Incarnation of the Son? Is it not rather with the redemptive sacrifice of the Cross, together with the Resurrection and the Ascension?—Christ's sacrifice on the Cross is the efficient cause of our Redemption and the "high point" of the glorification of God, which is continued perpetually through the risen Lord, who is the Lamb present "as though slain" before the throne of God; this is the supreme height of the heavenly liturgy (Apoc. 5,1ff.). The crib and the Cross cannot be divorced to the extent of proclaiming the Redemption a result of the Incarnation alone. If the latter were the case, then and only then could we say with the Encyclical, without reserve, that the Incarnation "marked the high point of the history of man." But is the Encyclical trying to say that the redemption and justification of all men is already accomplished through the Incarnation?

Of course we do not deny that the sole fact of the Incarnation gave human history a completely new dimension.[1] But the Encyclical claims that it is this dimension which God intended man to have from his first beginning, and further, *which God has granted definitively* (!)—"in the way that is peculiar to Him alone, in keeping with His eternal love and mercy." Does the Encyclical also claim that the effects of original and personal sin in human history cannot change the definitive character of this saving deed worked by God (= that all men are saved regardless of how they lead their lives)?

The wording of the Encyclical hardly allows any other interpretation than that already presented by Cardinal Wojtyla in *Sign of Contradiction* and constantly repeated by John Paul II in *Redemptor Hominis*[2]: The dimension which God not only intended for human life from the beginning, but also has given (!) through the Incarnation in a definitive manner proper to Him alone, is the formal union of the Son of God with each man, with all humanity.[3] The Encyclical re-affirms the same thesis: the thesis of universal salvation—only with different words.

This interpretation is corroborated by what the text omits, and should have included: There is no mention of the Cross, of the sacrifice in reparation for sin, of the necessity of applying the fruits of the Redemption to each individual, or of the subjective dispositions necessary to receive those fruits, namely penance, faith, and baptism. Therefore the liturgical praise of the Savior from the *Exsultet* of the Easter Vigil, which forms the conclusion and climax of the paragraph, is made in reference to the Incar-

---

[1] Cf. Matthias Joseph Scheeben, *Die Mysterien des Christentums* (Freiburg i. Br. 1951) [In English: *The Mysteries of Christianity*, trans. Cyril Vollert, S.J. (St. Louis, MO: B. Herder Book Co., 1946), p. 421]; Gesammelte Schriften [Complete Works], Vol. II, pp. 295-369. – See also Part I, pp. 67-78.

[2] E.g. *Redemptor Hominis*, 8,2; 13,1; 14,3; 16,1; 18,1.

[3] Cf. Part I, pp. 106ff.

nation of the Savior on Christmas.

We may conclude: As for Cardinal Wojtyla so also for Pope John Paul II, the Incarnation means not only the assumption of a human nature from the Virgin Mary by the Word begotten eternally of the Father, but also the formal union of the Son of God with all humanity–in the sense of a "more broad-minded Christology."[4] The Encyclical's seeming purely "Christ-centered" perspective becomes thereby purely man-centered, stemming from *the man-centered revelation a priori of the Pope's New Theology.–The Encyclical's first main principle is the axiom of universal salvation.*

b) The new Advent.

The "new Advent" is the second main principle of the Encyclical's theme. Years before, Pope Paul VI had already called our era a time of Advent.[5] Cardinal Wojtyla adopted this characterization of our era in *Sign of Contradiction.*[6] As Pope he makes the "new Advent" the all-embracing *category of his inaugural Encyclical in regard to salvation history.*

What does the Encyclical mean by a *"new Advent"?* Certainly not the first coming of Our Lord in His Incarnation!

The expression appears in the beginning (*RH* 1,2) and at the end (*RH* 22,6) of the Encyclical. Thus the "new Advent" forms almost the *central point of the Encyclical in regard to salvation history.* Moreover, the same expression comes up again in two other prominent passages (*RH* 7,1; 20,6).

The first mention is made with the initial sketch of the theme (*RH* 1,2):

> We also are in a certain way in a season of a new

---

4 Cf. Introduction, 7.4, pp. 32-36.
5 In *Populorum Progressio.*
6 Page 234.

Advent, a season of expectation: "In many and various
ways God spoke of old to our fathers by the prophets; but
in these last days he has spoken to us by a Son ..." (Heb.
1:1-2), by the Son, His Word, who became man and was
born of the Virgin Mary.

This expression from Hebrews reflects the New Testament's understanding of time: In that understanding, the
first Advent of the Son introduces the "last times," in
which Christians are living. They themselves are witnesses
to the coming of that great event of the transformation and
transition of the present world unto its perfection (Heb.
9:26; I Pet. 1:20; I Cor. 10:11). Since the Ascension, the
Church lives in expectation of the Lord's Parousia, the
Lord's second Advent (Acts 1:11). "Behold, I come
quickly," is the word of the Lord. "Amen. Come, Lord
Jesus!" (Apoc. 22:20), is the petition and *longing of early
Christianity*, but not just early Christianity. "*This word remains the yearning cry of the Church for all times.*"[7]

Early Christianity placed salvation history in the context
of world history as a time of expectation from the beginning to the Lord's first Advent, and from the Incarnation of
Christ until the His second Advent, which comprises the
Last Judgment at the end of history. This point of view on
salvation history prevailed uncontested in the Church's theology and liturgy–before Vatican II.

The Encyclical's "*new Advent*," however, presents a different view of salvation history, as becomes plain from
other relevant passages of the Encyclical. In the second
passage it is said (*RH* 7,1):

While the ways on which the Council of this century
has set the Church going, ways indicated by the late Pope
Paul VI in his first Encyclical, will continue to be for a
long time the ways that all of us must follow, we can at

---

7   Konstantin Rösch, *Das Neue Testament* [*The New Testament*] (Pad-
erborn 1953), p. 534, Footnote.

the same time rightly ask at this new stage: How, in what manner should we continue? What should we do, in order that this new advent of the Church connected with the approaching end of the second millennium may bring us closer to Him whom Sacred Scripture calls "Everlasting Father," *Pater futuri saeculi?* (Is. 9:6)

The third passage in the pastoral part of the Encyclical on the Eucharist and Penance runs (20,6): It is certain:

...that the Church of the new advent, the Church that is continually preparing for the new coming of the Lord, must be the Church of the Eucharist and of Penance. Only when viewed in this spiritual aspect of her life and activity is she seen to be the Church of the divine mission, the Church *in statu missionis*, as the Second Vatican Council has shown her to be.

The fourth passage is a "humble invitation to prayer," whereby the Encyclical reaches its final peak. It is said (*RH* 22,6):

We feel not only the need but even a categorical imperative for great, intense and growing prayer by all the Church. Only prayer can prevent all these great succeeding tasks and difficulties from becoming a source of crisis and make them instead the occasion and, as it were, the foundation for ever more mature achievements of the People of God's march towards the Promised Land in this stage of history approaching the end of the second millennium. Accordingly, as I end this meditation with a warm and humble call to prayer, together with Mary the Mother of Jesus (Acts 1:14), as the apostles and disciples of the Lord did in the Upper Room in Jerusalem after His ascension (Acts 1:13). Above all, I implore Mary, the heavenly Mother of the Church, to be so good as to devote herself to this prayer of humanity's new advent, together with us who make up the Church, that is to say the Mystical Body of her only Son. I hope that through this prayer we shall be able to receive the Holy Spirit coming upon us (Acts 1:8), and thus become Christ's witnesses "to the end of the earth" (*Ibid.*), like those who went forth from the Upper Room in Jerusalem on the day of Pentecost. With the apostolic blessing!

The Encyclical's most important statements on the new Advent are the following:

The new Advent is a characterization of the uniqueness of our present era. In that case, the traditional perspective of salvation history as expectation of the second Coming is automatically reduced to the present era, which begins with Vatican II and is "connected with the approaching end of the second millennium" (*RH* 7,1). *The new Advent includes thus a definite period of time, namely from Vatican II to the year 2000.*

The *nature of the expectation* in these last times is likewise specified: It is "a new stage of the journey," which should bring the People of God closer to the "*Pater futuri saeculi*" (*RH* 7,1). In the Vulgate this bible passage (Is. 9:6) announces the coming of the Messias with His kingdom of peace. The Encyclical says as much: May the people of God make "ever more mature achievements" in its "march towards the Promised Land in this stage of history approaching the end of the second millennium" (*RH* 22,6). The promised land is thus localized in our history. *Therefore the new Advent is the expectation of an essentially temporal objective, which the People of God are approaching.*

The "new Advent of the Church" suddenly becomes "the Church of the new Advent," which "must be the Church of the Eucharist and of Penance," which is "continually preparing for the new coming of the Lord" (20,6). "Only when viewed in this spiritual profile" is it "seen to be the Church of the divine mission" (*RH* 20,6):

Thus the "Church of the new Advent" includes also the expectation of a "new coming of the Lord"!

The "new coming of the Lord" has of course nothing to do with the traditional expectation of Our Lord's second coming, which comprises the Last Judgment at the end of history. But then what does it mean? The Encyclical says no more, except to affirm that the Church should be in constant–and sacramental–preparation for the "new coming of the Lord" (*RH* 20,6). This "new coming of the Lord" can only mean the establishment of the kingdom of world peace through the Messias in the third millennium. The context leaves room for no other interpretation.

The "Church of the new Advent" is a Church, *whose essence is determined by the expectations, nature and objectives of that new Advent*. But these are precisely in the context of the new perspective of salvation history, which is reduced to the present-day Church beginning with Vatican II and culminating with the year 2000, in other words the expectation of the "new coming of the Lord" and the promised messianic kingdom of peace in history. The Church, together with her sacraments and mission, changes course and sets out for this new Advent. The "Church of the new Advent" is a new Church: "Through the Second Vatican Council, she succeeded in re-defining her own essence."![8]

The "new Advent of the Church" is also the "new Advent of humanity" (*RH* 22,6). Both the Church and humanity share the same expectation with the same goals and purposes. In *Sign of Contradiction*, Cardinal Wojtyla already taught a "more broad-minded" idea of the Church, which includes all mankind.[9]

John Paul II likewise celebrates the Second Vatican Council as a "second" or "new Pentecost."[10] By that he means not only a pastoral, spiritual awakening, whereby Christianity entered a "new spring,"[11] but the "new Pentecost" also means, in the fullest sense, the rebirth of the

8 Karol Wojtyla, [*Sign of Contradiction*], p. 28.
9 *Ibid.*, pp. 26-28.
10 Cf. *Redemptor Hominis* 22,6.–In Santa Maria Maggiore, Dec. 8, 1990 (*OR*, dt., Dec. 14, 1990, p. 1) [*OR*, Eng. Dec. 10, 1990, p. 7].
11 John Paul II, *Redemptoris Missio* 2,2.

Church, therefore the Conciliar Church. *The "new Advent of the Church and humanity" and the "new coming of the Lord" also include the birth of the new "Church of the new Advent" with its new message and new mission* (cf. *RH* 20,6; 22,6).

The Encyclical closes with the grand vision of the Pope, in which he makes a connection between the "Church of the new Advent" and the early Christian community, between the "new Pentecost" and the first Pentecost (*RH* 22,6):

The present era as "the time of a new Advent of the Church and of humanity" is the subject of a "categorical imperative" for intense prayer. Prayer is the foundation upon which the Church should overcome all obstacles and make ever more mature achievements towards attaining "the Promised Land in this stage of history approaching the end of the second millennium." Then the Pope compares the present "new Advent of humanity" to early Christianity and extends the parallel to the early Christian community in Jerusalem, to the Ascension, to the Upper Room, and finally to Pentecost:

As Mary and the Apostles devoted themselves to prayer in the Upper Room after the Ascension to prepare for the "coming of the Holy Spirit from on high" at Pentecost, so also today should the Church pray with Mary for the coming of the Holy Ghost in the "new Advent of humanity."

Just as Mary and the Apostles, after receiving the Holy Ghost, "went forth from the Upper Room in Jerusalem on the day of Pentecost," so also should we who make up the Mystical Body of Christ–that is the "Church of the new Advent"!–"become Christ's witnesses 'to the end of the earth' (Acts 1:8)," after the reception of the Holy Ghost for which we have prayed. The new message of the witnesses of the "Church of the new Pentecost" is of course the same as the message of the "Church of the new Advent" in the "new Advent of humanity." To this cause the Pope gives his "apostolic blessing"!

It is obvious that the Pope's vision of the present era as the "time of a new Advent" has nothing in common with the New Testament's understanding of the expectation of Our Lord's second coming:

Up to Vatican II, the Incarnation of Christ, the first Advent of the Lord, and the manifestation of the Lord at the Last Judgment, the second Advent of the Lord, were accepted as fixed, immovable points in both world history and salvation history. After the Ascension, the Church, born on Pentecost and faithful to her mission, carried the message of expectation of the eschatological manifestation of the Lord "to the end of the earth." Both world history and salvation history were clearly understood as a sequence of objective, actual events, which took place at definite points in time. To speak of a "second Pentecost" or of a "new Advent of the Lord" as embodied in salvation history is simply not biblical.

Against the biblical view stands a new perspective of salvation history in the Encyclical: The "time of the new Advent" begins with the Second Vatican Council and ends with the year 2000, therefore with the anniversary of the Incarnation of the Son, with the "new coming of the Lord," with the establishment of the promised messianic kingdom of peace "in our history." The witness of the new message of the expectation of humanity is the "Church of the new Advent," which came into being and received a new "divine mission" through the Second Vatican Council, which was a "new Pentecost." She has been likewise sent to proclaim the "new coming of the Lord" and the message of the "new Advent," "to the end of the earth."

The traditional view of salvation history is not denied, but simply replaced by a new perspective. The question remains: How are we to understand the Pope's new perspective? Answer: As the fruit of existentialist hermeneutics.

According to this philosophy, the "historicity" of individuals and of our era is the basic structure of our understanding of history in general and of salvation history in particular. That means in our case: The sequence of objective, actual events, which took place at definite points in time, beginning with the "brute" historical event of the Incarnation and ending with the equally objective historical event of the second coming, in other words the "old" Advent of the Church, is absorbed into the "historicity" of the modern way of viewing history, is re-interpreted in light of its "relevance" for "today" as "something accomplished," and is finally re-oriented towards the "arrival of good things to come."[12] The basis for the existentialist hermeneutics in the Encyclical is therefore our present era, understood and presented as the "time of a new Advent," from which will emerge a new interpretation and understanding of revelation and salvation history.[13]

In this way the deposit of faith will be unhinged from its inviolable objectivity and cast afloat on the basis of existentialist "historicity," open to any "new interpretation," and all this on the pretext of the "spirit of the Council." From a "new awareness" of the Church, new "existentialist dogmas" can be processed at will. The Encyclical's new interpretation of the Advent of the Lord is an impressive exam-

---

12 Cf. Adolf Darlapp, Art. "Geschichtlichkeit," *LThK* IV, 780-783.–By the same author: *Fundamentale Theologie der Heilsgeschichte* [*Fundamental Theology of Salvation History*], Mysterium Salutis, I, 17-153.

13 Here are some characteristics of existentialist hermeneutics, which is based on the structure of historicity: The denial of the objective value of history, the absorption of the supernatural mysteries of Christianity into the realm of experience, the incorporation of the past into the present, the adapting of "what has been" to "what is to come," and the transformation of objective being into subjective consciousness. Cf. the lengthy dispute with existentialism from the standpoint of the *philosophia perennis*: Bernhard Lakebrink, *Die Wahrheit in Bedrängnis* [*The Truth in Distress*] (Stein a. Rhein 1986).

ple of the subtle, scarcely perceptible transformation and change in meaning of revelation and salvation history as a whole.

We may conclude: The final version of the Encyclical's two main points in the second statement of the theme runs: *The Incarnation of the Son in the sense of universal salvation and the uniqueness of our era as the "time of a new Advent."* Or to put it another way: Universal salvation in the new perspective of salvation history in general, and of the new Advent of humanity in particular.

1.3 Digression: Skillful arrangement and composition of the Encyclical.

Karol Wojtyla was a writer and poet. These he remained even as Pope. For an adequate understanding of the inaugural Encyclical, it is important to consider its skillful arrangement and composition. In order to grasp each sentence, one must consider the text as a whole. But we cannot show the skillful arrangement of each paragraph in detail here. Therefore let us show this aspect of the Encyclical in a specific instance, namely the paragraph we just quoted (*RH* 1,2).

In the Encyclical's second and final statement of the theme and main points, the quotation from Hebrews (*RH* 1,2) forms the starting point, the center and the reference point for the final version of its two main points. In order to grasp the full significance of the introduction to Hebrews in the Encyclical, we must have the entire text before us. The inspired text of Hebrews 1:1-4 runs as follows:

> God, who, at sundry times and in diverse manners, spoke in times past to the fathers by the prophets, last of all in these days hath spoken to us by His Son, whom He hath appointed heir of all things, by whom also He made the world. Who being the brightness of His glory, and the figure of His substance, and upholding all things by the word of His power, making purgation of sins, "sitteth on

the right hand" (Ps. 109) of the majesty on high. Being
made so much better than the angels, as he hath inherited
a more excellent name than they (Hebr. 1:1-4).

Traditional exegesis and dogmatic theology valued this
weighty introduction to Hebrews as the classical passage in
support of the Church's teaching on the inner relations in
the Trinity.[14] In the first sentence, the superiority of the
New Testament's revelation over that of the Old Testament
is emphasized, and the unique eminence of the Son, the
mediator of the New Covenant, is clearly presented: In the
messianic last times, revelation was proclaimed in its fulfillment through the Son (cf. Jn. 1:17). The divine dignity
and unique position of the Son is then set forth in three
relative clauses:

The Son is the Heir of the universe, because he is the
Son (Galatians). He is the Creator of the world. Two descriptions are given for illustration: "Brightness of His
glory" and "Figure of His substance." These express the
nature of the Son and his relationship to the Father. "As the
shining of the sunbeam to the sun, so the Son is related to
His Father: Both are equal, belong necessarily together for
eternity, and in such a way, that the nature of the Father is
not altered by the going forth of the Son. Just as the copy
produced through a seal is an exact duplicate of the original, so the Son is the perfect image of the Father; He is
generated by the Father, but entirely equal to Him. Both
descriptions express the Son's equality in nature with the
Father, while maintaining the distinction of persons. He
preserves and governs the world; He is the Savior of mankind, who sits at the right hand of the Father and has a
share in the divine power."[15]

---

14 Joseph Reuss, *Der Brief an die Hebräer* [*The Letter to the Hebrews*]
   (*Das Neue Testament* [*The New Testament*], Echter Bibel, Würzburg
   1952), pp. 39ff.

15 *Ibid.*

In accordance with the Church Fathers, this commentary on Hebrews 1:1-4 proceeds from the letter of the scriptural passage, and concludes with the Church's teaching on the "inner relations in the Trinity," namely the dogmatic statements on the nature of the Son and His relationship to the Father within the Trinity.

We find a totally different approach to the scriptural passage in the text of the Encyclical, which we quote again in full for the sake of comparison. Although *Redemptor Hominis* is supposed to be that part of the "trinitarian trilogy" which is "dedicated to the Son," the quotation from Hebrews is not the starting point for the Pope's teaching on the Trinity, but rather for his Redemption doctrine:

> We also are in a certain way in a season of a new Advent, a season of expectation: "In many and various ways God spoke of old to our fathers by the prophets; but in these last days he has spoken to us by a Son ..." (Heb. 1:1-2), by the Son, His Word, who became man and was born of the Virgin Mary (*RH* 1,2).

We cannot overlook the elegance of the style and the composition: The scriptural passage from Hebrews is encompassed by two statements: one on the present era as a "time of a new Advent" and the other on the Incarnation of the "Word, who was eternally begotten of the Father." The quotation from Hebrews (1:1-2) forms the nucleus of the two main points of the Encyclical, so that both have their common foundation in the same passage of Holy Scripture, from which they proceed. One and the same scriptural passage is therefore the theological starting point for the Encyclical's theme with its two main points, which through the quoted biblical passage are thus placed in direct relationship to each other. The fundamentally new version of the Encyclical's theme appears as a skillfully organized whole.

The Pope's subsequent remarks are an impressive development of the fundamental statement on the Incarnation of the Word, who was eternally begotten of the Father, a statement which finally reaches its climax with the words from the *Exsultet* of the Easter Vigil. What does this stylistic brilliance mean for the theological substance?

The comparison of the biblical text with that of the Encyclical clearly shows that the Pope does not faithfully reproduce the first sentence of the quoted text from Hebrews (...), but rather cuts it off before the important relative clauses involving the Son, "whom He (= the Father) hath appointed heir of all things, by whom also He made the world," despite the fact that these clauses would be best suited as a starting point for a trinitarian or Christ-centered exposition.

Instead the Encyclical supplements the interrupted biblical text by adding a personal reflection on the Son through the relative clause: "by the Son, His Word, who became man and was born of the Virgin Mary." The fact is, however, that not one of the numerous expressions on the Son in Hebrews (1:1-4) refers to His Incarnation. Why make an addition to the biblical text, so as to give the line of thought another twist? The obvious reason is the literary composition: By stating the Encyclical's theme, the Pope intends to delineate its main points in the process. And these are: the "new Advent" and the "Incarnation of the Word." Through the addition to the biblical text, the Encyclical's theme takes on its final shape.

For a correct understanding of the Encyclical's basic thrust, we must observe the remarks which directly follow, and which exclusively refer to the addition to the scriptural passage, that is to the "saving deed of the Incarnation of the Word" (see above 1.2 a, pp. 46-49). They are merely *an explanation of the addition, not of the scriptural passage itself.* And this explanation leads to the thesis on the Incarnation as a supernatural union of the God the Son with each human being, thus the axiom of universal salvation.

What, therefore, does this literary brilliance mean for the theological substance? By quoting Hebrews, the Encyclical skillfully makes a connection between its own main points and the Bible, and announces its theme at the outset with biblical impact. But neither of the two main points of the inaugural Encyclical is theologically warranted by the scriptural passage; nor has either principle anything to do with the genuine biblical sense. Nevertheless, the scriptural passage bears an outer resemblance to the Encyclical's main points.

The same holds for the literary arrangement of the entire paragraph, which culminates in the liturgical *Exsultet* of the Easter Vigil, but in praise of Christmas.

The understanding of the Encyclical results not only from its basic structure of existentialist historicity. We must likewise consider the skillful display and impeccable choice of texts, even those of Holy Scripture and the Liturgy. The latter are employed as mere instruments of composition in support of the writer's personal theological views, namely his *New Theology*. The literary brilliance of the presentation is acquired at the expense of theological precision and conceptual clarity.

2.   Theological orientation of the new pontificate.*

After the statement of the theme and main points (*RH* 1), there follows the theological orientation of the new pontificate (*RH* 2).

2.1 In service of the first fundamental truth of the Incarnation.

John Paul II describes the theological orientation of his pontificate in the form of a personal testimony (*RH* 2,1):

---

* Heading in the English translation="The First Words of the New Pontificate."

It was to Christ the Redeemer that my feelings and my thoughts were directed on October 16 of last year, when, after the canonical election, I was asked: "Do you accept?" I then replied: "With obedience in faith to Christ, my Lord, and with trust in the Mother of Christ and of the Church, in spite of the great difficulties, I accept." Today I wish to make that reply known publicly to all without exception, thus showing that there is a link between the first fundamental truth of the Incarnation, already mentioned, and the ministry that, with my acceptance of my election as Bishop of Rome and Successor of the Apostle Peter, has become my specific duty in his See.

The Pope is telling us that, at the conclave, he directed his "feelings and thoughts to Christ the Redeemer" and that he accepted his election to the papacy "with obedience in faith to Christ." In the public declaration, he makes sudden reference to "the first fundamental truth of the Incarnation, already mentioned (thus in the answer given at the conclave)." *But this truth of the Incarnation is nowhere mentioned at the conclave!*

There is really something novel about the solemn declaration of a statement which was never made at the conclave: The (new Pope's) "obedience in faith to Christ" is not the same as the service which is linked to the "first fundamental truth of the Incarnation."

One could easily pass over this kind of personal testimony as unimportant, were it not a question of such a significant fact as *the solemn declaration, by the Pope himself, of the fundamental theological orientation of the new pontificate.* We could paraphrase this orientation–without reference to the conclave–as the Pope's "personal testimony" in the following words:

I would like to proclaim to everyone publicly and hereby attest, that the service of the first fundamental truth of the Incarnation is the purpose of my entire activity on the Chair of Peter.

We may conclude: In the line of successors to the Apostle Peter in the Roman See, John Paul II considers it his prime responsibility to serve the "first fundamental truth of the Incarnation." But, for the Pope, the Incarnation means not just the union of a human nature with the Word, who was eternally begotten of the Father and born of the Virgin Mary, but rather the supernatural union of the Son with all humanity, in the sense of a "more broad-minded Christology," therefore the thesis of universal salvation.

The fundamental theological orientation of the new pontificate is therefore identical with the first main principle of the Encyclical's theme.

2.2 Recognition of the inheritance left by the Council Popes; attachment to the Tradition of the Roman See.

A further statement of the theological orientation of the new pontificate is contained in the Pope's likewise personal explanation of his choosing the double name John Paul II (*RH* 2,2):

> Through these two names and two pontificates I am linked with the whole tradition of the Apostolic See and with all my predecessors in the expanse of the twentieth century and of the preceding centuries.
> I am connected, through one after another of the various ages back to the most remote, with the line of the mission and ministry that confers on Peter's See an altogether special place in the Church. John XXIII and Paul VI are a stage to which I wish to refer directly as a threshold from which I intend to continue, in a certain sense together with John Paul I, into the future, letting myself be guided by unlimited trust in and obedience to the Spirit that Christ promised and sent to His Church.

There follows a series of scriptural passages on the Holy Ghost from the Gospel of St. John (16:7; 15:26; 16:13), which forms the stylistically effective climax and conclusion of the whole paragraph of the Encyclical (*RH* 2).

With two statements the Pope outlines the orientation of his pontificate:

a) Through both names and both pontificates, namely of John XXIII and Paul VI, he is linked to the entire tradition of the Roman See, all the way back to St. Peter.

To manifest this solidarity, John Paul II deems it sufficient to refer to the "two names and two pontificates" of the Council Popes. Period! End of discussion! The Encyclical practically ignores two thousand years of Church Tradition. And yet the reference to both Popes and both pontificates pretends to include the Church's entire tradition from St. Peter up to and including Vatican II.

b) In the same breath, the Pope himself gives the reason for what is in fact the divorce of his pontificate from the Church's entire tradition:

John XXIII and Paul VI represented a historic era, which for him is the immediate threshold, from which he is called upon to forge ahead into the future. The historic central point of his pontificate includes therefore precisely the "new stage" of the Church's course, which begins with Vatican II and approaches the end of the second millennium: It is "the time of the new Advent of the Church."

Coming from a Polish Pope with a distinct historical awareness, the reduction of two thousand years of tradition of the Roman See to the conciliar era is simply astonishing—and very suggestive!

John Paul II clearly intends to align his pontificate on the unique inheritance of the Council Popes, in order to preserve it and to develop it further. The new Pontiff understands himself decidedly and unconditionally as a Pope of the Conciliar Church. He considers Vatican II as a "new Pentecost" and sees the post-conciliar era as the time of a special outpouring of the Holy Ghost.

This article of the Encyclical, which clearly sets the theological orientation of the new pontificate (*RH* 2), culminates with stylistic effectiveness in three scriptural passages on the Holy Ghost from the Gospel of St. John. The last of them seems like a prophecy spoken especially for our time (Jn. 16:13): "When the Spirit of truth comes, he will guide you into all the truth; for he will not speak on his own authority, but whatever he hears he will speak, and he will declare to you the things that are to come."–What is "all the truth" and "the things that are to come" in the perspective of the "new Advent of the Church"?

We may conclude: The theological and pastoral orientation of John Paul II's new pontificate can be summed up in one sentence: The foundation is the unique inheritance of the Council Popes, which at the same time is the threshold, from which the Pope intends to forge ahead into the future, in order to "develop it further." *The Encyclical's temporal perspective of the new pontificate is the "new Advent of the Church," the second main principle of the Encyclical.*

3. The inheritance left by the Council Popes and the "present-day consciousness of the Church."*

In the Encyclical, the recognition of the person and work of the Council Popes, the description of the "present-day consciousness of the Church," and the judgment of the current situation in the Church are several points which are intertwined (*RH* 3; 4). Each point, however, will be treated here individually.

3.1 Recognition of the Council Popes.

On the list of his predecessors in the office of Peter, John Paul II only acknowledges the inheritance of the Council Popes, but the person and achievements of Paul VI receive more special treatment. That is understandable, since John XXIII convened the Council, but died soon after on Pente-

---

* Heading in the English translation="Trust in the Spirit of Truth and of Love."

cost 1963, and since John Paul I reigned for little more than a month.

Paul VI is judged exclusively on his merits for bringing the Council to a successful close and for implementing the Council's decisions in the life of the Church. He is praised for his wisdom, his courage, his constancy and his patience in the implementation of the Council's decisions (*RH* 3,1). Special emphasis is given to Paul VI's respect for "every particle of truth contained in the various human opinions" (*RH* 4,2).

John Paul II attaches great importance to Paul VI's first Encyclical *Ecclesiam Suam*, to which he refers and on which he aligns his own Encyclical *Redemptor Hominis*. The particular reference points are Paul VI's remarks on the "dialogue of salvation" and the "present-day consciousness of the Church" (*RH* 3,2; 4,1).

3.2 The "present-day consciousness of the Church."

In an idealist existentialism, *time and consciousness* are in a sense Siamese twins. The influence of existentialism on Karol Wojtyla's thinking is suggested by his frequent reference not only to time (see above 1.2 b, pp. 49-57), but also to "consciousness." By the mere fact that John Paul II defines the inheritance of the Council Popes *with respect to the "consciousness of the Church,"* he betrays his existentialist thinking.

After John Paul II has clearly stated that the inheritance of the Council Popes is the foundation of his pontificate and at the same time represents the threshold, from which he intends to continue the implementation of Vatican II, *he shows the extent to which this inheritance has taken root in the consciousness of the Church* (*RH* 3,1):

> Entrusting myself fully to the Spirit of truth, therefore, I am entering into the rich inheritance of the recent pontificates. This inheritance has struck deep roots in the

awareness of the Church in an utterly new way, quite unknown previously, thanks to the Second Vatican Council, which John XXIII convened and opened and which was later successfully concluded and perseveringly put into effect by Paul VI, whose activity I was myself able to watch from close at hand. I was constantly amazed at his profound wisdom and his courage and also by his constancy and patience in the difficult post-conciliar period of his pontificate. As helmsman of the Church, the bark of Peter, he knew how to preserve a providential tranquillity and balance even in the most critical moments, when the Church seemed to be shaken from within, and he always maintained unhesitating hope in the Church's solidity. What the Spirit said to the Church through the Council of our time, what the Spirit says in this Church to all the Churches (cf. Apoc. 2:7) cannot lead to anything else–in spite of momentary uneasiness–but still more mature solidity of the whole People of God, aware of their salvific mission.

The paragraph goes on to say (*RH* 3,2):

Paul VI selected this present-day consciousness of the Church as the first theme in his fundamental Encyclical beginning with the words *Ecclesiam Suam.* Let me refer first of all to this Encyclical and link myself with it in this first document that, so to speak, inaugurates the present pontificate. The Church's consciousness, enlightened and supported by the Holy Spirit and fathoming more and more deeply both her divine mystery and her human mission, and even her human weaknesses–this consciousness is and must remain the first source of the Church's love, as love in turn helps to strengthen and deepen her consciousness. Paul VI left us a witness of such an extremely acute consciousness of the Church. Through the many things, often causing suffering, that went to make up his pontificate he taught us intrepid love for the Church, which is, as the Council states, a "sacrament or sign and means of intimate union with God, and of the unity of all mankind" (*Lumen Gentium* 1).

Within 33 lines of the quoted text, the "consciousness of

the Church" or of the "People of God" is mentioned no less than six times! This is characteristic of the important role which "consciousness" plays in the Pope's theology.

The most important statements on the "consciousness of the Church" give us the following general picture:

– Thanks to Vatican II and its realization in the life of the Church, the inheritance of the Council Popes has "struck deep roots in the awareness of the Church" in a completely new way, which was previously unknown. This is an admission to the sheer revolutionary effect of the conciliar inheritance on the consciousness of the Church.

– As the Holy Ghost spoke through the Council, so today he continues to speak to the Church, the people of God, who are "aware of their salvific mission," and he gives them "still more mature solidity,"–"in spite of momentary uneasiness." The Pope is here saying three things:

– Firstly, the Council is acclaimed as the voice of the Holy Ghost. This acclaim raises a self-professed pastoral Council, twenty years after the fact, to the highest conceivable theological status. It is declared a "super dogma," which it by no means is (cf. Ratzinger).

– Secondly, what holds for the Council still holds for us "today," thus for the post-conciliar era. Hence the implementation of the Council in the post-conciliar period is sanctioned with the same divine authority.

– Thirdly, the message of the Holy Ghost, spoken at the Council, gives more firm solidity to the People of God, who are "aware of their salvific mission."

Is that really the case? It was before Vatican II that the Catholic Church enjoyed a unique status of firm stability, both in her ecumenical conversations and in her missionary activity, thanks to the clear and unyielding position of the Roman authorities, who were "aware of their salvific mission."[16] Does the post-conciliar practice of pluralism, ecu-

---

16 Cf. my essay, "Das II. Vatikanum: Radikale Zäsur in der Missions-

menism and interfaith dialogue really indicate a "still more mature solidity," when coupled with the timid qualification "in spite of momentary uneasiness"? But the "momentary uneasiness" means nothing less than the revolutionary impact of the Council on the entire faith and practice of the Church!

We can now attempt–by way of intermediate summary– a basic, general definition of the nature and extent of the new "consciousness of the Church": It is and includes, across the board, what the Holy Ghost has spoken, and still speaks today, to the Church through the Council. Thus the "new consciousness" is the "conciliar consciousness of the Church." Because of its divine origin, it assumes a pretentious air. But nothing concrete has been said yet about its exact nature.

The new conciliar consciousness, of course, differs from the old pre-conciliar consciousness of the Church. But the latter must, "in spite of momentary uneasiness," be brought up to date with the new conciliar consciousness according to the principle of the *accommodata renovatio Ecclesiae*.[17]

– The new conciliar consciousness is simply referred to as the "present-day consciousness of the Church," which Pope Paul VI "selected ... as the first theme in his fundamental Encyclical ... *Ecclesiam Suam.*"

"Present-day" consciousness? How can an Encyclical from the year 1964 speak of the "present-day consciousness of the Church" which *Redemptor Hominis* (1979) mentions, when the latter was promulgated fifteen years after the former? The wording of the Latin original bridges the gap: The "present-day" consciousness (*hac aetate!*) really

---

geschichte?," in: *Die eine Wahrheit und die vielen Religionen* [*One Truth and Many Religions*] (Abensberg 1988), *Respondeo* 8, 111-128.

[17] Cf. 4,2, pp. 81-87: Evaluation of the *accommodata renovatio Ecclesiae*.

means the consciousness "of these times," "of this era." The present-day consciousness is therefore an *epoch-making consciousness.*

Nevertheless: How could Paul VI claim to expound on the "epoch-making, conciliar consciousness of the Church" in *Ecclesiam Suam,* since the Encyclical was promulgated (Aug. 6, 1964) before he even saw either the final text of *Lumen Gentium* (Nov. 21, 1964), or of *Gaudium et Spes* (Dec. 7, 1965), or of *Nostra Aetate* (Oct. 28, 1965), or of *Dignitatis Humanae* (Dec. 7, 1965), or before he even experienced the revolutionary consequences of the Council for the stability of the faith and of missionary activity in the Church up to the inaugural Encyclical of John Paul II in the year 1979? How could Paul VI give an adequate treatment of the "conciliar consciousness" in *Ecclesiam Suam,* before the Council even promulgated the final draft of its major documents?

Therefore the question remains: What can possibly be meant by the "present-day conciliar consciousness of the Church"?

There can be no question of an actual, historically verifiable "present-day consciousness" of the universal Church, nor for that matter of a "conciliar consciousness of the Church" in light of Council documents already promulgated. The "present-day conciliar consciousness of the Church" must therefore be *a buzzword behind which lurks an updated understanding of the Church, which will soon begin to take shape, like the famous slogan "spirit of the Council,"* and which everyone can interpret as he pleases. What specifically does the Pope mean by the "present-day conciliar consciousness of the Church"?

– John Paul II declares *Ecclesiam Suam* as the basis of his own Encyclical, in which he further develops the idea of the "present-day consciousness of the Church."

There he gives us further characteristics of this consciousness: It is "enlightened and supported by the Holy

Spirit." By these words, the Pope invests the present-day consciousness of the Church *with an absolute and unquestionable status.*

– This "conciliar present-day consciousness of the Church," which is "enlightened and supported by the Holy Spirit," is also claimed to be "fathoming more and more deeply both her divine mystery and her human mission." *The buzzword: "Present-day consciousness of the Church," develops a spiritual momentum by which it becomes personified* (cf. "Sapientia" in the book of Wisdom).

– If we now ask what is the function and purpose of the conciliar "present-day consciousness of the Church" in the faith and practice of the People of God, we receive the following answer: It "is and must remain the first source of the Church's love"–and this love, from which the "present-day consciousness of the Church" springs (!), "helps to strengthen and deepen" that consciousness.

Hence the "present-day consciousness of the Church," which is produced, enlightened, and supported by the Holy Ghost, is also *the principle ("source") and the abiding norm ("is and must remain") of love for the Church.* Because of its divine origin, it has an *absolute, normative character.*

What kind of Catholic regards the "present-day consciousness of the Church" as the first and abiding source of his love for the Church? The first and abiding source of his love for the Church should be no vague "present-day consciousness of the Church," but simply his faith in Christ and in the One, Holy, Catholic, and Apostolic Church founded by Christ. His love for the Church does not spring from a "conciliar consciousness," but rather from his faith in an objectively revealed reality, namely the Church, which exists quite independently of our consciousness. Now the Pope is calling upon Catholics to acknowledge the conciliar "present-day consciousness of the Church" as the first, abiding source and norm of their love for the Church.

– Finally it is said: Paul VI "left us a witness of such an extremely acute (!) consciousness of the Church." Whether John Paul II understood his predecessor correctly is an open question.

Are we ever going to find out specifically what *dogmatic importance* this present-day consciousness of the Church has, which is said to be extremely acute, was produced, enlightened, and supported by the Holy Ghost, and took up roots in the inheritance of the Council Popes in an entirely new way, never known before? This question is answered in the last sentence: The Church has come to realize–through the Council–that she is the "sacrament or sign and means of intimate union with God, and of the unity of all mankind" (*Lumen Gentium* 1,1).

For the Pope, it is through this "realization" at the Council that the "present-day consciousness of the Church" has found its doctrinally adequate expression. Or conversely: In the context of the Encyclical, the "present-day consciousness of the Church" is the adequate expression of that dogmatic realization at the Council.

As a matter of fact, the quotation from *Lumen Gentium* 1,1 is the key text *not only for the Council's, but also for the Encyclical's concept of the Church.*[18] It forms the stylistically suspenseful climax and conclusion of the entire article of the Encyclical (*RH* 3), while at the same time serving as the direct starting point for the Pope's further reflections on the "consciousness of the Church" (*RH* 4). Up until now, it is the only concrete statement on the dogmatic importance of that consciousness. Apparently, this dogmatic statement is plain and clear for the Pope. That is why he is content with the mere indication of the Council's realization without

---

[18] Cf. Aloys Grillmeier, Herder-Kommentar zu *Lumen Gentium*, *LThK* XIII, 157: "This vocation of the Church, namely to be a light for the Gentiles in Christ, is contained in a sentence which is the very heart of the Constitution's ecclesiology: 'The Church in Christ is in the nature of sacrament ...'"

any commentary, in order to continue from there with a deeper explanation of the consciousness of the Church (*RH* 4).

But the sense of the key text from *Lumen Gentium* 1,1 is not so clear and simple for us, neither in the Council document nor in the Encyclical. Therefore we must discover the precise dogmatic import of that key text before going into the Pope's subsequent remarks on the consciousness of the Church.

3.3 Digression: The Church as the sacrament of unity in the consciousness of the people of God.

In the Pope's vocabulary, "consciousness" comes to the forefront so often (*RH* 3), that one cannot help reducing the "new outlook on the Church," which Vatican II gave us,[19] to a mere question of consciousness and not of dogma. According to the classical teaching, there can always be a new, more broad-minded consciousness of the Church, but not a more broad-minded dogma of the Church. *But the crucial point is dogma.*

As for the question of the dogmatic import of the "present-day consciousness of the Church," the Pope (*RH* 3,2) answers by pointing out the "realization" of the Council:

> The Church is "a sacrament or sign and means of intimate union with God, and of the unity of all mankind" (*Lumen Gentium* 1,1).

This sentence is of capital importance not only for the entire ecclesiology of the Dogmatic Constitution on the Church,[20] but also for that of the Encyclical *Redemptor*

---

19 John Paul II, Address to the clergy of Rome, where the conciliar "new outlook of the Church" is stressed as "an outlook which is more open for the universality of the people of God" (*OR*, dt. Mar. 8, 1991).

20 See footnote 18.

Hominis. The Council's definition gives us the key to the adequate dogmatic understanding of the "present-day consciousness of the Church," even if the Pope's hymn of praise for that consciousness virtually drowns out the Council's definition.

The Council text is rather vague; it is neither plain nor clear. The use of the term "sacrament" is unusual. Since when is the Church simply a sign or instrument "of the unity of all mankind"? Since Vatican II! With this definition, the Council follows the "signs of the times," which point "in the direction of the unity of all mankind."[21]

The majority of the Council Fathers most likely understood and interpreted the definition according to the Church's traditional teaching. And many commentaries strive to uphold that traditional understanding.

Thus says the Herder commentary (Aloys Grillmeier): The Council text is somewhat reserved in its expression. It gives no definition or explanation of "sacrament," nor any indication as to how this idea should be applied to the Church. But then again, the idea of the Church as sacrament of salvation has an intimate connection to the patristic and modern ecclesiology. This idea has its ultimate foundation in the biblical expression *Mysterion*, which means God's entire economy of salvation. Through the Latin translation of the Bible, which renders the term *Mysterion* by *Sacramentum*, it became standard usage in the theology of the Fathers to designate the Church also as *Mysterion-Sacramentum*. The Constitution therefore intends to restore the ancient usage of "referring to the Church in its sacramental signification and instrumentality in the entire divine economy of salvation for all mankind throughout history. It is the 'universal sacrament of salvation' (Art. 48,2)."[22]

---

21 Aloys Grillmeier, *op. cit.*, p. 158.
22 *Ibid.*, p. 157.

As for the crucial question of how the unity of all mankind is accomplished by the Church, the commentary answers: Through the incorporation of mankind into the Church. In that case, salvation in Christ was likewise communicated to all mankind, who all belong to the eschatological family of the children of God. The commentary goes on to interpret the Council text on the Church as sacrament of unity in this very sense: "Since this Church of perfection is mankind's sole objective, it is the Council's duty to proclaim with all her might the universal meaning of this sacrament of salvation."[23] The attempt to give the Council text an orthodox interpretation is rather obvious, but is it also a faithful interpretation of the text?

It is simply not true that the Council text–"reserved in its expression"–gives no definition or explanation of the term sacrament, nor any indication for its application. Quite the contrary, the text loses no time in giving the definition and application of the term: The Church is "a sacrament or sign and means of intimate union with God, and of the unity of all mankind." That describes "the function of the Church," as the commentary of Rahner-Vorgrimler correctly observes.[24] But even that is only half the truth: The crucial point of the sentence is precisely the fact that the Church calls herself a sacrament (i.e. by her very nature), which she then defines as her function. That means: The Church's "function" is to be a sacrament, that is, a "sign and means." There is no mention of incorporation into the Church; the Council's definition speaks only of the Church as a sacrament for the unity of all mankind. Up to Vatican II, however, the Church never identified the community of those redeemed in Christ with the community of all mankind; she never understood herself as simply

---

23 *Ibid.*, p. 158.
24 Karl Rahner, Herbert Vorgrimler, *Kleines Konzilskompendium* [*A Small Compendium of the Council*] (Freiburg i. Br. 1966), p. 106.

an instrument for the unity of all mankind. Instead, her missionary activity was aimed at the union of all nations in the new people of God. The purpose of her mission was therefore *the new supernatural unity of mankind in the Mystical Body of Christ, in the Church with her marks, which St. Paul defines with the following words*: "One body and one spirit ... One Lord, one faith, one baptism, one God and Father of all" (Eph. 4:4ff). Through Christ and the mission of the Church, mankind is in a state of "krísis," i.e. judgment, having to make a decision for or against the faith.

In contrast, the Council text as it stands can easily be understood and interpreted *in the sense of the thesis of universal salvation.*

It is obvious that the term "sacrament" in *Lumen Gentium* 1,1 does not correspond to the biblical *Mysterion*, nor has it anything to do with the patristic *Mysterion-Sacramentum*, but it is *the expression of modern ecclesiology.*

The recognition of non-Christian religions as legitimate means of salvation, instituted by God, the proclamation of the universality of the Redemption and divine grace in the context of "anonymous Christianity," both of these represent a theological breakthrough which was made even before the Council. In this light, the Church was regarded as a "sign"of universal salvation and as an "instrument" to make anonymous Christians conscious of their Christianity.[25]

If the non-Christian world is "anonymous Christianity," then there exist *a priori* an unconscious union of all persons with Christ and a hidden "ontological" unity of the Church and mankind, then we can regard all mankind as a "hidden" Church. Thus what we call the Church is the "sign"of universal salvation and at the same time the "in-

---

25 Heinz Robert Schlette, *Die Religionen als Thema der Theologie* [*Religion as the Theme of Theology*] (Freiburg i. Br. 1963).–Eugen Hillman, *The Wider Ecumenism* (London 1968).–Et al.

strument" for the unity of all mankind, and acts in that capacity by her "missionary dynamism," whereby she makes all men aware of the unconscious, hidden, yet real unity of all mankind in Christ, and, by proclaiming revelation *a posteriori* to all mankind, announces the grace of God given to everyone *a priori–then the mission of the Church to bring about "the unity of all mankind" in God and in Christ is merely a question of consciousness.*

In the present stage of theology, there is a strong consensus: The Council text on the Church as sacrament of unity in *Lumen Gentium* 1,1 is understood in the sense of universal salvation. That holds also for Cardinal Wojtyla, even as Pope. In *Sign of Contradiction*, his commentary on this Council text is succinct: "All men are included in this sacrament of unity" (p. 37). The new more broad-minded idea of the Church is also defined there: "The Church of the living God unites all men" (p. 27).

We may conclude: The sentence: The Church is "a sacrament or sign and means of intimate union with God, and of the unity of all mankind," sentence which is essential for the entire ecclesiology of the constitution *Lumen Gentium* and for the Encyclical *Redemptor Hominis*, is tantamount in the Encyclical to the thesis of universal salvation, to the more broad-minded Christology and ecclesiology. This is how he defines the dogmatic import of the "present-day consciousness of the Church."

4. Worldwide broadening of the Church's consciousness and the *accommodata renovatio Ecclesiae.**

In the fourth article, the Pope locks into the Council text on the Church as sacrament of unity (LG 1,1), develops his meditation on the "present-day consciousness of the Church" (4,1), and closes with a brief assessment of the *accommodata renovatio Ecclesiae* (4,2).

---

* Heading in the English translation="Reference to Paul VI's First Encyclical."

4.1 Broadening of the Church's consciousness to all persons.

Following the Council's definition: The Church is, in Christ, the "sacrament ... for the unity of all mankind," the Pope continues (*RH* 4,1):

> Precisely for this reason, the Church's consciousness must go with universal openness, in order that all may be able to find in her "the unsearchable riches of Christ" (Eph. 3:8) spoken of by the Apostle of the Gentiles. Such openness, organically joined with the awareness of her own nature and certainty of her own truth, of which Christ said: "The word which you hear is not mine but the Father's who sent me" (Jn. 14:24), is what gives the Church her apostolic, or in other words her missionary, dynamism, professing and proclaiming in its integrity the whole of the truth transmitted by Christ. At the same time she must carry on the dialogue that Paul VI, in his Encyclical *Ecclesiam Suam* called "the dialogue of salvation," distinguishing with precision the various circles within which it was to be carried on (AAS 56,650 ff).

The text offers a self-contained line of reasoning, which proves that, from the new *dogmatic self-image* of the Church, the *postulate* of the worldwide broadening of her consciousness emerges, which determines the character of her new, more broad-minded mission:

Since "the Church is the sacrament ... for the unity of all mankind," "the Church's consciousness must go with universal openness" (*Hac ipsa de causa conscientia Ecclesiae coniungatur oportet cum animo cunctis patente*), "in order that all may be able to find in her 'the unsearchable riches of Christ.'" And this spiritual outlook of openness to all (*Eiusmodi animus universis patens*) is in turn "what gives the Church her apostolic, or in other words her missionary, dynamism."

To the extremely acute, epoch-making, conciliar "present-day consciousness of the Church," which is produced, enlightened, and supported by the Holy Ghost, the Pope adds yet another feature: It is open for all, so that all can find in the Church the riches of Christ. *This openness is the missionary dimension of the present-day consciousness of the Church.*

We can summarize as follows the Pope's missionary theology, as manifested in his pontificate:

– Firstly, the "present-day consciousness of the Church" has a clearly definable dogmatic import, namely the "realization" of the Council:

> The Church is "a sacrament or sign and means of intimate union with God, and of the unity of all mankind" (Lumen Gentium 1,1).

In the Encyclical, this "fact" should be understood in light of the more broad-minded Christology and ecclesiology (cf. Digression, pp. 73-77). That means the dogmatic widening of the Church's traditional teaching. Never before did the Church understand herself and the mystery of the Redemption in the sense of universal salvation, or "anonymous Christianity."

The new definition of the Church's nature by the Second Vatican Council is a new dogma of the new Church, the "Conciliar Church."[26]

– Secondly, *the reason for demanding the worldwide broadening of consciousness is the broadening in the area of dogma: Since* the Church is the "sacrament ... for the unity of all mankind," "the Church's consciousness *must* go with universal openness" (*cum animo cunctis patente*). That stands to reason: For the "present-day consciousness of the Church" is the mainspring for the widening of dogma. We are in fact dealing with an *authentically new more broadminded consciousness of a new Church*, thanks to its recent, more broad-minded dogmatic origin.

---

26 Karol Wojtyla, [*Sign of Contradiction*], p. 28.

The Church of Christ was always synonymous with the Catholic Church, which was essentially open to everyone, to all mankind from the beginning. Any misunderstandings in the early Church were cleared up once and for all through St. Paul's struggle for freedom from the law: The new covenant is a covenant for Jews and Gentiles, that is to say for all men (Eph. 2:11-22). Did the Church need a further broadening of her consciousness? The Pope seems to think so (cf. *RH* 11,1).

– Thirdly, the widening of dogma and the broadening of the Church's consciousness has a definite goal: so that all men can find in her the riches of Christ. This purpose results from the nature of the Church, which is a sign and instrument for the unity of all mankind. *The Conciliar Church is "by its very nature" missionary.*[27]

– Fourthly, the Church strives after this missionary goal through her *"missionary dynamism."* This is what characterizes the Pope's *"missionary method"*:

This missionary dynamism bursts forth from the conciliar broadening of dogma and of the Church's consciousness. It is therefore of the same nature. For so we read: The worldwide broadening of the Church's consciousness, which is "organically joined with the awareness of her own nature and certainty of her own truth," also determines the nature of the Church's missionary dynamism. That awareness of her own nature and that certainty of her own truth are of course to be understood in light of the new definition of the Church's nature, which is to be, in Christ, a "sacrament for the unity of all mankind."

This missionary dynamism becomes manifest in two ways:

On the one hand through preaching: The Church professes the "whole truth," the truth of the Father, "transmit-

---

[27] The Church was always missionary by her very nature. Cf. *Ad Gentes* 2.

ted (!) by Christ." – Of course the Pope does not mean the old (incomplete) truth, but the new "more complete awareness of the mystery of Christ," which was bestowed on Christianity for the first time with Vatican II (cf. *RH* 11,3). The Church's more complete message on the mystery of Christ is universal salvation.

On the other hand through dialogue: Through the interfaith "dialogue of salvation," the Church overcomes her old narrow-minded consciousness and matures to a "full, universal self-awareness" (*RH* 11,1).–Thus she finds the work of the Holy Ghost in all men and in all religions (cf. *RH* 6,3 et al.).

The Pope's missionary theology possesses the inner unity of a broad-minded *progress of consciousness*: If the Son of God, through his Incarnation, has formally united himself with each person (see above 1.2, pp. 45-57), and if each man possesses *a priori* being in Christ as an essential part of human nature, then mankind's "coming unto himself" is a question of consciousness. If all men *a priori* "are included in the Church as the sacrament of unity,"[28] then the discovery of the riches of Christ in the Church is also a question of consciousness, then the mission of the Church to realize in Christ the unity of all mankind is likewise a question of consciousness.

Thus John Paul II has clearly outlined the missionary theology of his pontificate.

In the text quoted above, the Pope mentions the Apostle of the Gentiles as well. But St. Paul's mission was not founded on the axiom of universal salvation. For him, the discovery of the riches of Christ was not a mere question of consciousness, but of faith in Christ crucified.

4.2 Evaluation of the *accommodata renovatio Ecclesiae*.

---

[28] Karol Wojtyla, [*Sign of Contradiction*], p. 37.

For John Paul II, the chief exponent and model for the realization of the Church's missionary dynamism is the Council Pope Paul VI, who in *Ecclesiam Suam* demonstrated and successfully embarked on the way of dialogue (*RH* 4,2):

> In referring today to this document that gave the program of Paul VI's pontificate, I keep thanking God that this great predecessor of mine, who was also truly my father, knew how to display *ad extra*, externally, the true countenance of the Church, in spite of the various internal weaknesses that affected her in the post-conciliar period. In this way much of the human family has become, it seems, more aware, in all humanity's various spheres of existence, of how really necessary the Church of Christ, her mission and her service are to humanity. At times this awareness has proved stronger than the various critical attitudes attacking *ab intra*, internally, the Church, her institutions and structures, and ecclesiastics and their activities.

The Pope further mentions the criticism of "triumphalism," recalls the duties of love of the Church and what he calls "the attitude of service," and finally thanks Paul VI, "because, while respecting every particle of truth contained in the various human opinions, he preserved at the same time the providential balance of the bark's helmsman."

From the Encyclical's point of view—whether founded or unfounded—Paul VI understood how to display "the true countenance of the Church" outwardly, and to make her known and loved as such to most of the world. Of course the Pope is here referring to the new countenance of the Conciliar Church, as she has manifested herself since Vatican II, above all in the interfaith congresses and prayer meetings. Unquestionably the non-Christian world finds this countenance more sympathetic than that of the Catholic Church before the Council. But is the new countenance of the Conciliar Church the "true countenance" of the

Church, especially when she leads the prayer dance of all religions?

From her foundation, the Church displayed her "true countenance" *ad extra* by proclaiming to everyone their obligation to enter the Church in order to be saved, since the Church's mission is to make disciples of all nations, by leading all men to be disciples of Christ through faith and baptism (cf. Matt. 28:18-20). Has all this been preached to mankind? And if so, has "much of the (non-Christian) human family," which has for quite some time experienced a renaissance of their religions,[29] really become *"more aware" of this obligation, this mission and this service of the Church?*

As we know, the display of the Conciliar Church's countenance has also led to critical reactions "from the inside." But we are told that the new conciliar consciousness "has proved stronger."

These expressions give rise to the idea *that the accommodata renovatio Ecclesiae ad intra and ad extra is the principle* by which the Pope judges the missionary proclamation of Paul VI.

As far back as the year 1968, the Council Father Karol Wojtyla put this principle into an essay with the following words:

> In the course of theological study of the Council documents, one must bear in mind the general picture and thereby refer constantly to certain ideas or even guiding principles, such as *accommodata renovatio*, ecumenism, or dialogue.[30]

These guiding principles of his study become later the main ideas of his pontificate. The most far-reaching of the

---

29 Georg Vicedom, *Die Weltreligionen im Angriff auf die Christenheit* [*The World Religion's Attack on Christianity*] (Munich 1961).

30 Karol Wojtyla, *Von der Königswürde des Menschen* [*On the Kingly Dignity of Men*] (Stuttgart 1980), p. 153. Cf. Part I, pp. 20-24.

three main ideas is the *accommodata renovatio Ecclesiae*. *It presents the practical guidelines for conciliar renewal in the Church.* This renewal is understood as a dynamic transformation of the consciousness, which, on the basis of the "present-day conciliar consciousness of the Church," transforms the life of the Church on a wide scale. This comes about as follows:

The basis for the process of renewal within the Church is the "stage of consciousness which the Church has reached through the Council."[31] But that is precisely what we described above, namely the "epoch-making, conciliar, missionary, present-day consciousness of the Church," which comes from the Holy Ghost and is therefore also an absolute norm. On this basis follows the transformation of the consciousness both *ad intra*, i.e. renewal within the Church, and *ad extra*, i.e. the adaptation of the conciliar consciousness to the world. The whole program of the *accommodata renovatio Ecclesiae* can be reduced to the formula: Adaptation of the pre-conciliar to the conciliar present-day consciousness of the Church, and adaptation of the conciliar consciousness to the "modern world." The absolute status given to the "present-day conciliar consciousness" shows the intolerant character of the principle of the *accommodata renovatio*, which in the modern Church is apt to become an instrument for the suppression of the "pre-conciliar consciousness" of the Church. In that perspective, nothing seems worse than the "relapse into pre-conciliar thinking"!

It is significant that the process of updating the Church consciousness *ad intra* and *ad extra* is considered in terms of "stronger" or "weaker," as though the conflict with the Church's pre-conciliar position did not involve serious issues and dogmatic truths. But this process will be imposed by force under the name of conciliar consciousness.

---

[31] Cf. Part I, pp. 15-19.

– Considering the post-conciliar crisis of faith which has affected the whole Church, it is very interesting, and revealing for the new pontificate, to see how John Paul II views and judges the current condition of the Church in his inaugural Encyclical. Here is his assessment (*RH* 4,2):

> The Church that I–through John Paul I–have had entrusted to me almost immediately after him is admittedly not free of internal difficulties and tension. At the same time, however, she is internally more strengthened against the excesses of self-criticism ...more resistant with respect to the various "novelties," more mature in her spirit of discerning, better able to bring out of her everlasting treasure "what is new and what is old" (Matt. 13:52), more intent on her own mystery, and because of all that more serviceable for her own mission of salvation for all: God "desires all men to be saved and to come to the knowledge of the truth" (I Tim. 2:4).

The article closes with I Tim. 2:4, the catch-all phrase for any version of the thesis of universal salvation! – The assessment is overwhelmingly positive.

Paul VI gave a more sober analysis of the post-conciliar condition of the Church: Already three years after the Council, in the famous address of June 30, 1968 which proclaimed the "Credo of the People of God," he tried to put a stop to the collapse of the faith and the "self-destruction of the Church." Without success! On the feast of Saints Peter and Paul in 1972, he gave a shocking description of the internal condition of the Church: "The smoke of Satan has entered through a crack into the temple of God: Doubts, uncertainty, calling into question, uneasiness, discontent, confrontations have become prevalent ... Doubt has entered into our conscience."[32] A shocking admission!

No less critical is Joseph Ratzinger's assessment of the

---

[32] Cf. *Ibid.*, pp. 43-46.

Church's situation. Formerly a *peritus* at the Council, he says the following in his book *The New People of God*, which appeared in 1969 (p. 325):

> The image of the Church of modern times has changed, and is characterized by the fact that it has become, and will continue to become still more, the Church of pagans: no longer the Church of pagans who have become Christians, as she used to be, but the Church of pagans who still call themselves Christians. Paganism is at home today in the Church, and that is typical of the Church of modern times as well as of the new paganism, which both involve a paganism in the Church and a Church in whose hearts paganism dwells. We are not speaking here of that paganism which has become a united front against the Church in the Eastern countries....But we mean that much more typical phenomenon of our time which constitutes the real threat for Christians, namely paganism within the Church, the "abomination of desolation in the holy place" (Mk. 13:14).

Later on as Prefect of the Congregation for the Faith, Joseph Ratzinger, in his book *The Ratzinger Report* (1985), unrolls before our eyes the whole panorama of theological currents, which threaten the Catholic faith and water down the foundation of the Church. His analysis ran up against the most vehement opposition: The opposition accused him of relapsing into pre-conciliar thinking. At that time, it was still taboo even to suggest a crisis of faith in the Church!

In light of the current situation, John Paul II's view appears simply preposterous. He mentions "difficulties and tensions," but does not speak of the crisis of faith, let alone its causes. Nevertheless, the Pope's judgment is fully understandable from the point of view of the *accommodata renovatio Ecclesiae*.

The conciliar renewal of the Church is thus understood as a gradual transformation of the Church's consciousness as a whole, in which the present-day consciousness of the Church, supported by the Holy Ghost, enjoys absolute status. For the advance of this process, the main element is the forced imposition of the genuinely new conciliar consciousness. Therefore the inaugural Encyclical is not a rebuttal of the "dogmatically outdated stage of consciousness of the pre-conciliar Church," but simply the positive presentation and defense of the novel, progressive tendencies of Vatican II.

In this respect, the Encyclical's positive assessment of the current situation in the Church is fully consistent: The conciliar inheritance had in fact "struck deep roots in the awareness of the Church in an utterly new way, quite unknown previously" and furthermore, in all areas of the Church's life, had developed its progressive transforming power within the Church and in the Church's relations to the modern world. The purpose of the process of renewal is precisely the wide-scale transformation of the old Church, which re-defined her own essence at the Second Vatican Council.

John Paul II completely approves of the development begun by Vatican II with its broadening of dogmatic horizons. He deems it his task to help the Church's "apostolic, or in other words, missionary dynamism" to achieve a radical breakthrough, inspired by the main ideas of ecumenism and interfaith dialogue.

5. The main objective of the pontificate: the unity of all mankind.*

The main objective of the new pontificate is the unity of all mankind. It is no individual initiative. John Paul II is determined to follow in the footsteps marked out by the Council and Paul VI (*RH* 7).

The objective is clearly defined: It is the broadening of the consciousness of the Church, especially in her doctrine, which produces her missionary dynamism, which *per se* is

---

* Heading in the English translation="Collegiality and Apostolate."

designed to achieve the unity of all mankind. The basic tenet for the Church's entire ecclesiology: The Church is "a sacrament or sign and means of intimate union with God, and of the unity of all mankind" (LG 1,1), already expresses this clear statement of purpose: The unity of all mankind.

The Encyclical indicates the means to attain this objective: the main ideas of ecumenism and dialogue (*RH* 5 & 6). The starting point is the unity of the Church (*RH* 5). From thence proceed all efforts of the ecumenical, more broad-minded Church in search of "Christian unity" (*RH* 6,1.2). The ecumenical unity of Christianity is in turn the starting point for all efforts in search of the unity of all religions (*RH* 6,3).

5.1 Church unity.

On assuming office, John Paul II sees no dangers for the unity of the Church. On the contrary! He says (*RH* 5,1):

> In spite of all appearances, the Church is now more united in the fellowship of service and in the awareness of apostolate. This unity springs from the principle of collegiality, mentioned by the Second Vatican Council. Christ Himself made this principle a living part of the apostolic college of the Twelve with Peter at their head...

Hence the *unity of the Church* springs from the newly discovered *"principle of collegiality."*

This principle, bestowed by Christ on the college of the apostles, marks the *Church's entire juridical structure.* The Encyclical elaborates on this point (*RH* 5,1-2):

> The Second Vatican Council not only recalled the "principle of the collegiality of bishops," but also animated and developed it in new way, e.g. in the Roman synod of bishops, in the national episcopal conferences and other collegial structures whether international or continental, in the various diocesan and provincial syn-

ods, and in the collaboration with the metropolitan structure.
The same spirit of collaboration and shared responsibility is also spreading in priestly organizations, organizations for lay apostolate, in conjunction with the Pastors and representatives of the Institutes of consecrated life, and in the spheres of diocesan synods and of the pastoral councils in the parishes and dioceses.

The Pope welcomes this development, encourages everyone to continue in it, and recalls (*RH* 5,3):

> with heartfelt gratitude the work of the Second Vatican Council and my great predecessors, who set in motion this new surge of life for the Church, a movement that is much stronger than the symptoms of doubt, collapse and crisis.

Thus the Church, which, thanks to the *principle of the collegiality*, is "united in the fellowship of service and in the awareness of apostolate," is fully equipped to pursue the important ecumenical objectives of the pontificate and to fulfill her mission as a "sign and instrument for the unity of all mankind."

The singular feature of this starting point is its clash with traditional teaching:

The Encyclical mentions only the "principle of collegiality," from which the unity of the Church springs. *But there is no mention of the unity of faith and worship!*

With the First Vatican Council, classical theology distinguishes between *two kinds of unity in the Church*: the *unity of faith* (*unitas fidei*) and the *unity of communion* (*unitas communionis*). The unity of faith consists in the acknowledgement of those truths clearly defined by the Church and presented in the Catholic creed (= symbolic unity); the unity of the community consists in the unity of government (= hierarchical unity) and worship (= liturgical unity).[33] *The unity of faith is fundamental. The unity of*

___
33 Ludwig Ott, *Fundamentals of Catholic Dogma* (St. Louis: Herder

communion cannot exist without the unity of faith.

The unity of faith is destroyed through heresy; the unity of communion is broken through schism.[34] Hence the non-Catholic "confessions" are institutionalized heresies or schisms. On this basis, the only hope for restoration of the ruptured unity among Christians lay in conversion, in the return to the fold of the Catholic Church. From this teaching followed also the practice of the Catholic Church, up to Vatican II, in her relations with non-Catholics and with non-Christians (cf. *Mortalium Animos*, see Part I, pp. 1-7).

Vatican II was a startling breach of the Catholic Church's pre-conciliar doctrine and practice. The Council's ecumenical broadening of horizons represents the beginning of a novel development on a novel dogmatic basis: *The theological basis for the Church's "new ecumenical orientation" is the widening of Church dogma.*

In front of this backdrop, the Encyclical's *dogmatic position* (*RH* 5) is clear: The *unity of the Church* is reduced to the *unity of communion*, which in turn is reduced to the *"hierarchical unity,"* which is defined as the "principle of the collegiality." The *unity of faith* is entirely left out.

Considering the main ecumenical objectives of the pontificate, that means that the defined, traditional articles of the Catholic faith are blurred out *a priori*. Thus the faith is no major criterion in the Church's "new ecumenical orientation," which seeks after the all-embracing unity of all mankind.

This downplaying of the faith results from the silent refusal of the traditional concept of the Church, which is unobtrusively replaced by that of *Lumen Gentium* 1,1. That might account for the astonishing fact that, *in the entire Encyclical, the Church is never once called by her name: Catholic or Roman-Catholic Church.*

Book Company, 1954), p. 303f.

34 *Ibid.*, p. 304.

Since the Pope establishes "collegiality" as the only "principle of Church unity," it is now possible, on the basis of the new concept of the Church: The Church is "a sacrament or sign and means of intimate union with God, and of the unity of all mankind," that is to say based on the thesis of universal salvation, to strive for the main objective of the pontificate. And no one need trouble himself about unity in the faith of the Catholic Church.

6. Christian unity.*

The first main objective of the pontificate ad extra is universal "Christian unity."

John Paul II is determined to seize upon and pursue the course of ecumenism, which John XXIII expressed with "evangelical clarity," which Vatican II covered "in its *Decree on Ecumenism,*" and for the attainment of which Pope Paul VI began the first difficult steps, "availing himself of the activities of the Secretariat for Promoting Christian Unity" (*RH* 6,1). He begins with a question on the progress of that development:

> And what shall I say of all the initiatives that have sprung from the new ecumenical orientation? (*RH* 6,1)

His assessment of the "new ecumenical orientation" is positive. The fruits are judged as "real and important advances" (*RH* 6,1). Therefore the quest for that unity must continue at all costs (*RH* 6,1):

> For it is certain "that in the present historical situation of Christianity and the world the only possibility we see of fulfilling the Church's universal mission, with regard to ecumenical questions, is that of seeking sincerely, perseveringly, humbly and also courageously the ways of drawing closer and of union. Pope Paul VI gave us his personal example for this."

---

* Heading in the English translation="The Road to Christian Unity."

These ecumenical initiatives, to which there is no alternative, are thus a fulfillment of the will of Christ and a
demonstration of loyalty to His words (*RH* 6,1). Nevertheless the Church encounters strong reactions from within
(*RH* 6,2):

> There are people who in the face of the difficulties or
> because they consider that the first ecumenical endeavors
> have brought negative results would have liked to turn
> back. Some even express the opinion that these efforts are
> harmful to the cause of the Gospel, are leading to a fur-
> ther rupture in the Church, are causing confusion of ideas
> in questions of faith and morals and are ending up with a
> specific indifferentism. It is perhaps a good thing that the
> spokesmen for these opinions should express their fears.
> However, in this respect also, correct limits must be main-
> tained.

Thus not everyone views the fruits of ecumenism as "real
and important advances." The most serious biblical, dogmatic, and moral concerns against "the new ecumenical
orientation," which had by then already led to an indisputable protestantizing of the Catholic Church, were of course
rated as false alarms, and rejected on the whole.

There are many Catholics who feel that the substance of
their faith is in danger, especially with the clearly expressed
guidelines of the pre-conciliar Popes in mind (cf. Pius XI,
Mortalium Animos). The Pope admonishes these Catholics
to maintain "correct limits," and he gives them a brief
lesson on the nature of "true ecumenical activity" (*RH*
6,2):

> It is obvious that this new stage in the Church's life
> demands of us a faith that is particularly aware, profound
> and responsible. True ecumenical activity means open-
> ness, drawing closer, availability for dialogue, and a shared
> investigation of the truth in the full evangelical and Chris-
> tian sense; but in no way does it or can it mean giving up

or in any way diminishing the treasures of divine truth that the Church has constantly confessed and taught.

The instruction on "true ecumenical activity" follows the well-known scheme of the Church's "apostolic, or in other words missionary dynamism" (*RH* 4,1) in its double aspect: On the one hand, the Pope demands a deep faith and adherence to the Church's constant teaching; on the other hand, he demands "openness" and a "shared investigation of the truth in the full evangelical and Christian sense." This paradox of the Pope's ecumenism should suffice to assuage the doubts of those who express concern.

The following, final "argument" leaves no grounds for opposition to ecumenism by those inside the Church (*RH* 6,2):

> To all who, for whatever motive, would wish to dissuade the Church from seeking the universal unity of Christians the question must once again be put: Have we the right not to do it? Can we fail to have trust—in spite of all human weakness and all the faults of past centuries—in our Lord's grace as revealed recently through what the Holy Spirit said and we heard during the Council? If we were to do so, we would deny the truth concerning ourselves that was so eloquently expressed by the Apostle: "By the grace of God I am what I am, and his grace towards me was not in vain" (I Cor. 15,10).

Is the Church allowed to resist the grace of Christ and the word of the Holy Ghost? All who have problems with "the new ecumenical orientation" are confronted with this truly disarming question! The ecumenical "openness" is a divine mandate which allays all fears and leaves no other alternative! A quote from the Bible marks the persuasive climax.

The Encyclical's remarks express the theological orientation of the new pontificate on the question of ecumenism! They give us the following *general outline*:

– Firstly, conciliar ecumenism admittedly represents "a new orientation," "a new stage in the Church's life." How can this be justified?

The *theological justification* runs as follows: The Church's "new ecumenical orientation" is simply a consequence of Our Lord's words expressed in the Upper Room at the Last Supper (*RH* 6,1). The Church set out on the road to ecumenism in virtue of "Our Lord's grace as revealed recently through what the Holy Spirit said and we heard during the Council."

There is no recourse against this "final court of appeal"!

The Pope does not tell us the exact nature of that eschatological revelation. But one thing is clear: The new revelation of the grace of Christ is the axiom of universal salvation, of which the Church has "recently" become aware through the word of the Holy Ghost during the Council.

Hence the connection with the two main points of the Encyclical's theme: with the axiom of universal salvation and with the "last times," the "season of a new Advent."

– Secondly, in this "new stage in the Church's life," she has made "real and important advances." The conciliar assessment is always positive! It is therefore imperative to continue in that course, to the exclusion of all alternatives–despite all protests and concerns expressed within the Church.

Those opposed to ecumenism are told what "true ecumenical activity" is, namely two things: On the one hand, "openness, drawing closer, availability for dialogue, and a shared investigation of the truth in the full evangelical and Christian sense"; on the other hand, adherence to the "divine truth that the Church has constantly confessed and taught."–The contradiction is unmistakable:

The *shared investigation of all Christians* for the truth means per se that no special denomination may claim to possess the truth. Everyone is in search of the truth, including the Catholic Church.

In search of which truth?—Answer: "the truth in the full evangelical and Christian sense"! Therefore not in *the full Catholic sense of doctrines infallibly preserved and taught by the magisterium (fides quae creditur)*. The truth after which all aspire "in the full biblical and Christian sense" is of course not identical with the defined truth in the full sense of the Catholic faith, which most men do not want anyway.

Up to Vatican II, the believing Catholic was by no means part of a shared investigation with all non-Catholics on a constant search for an undefined truth in the full evangelical and Christian sense, but he was devoted and attached to the faith of the Catholic Church. The Catholic faith was the confident acceptance of doctrines defined by the Church with the claim of infallibility. Thus the Catholic faith was obedience in the faith.

To define the common search of Christians of all denominations for the truth in the full evangelical and Christian sense as the basis of "true ecumenical activity" is for the believing Catholic an *absolute novelty*, both with regard to the act of faith (*fides qua*) and with regard to the objective truths of the faith (*fides quae*). *Yes, we are looking at the new foundation of a new ecumenical Church and theology.*

After the Pope has urged Catholics to take part in the shared investigation of the truth in the full evangelical and Christian sense, he urges them in the same breath to protest their *unwavering adherence* to the "divine truth that the Church has constantly confessed and taught."

The contradiction is striking—as well it should be for the Pope! For the Catholic Church up to Vatican II has "constantly confessed and taught" that she is the one and only Church founded by Christ, and the sole divinely invested, infallible guardian of revealed truth. Up to Vatican II, she laid an exclusive, "intolerant" claim to teach the truth and to govern in the name of Christ. The purpose of her "true ecumenical activity" (*Una Sancta*) was the unity of all Christians in *the truth of the Catholic faith*, therefore the return of all those separated from her to the fold of the One, Holy, Catholic, and Apostolic Church. The Pope has thus clearly abandoned the pre-conciliar teaching of the Catholic Church (cf. *Mortalium Animos*).

The new path to universal Christian unity: the shared investigation of the truth in the full evangelical and Christian sense, means the abandonment of the Catholic Church's claim to teach and to govern in the name of Christ. It also means the watering down of Catholic dogma and the self-destruction of the infallible magisterium by the Pope himself.

This "true ecumenical activity," which of course includes common ecumenical services and activities at all levels, has led to the protestantizing of the Church and produced the consciousness of imperfect unity among Christians. The Encyclical speaks of "real and important advances"! This assessment follows from the conciliar standpoint of the *accommodata renovatio Ecclesiae*.

Thanks to "true ecumenical activity," the pre-conciliar consciousness of the Church was transformed into the conciliar, epoch-making, missionary, ecumenical, present-day consciousness, which was produced and supported by the Holy Ghost, and to which there is no alternative! The absolutism in this line of reasoning is typical of existentialist thinking and also of the intolerance in the process of updating: The serious objections against post-conciliar ecumenism are not refuted by sound arguments, but simply dismissed as expressions of needless worry and totally pushed aside by the continuation of ecumenical practice, with an appeal to the eschatological revelation of the Holy Ghost.

The "new ecumenical orientation" is an *absolute novelty in the history of the Catholic Church and represents an undeniable break with pre-conciliar doctrine and practice*. At least the Encyclical is consistent when it discreetly regrets the pre-conciliar Church's attitude as "faults of past centuries" (cf. *RH* 6,2), but it is intellectually dishonest to disguise an obvious break with tradition by pretending to uphold the "divine truth that the Church has constantly confessed and taught" (cf. *RH* 6,2).

In the spirit of sincerity, the Encyclical claims to continue the path of "true ecumenical activity" (*RH* 6,1). But we are witnessing intellectual bankruptcy when an indisputable break with tradition is flatly denied and when at the same time the novelty of the Church's ecumenical orientation is maintained, with an appeal to a new eschatological revelation of the grace of Christ and to the word of the Holy Ghost in favor of the Church's new path. A "pastoral Council" suddenly becomes a dogmatic "Super-Council," which succeeded in "re-defining" the nature of the Church.[35]

What the Encyclical says about the path to universal Christian unity can also be applied, "although in another way," to the path towards the unity of all religions.

6.1 Unity of all religions.

The second main objective ad extra of the pontificate of John Paul II is the unity of all religions.

In addition to the *accommodata renovatio* and ecumenism, dialogue is the third main idea for achieving the unity of all mankind. The dogmatic foundation for conciliar ecumenism and interfaith dialogue is the same in both cases: the thesis of universal salvation. The same main ideas will be achieved therefore, "although in another way." Everything that the Encyclical says about ecumenism holds also, *mutatis mutandis*, for interfaith dialogue, with the unity of all religions in view. Thus it is said (*RH* 6,3):

---

[35] Karol Wojtyla, [*Sign of Contradiction*], p. 28.

What we have just said [about ecumenism] must also be applied–although in another way and with the due differences–to activity for coming closer together with the representatives of the non-Christian religions, an activity expressed through dialogue, contacts, prayer in common, investigation of the treasures of human spirituality, in which, as we know well, the members of these religions also are not lacking. Does it not sometimes happen that the firm belief of the followers of the non-Christian relig-ions–a belief that is also an effect of the Spirit of truth operating outside the visible confines of the Mystical Body–can make Christians ashamed at being often them-selves so disposed to doubt concerning the truths revealed by God and proclaimed by the Church and so prone to relax moral principles and open the way to ethical permis-siveness. It is a noble thing to have a predisposition for understanding every person, analyzing every system and recognizing what is right; this does not at all mean losing certitude about one's own faith or weakening the princi-ples of morality, the lack of which will soon make itself felt in the life of the whole societies with deplorable con-sequences besides.

The Pope's fundamental thesis, which comes out more clearly in the Latin original than in the English translation, runs as follows: The firm conviction of non-Christian be-lievers proceeds from the Spirit of truth, who operates out-side the visible confines of the Mystical Body (*firma persua-sio non christianas religiones profitentium–quae et ipsa procedit a Spiritu veritatis, extra fines aspectabiles Corporis mystici operante*). The theological reference to the "firm (religious) belief of the followers of the non-Christian relig-ions" is unusual: It is the fruit of the "Spirit of truth" operating in non-Christian religions, that very Spirit, *whom Our Lord in the Upper Room* (Jn. 15:26f) *specifically promises to the Apostles alone.* Thus the Encyclical makes the general statement in such an offhand manner (in parenthe-ses!): The "Spirit of truth," which was bestowed on the Church at Pentecost, operates "outside the visible confines of the Mystical Body," therefore also in non-Christian religions. He is not only in the Church, but operates in all religions. The existence of "visible" confines is unquestionable. But in this perspective, on a deeper plane, "ontologically" considered, can such "visible confines of the Mystical Body" still exist? Does not everyone belong to the "invisible" Mystical Body?

On this dogmatic foundation, the Encyclical clearly sets its goal: the unity of all religions. The way to get there is by mutually drawing closer. It comes about, just as with ecumenism, in the context of the Church's "missionary dynamism" in its double aspect: On the one hand, the process of coming closer together is accomplished "through dialogue, contacts, prayer in common, investigation of the treasures of human spirituality." If "true ecumenical activity" consisted in "the shared investigation of the truth in the full evangelical and Christian sense," here in the case of non-Christians religions, there is "the search after the treasures of human spirituality," which is also produced by the "Spirit of truth," therefore by the Holy Ghost.–On the other hand, Christians are urged to conduct this search "without losing certitude about one's own faith or weakening the principles of morality." Of course, the certitude about one's own faith implies the new dogma of universal salvation. This is the only conceivable explanation for such a paradoxical process of coming together, but then the paradox is only apparent.

The Pope's general theological and psychological line of reasoning is remarkable: We are given only a partial, rather selectively positive view of non-Christian religions. The high opinion of the non-Christian religions is further accentuated by the fact that their firm beliefs, inspired by the Spirit of truth, are extolled to the skies, to the shame of Christian believers. In relationship to the non-Christian religions, the Christians are expected to show a new openness, a new kind of virtue: The noble predisposition "for understanding every person, analyzing every system and recognizing what is right." The sharp contrast, which exists between the truths of Christianity and precisely those firm religious convictions of non-Christians, is swept under the carpet. The same for the Church's duty to preach the Gospel and to baptize all nations in the Catholic faith: it is simply ignored.

The Encyclical's "theology of religions" brushes aside the pre-conciliar point of discussion: The possibility of non-Christians to be saved was never denied in the pre-conciliar Church; the point is that non-Christian religions as such are not means of salvation. Moreover, the largely differing central views of these religions were taken into account: Judaism with its denial of Christ; Islam with its denial of the Trinity, the Incarnation and the Redemption; Buddhism and Hinduism with their versions of pantheism. In the Pope's New Theology, distinctions and analyses of this kind simply do not seem to apply. The subjective principle of revelation *a priori* is finally the sole criterion for the assessment of non-Christian religions.

We may conclude: The Conciliar Church's openness aims at "*coming closer together with the representatives of the non-Christian religions, an activity expressed through dialogue, contacts, prayer in common, investigation of the treasures of human spirituality.*" There we have the clear marking of John Paul II's theological journey to the prayer meeting of religions in Assisi—and to the unity of all religions!

Hence, already in his inaugural Encyclical *Redemptor Hominis*, the Pope considers prayer in common with the representatives of all religions as the main objective of his pontificate. The text quoted above sounds like the theological overture to Assisi—and like the burial service for the Church's mission to teach and baptize all nations, which is not even mentioned once.

CHAPTER II

THE MYSTERY OF THE REDEMPTION

The second Chapter (*RH* 7-12) is wholly dedicated to the Encyclical's central theme, the mystery of Redemption. So it contains the Encyclical's doctrine of Redemption.

7. The Redeemer of man in the present-day consciousness of the Church.*

John Paul II states his determination to move forward along the path shown by the Council and by Paul VI in his Encyclical *Ecclesiam Suam* (*RH* 7,1).

> What should we do, in order that this new advent of the Church connected with the approaching end of the second millennium may bring us closer to Him whom Sacred Scripture calls "Everlasting Father," *Pater futuri saeculi* (Is. 9:6)?

To this question there is "only one fundamental and essential response" (*RH* 7,2):

> Our response must be: Our spirit is set in one direction, the only direction for our intellect, will and heart is – towards Christ our Redeemer, towards Christ, the Redeemer of man.[1] We wish to look towards Him – because there is salvation in no one else but Him, the Son of God – repeating what Peter said: "Lord, to whom shall we go? You have the words of eternal life" (Jn. 6:68; cf. Acts

---

[1] Latin text: "*intellectus, voluntas, cor ad unum Christum, Redemptorem nostrum, sunt dirigenda, ad Christum, hominis Redemptorem.*"

* Heading in the English translation="Within the Mystery of Christ."

4:8-12).

The formulation of the start of the doctrine of Redemption and that of the theme at the beginning of the Encyclical are similar (cf. *RH* 1). The two openings are in content identical. In both cases the main points are: Jesus Christ, the Redeemer of man, and the uniqueness of our era (cf. *RH* 1;1,2).

The context in which the "basic question" and the "fundamental answer" are set, give the reader from the outset clearly to understand that the Encyclical is developing its theology of the Redemption in the perspective of the "new Advent of the Church," as part of salvation history.

In the Pope's thinking, time and consciousness belong inseparably together. Together with the time of the new Advent goes the "present-day consciousness of the Church" (cf. *RH* 3;4). Hence we are now called upon to make the turning of our thoughts to the Redeemer of man not only in the perspective of the "new Advent," but also within the present-day conciliar consciousness of the Church. Thus he says (*RH* 7,3):

> Through the Church's consciousness, which the Council considerably developed, through all levels of this self-awareness, and through all the fields of activity in which the Church expresses, finds and confirms herself, we must constantly aim at Him "who is the head" (cf. Eph. 1:10, 22; 4:25; Col. 1:18), through whom are all things and through whom we exist (I Cor. 8:6; cf. Col. 1:17), who is both "the way, and the truth" (Jn. 14:6), and "the resurrection and the life" (Jn. 11:25), seeing whom, we see the Father (Jn. 14:9), and who had to go away from us – that is, by His death on the cross and then by His ascension into heaven – in order that the Counselor should come to us and should keep coming to us as the Spirit of truth (cf. Jn. 16:7,13). In Him are "all the treasures of wisdom and knowledge" (Col. 2:3), and the Church is His Body (cf. Rom. 12:5; I Cor. 6:15; 10:17; 12:12; 12:27; Eph. 1:23; 2:16; 4:4; Col. 1:24; 3:15). "By her relationship with

Christ, the Church is a kind of sacrament or sign and means of intimate union with God, and of the unity of all mankind" (*LG* 1), and the source of this is He, He Himself, He the Redeemer.

The Encyclical begins its theology of the Redemption with the *Redeemer himself* and from there goes straight on to the *Church*: it "is his body." Insofar as it is founded on Christ and has in him the source of its life, it is the sacrament for the innermost union with God, as for the union of all mankind.

All these Scripture quotations concerning the Redeemer could be understood in the sense of the New Testament and Tradition. However, as the text (7,3) emphasized at the outset, it is in the perspective of the "new Advent" and in the "consciousness that the Council considerably developed" that we must constantly aim at Christ. That means, that the quotations concerning the Redeemer are also to be understood and interpreted in the perspective of the new Advent and the new conciliar consciousness of the Church.

Thereby St. Paul's phrase: "The Church is the body of Christ" also acquires a new content in the Encyclical. Since the Church is directly founded on Christ the Redeemer of all men, who through the Incarnation has formally united himself with every man, then it follows that Christ the Universal Redeemer is the content and source of the Church's life, that in Christ the Universal Redeemer the Church is the sacrament of universal salvation embracing all men,[2] that in the sense of universal salvation the Church is sign and instrument for the unity of all mankind, which is also, in a hidden manner, the body of the Universal Redeemer.[3]

---

2   Karol Wojtyla, [Sign of Contradiction] (Freiburg i.Br. 1979), p. 37.

3   *Ibid.*, pp. 37ff, 52-54, 78ff, 98-101. See further, Part I, pp. 67-78. – On the Incarnation of the Son, we read in *Dominum et Vivificantem* (50,3): "By means of this 'humanization' of the Word-Son the self-communication of God reaches its definitive fullness in the history

of creation and salvation. This fullness acquires a special wealth and expressiveness in the text of John's Gospel: 'The Word became flesh' (Jn. 1:14). The Incarnation of God the Son signifies the taking up into unity with God not only of human nature, but in this human nature, in a sense, *of everything that is 'flesh'*: the whole of humanity, the entire visible and material world. The Incarnation, then, also has a cosmic significance, a cosmic dimension. The 'firstborn of all creation' (Col. 1:15), becoming incarnate in the individual humanity of Christ, unites himself in some way with the entire reality of man, which is also 'flesh' (cf. Gen. 9:11; ... Lk. 3:6; I Pet. 1:24), – and in this reality with all 'flesh,' with the whole of creation."

What exactly does he mean by: "the taking up into unity with God ... human nature and ... the whole of humanity"? In any case, already in the Incarnation of the Son, the self-communication of God reaches its definitive fullness in the history of creation and salvation (cf. *RH* 1,2). Or again: "In the mystery of the Incarnation the work of the Spirit 'who gives life' reaches its highest point" (*DeV* 52,1).

Man becomes a supernatural, adopted child of God through the Incarnation: "The filiation of divine adoption is born in man on the basis of the mystery of the Incarnation, therefore through Christ the eternal Son. But the birth, or rebirth, happens when God the Father 'sends the Spirit of His Son into our hearts'" (*DeV* 52,2).

Just as the Incarnation is the formal union of the Son with every man, so all men receive the gift of the Holy Ghost. On that point, see in *Dominum et Vivificantem* (52,3): "This is what we are told by St. Paul, whose cosmic and theological vision seems to repeat the words of the ancient Psalm: creation 'waits with eager longing for the revealing of the sons of God' (Rom. 8:29), that is, those whom God has 'foreknown' and whom he 'has predestined to be confirmed to the image of his Son.' Thus there is a supernatural 'adoption,' of which the source is the Holy Spirit, love and gift. *As such he is given to man.* And in *the superabundance of the uncreated gift* there begins in the heart of all human beings (!) that particular *created gift* whereby they 'become partakers of the divine nature' (cf. II Pet. 1:4). Thus human life becomes permeated, through participation, by the divine life, and itself acquires a divine, supernatural dimension. There is granted the *new* life, in which as a sharer in the mystery of Incarnation 'man has access to the Father in the Holy Spirit' (cf. Eph. 2:18; *Dei Verbum* 2). Thus there is a close relationship *between the Spirit* who gives life and sanctifying grace and *the manifold supernatural vitality* which derives from it in man: between the uncreated Spirit and the created human spirit." See also, *Sign of Contradiction*, pp. 27ff. The dogmatic axiom of the prayer meeting at Assisi is the effective, working presence of the Holy Ghost in the hearts of all men as a consequence of the Incarnation. Thus John

Thereon follows a change of the relationship of Church and non-Christians to the Redeemer, as also a strange new concept of the Church's mission. Concerning the first the Pope says (*RH* 7,4):

> The Church does not cease to listen to His words. She rereads them continually. With the greatest devotion she reconstructs every detail of His life. These words are listened to also by non-Christians. The life of Christ speaks, also, to many who are not capable of repeating with Peter: "You are the Christ, the Son of the living God" (Matt. 16:16). He, the Son of the living God, speaks to people also as man: it is His life that speaks, His humanity, His fidelity to the truth, His all-embracing love. Furthermore, His death on the cross speaks – that is to say the inscrutable depth of His suffering and abandonment ...

The Encyclical's words concerning the relationship of non-Christians to Christ remain *within the frame of the purely human*. To be sure, the word of Christ reaches also to the ears of non-Christians; to be sure, his life speaks to many of them, even as man speaks to man.[4] But the same can be said of all great personalities of mankind: Socrates, Buddha, Confucius, Gandhi and so on. However, Jesus was not content with merely human admiration. He demanded the faith, which Simon Peter professes. But concerning this faith, the Pope says (apologetically?) that many non-Christians, who are drawn by the life of Christ, are "not yet capable" of it. Such a situation is well-known in the New

Paul II: "The meeting of religions in Assisi was meant to be a clear confirmation of the fact that 'every genuine prayer is inspired by the Holy Ghost, who is mysteriously present in the heart of every man (!)'" (Address to the Cardinals on December 22, 1986 [AAS 79, 1987, 1089]; *Redemptoris Missio* 28). Therefore it does not matter to which god one's genuine prayer is addressed. Thus in *Sign of Contradiction*, pp. 26ff.

4 Cf. my essay: "Assisi: Beginning of a New Age," in *Respondeo* 8 (Abensberg.1988), pp. 126-141.

Testament: very many Jewish contemporaries of Jesus, who admired his words and deeds and the man himself, were "not yet capable" of making Simon Peter's profession of faith. To them the words of Scripture applied: "Seeing they do not see, hearing they do not understand!" (cf. Matt. 13:13ff). But Christ puts men before the decision, and demands of them precisely the faith of Peter in the Son of God. This faith, upon which eternal salvation depends, is what the Church is bound to proclaim (cf. Mk. 16:16).

On this point, the Church's mission, the Encyclical says as follows (*RH* 7,4):

> The Church lives His mystery, draws unwearyingly from it and continually seeks ways of bringing this mystery of her Master and Lord to humanity (*propius adducere possit ad hominum genus*) – to the peoples, the nations, the succeeding generations, and every individual human being – as if she were repeating, as the Apostle did: "For I decided to know nothing among you except Jesus Christ and Him crucified" (I Cor. 2:2). The Church stays within the sphere of the mystery of the Redemption, which has become the fundamental principle of her life and mission.

What conclusion does the Encyclical accordingly draw from the confrontation of the non-Christian world with its Redeemer, concerning the Church's mission? The Church is constantly seeking for ways "of bringing to humanity" the "mystery of her Master and Lord" from which it draws its own life. However, in the Encyclical this "mystery" is universal salvation! Hence the mission of this Church too as sign and instrument for the unity of all mankind can only consist in "manifesting" to man the deepest essence of his being as man, namely his "being in Christ," this through the revelation of the Father and his love. The Encyclical lays out how from the "mystery of the Redemption" (= universal salvation), the basic principle of the Church's life and mission, the Church's mission derives and is to be understood.

The complete text of the Encyclical's Article 7 gives us the following picture: in the perspective of the new Advent and the Church's new conciliar consciousness, the Pope demands that we turn decisively to Christ, the Redeemer of man and of the world, who through the Incarnation is formally united with every man. That is the basic principle of the "more broad-minded Christianity."

In the universal Redeemer Jesus Christ, the Church is the universal sacrament of salvation, embracing *all* men, Christians and non-Christians alike.[5] It is in this sense that the Church in Christ is the sign and instrument for the unity of all mankind. That is the basic principle of the "more broad-minded ecclesiology."

The Church lives the mystery of Christ, the Universal Redeemer. This prime principle of its life is also the prime principle of its mission. The Church's mission consists accordingly in further "bringing" to all men, "revealing" to them and making them "aware" of the mystery of its Maker and Lord, the Universal Redeemer. That is the Encyclical's basic outline of the Church's mission. – Obviously, the Church's mission as thus formulated in the Encyclical, "constantly seeking for ways" "to bring to mankind" the mystery of the Redeemer, is not the same as Christ's clear mandate to His Church in the Gospel (Matt. 28:18-20).

The outlines of the theological position taken by the Encyclical are highlighted even more clearly by what the Encyclical does not say: there is no mention of God's demanding the faith in Christ that leads to justification; no mention of God's demanding baptism that incorporates men (sacramentally) in Christ's work of Redemption and his Resurrection, and that applies the fruits of the Redemption to individuals (cf. Rom. 6). Why does the Encyclical

---

5 Karol Wojtyla, [*Sign of Contradiction*], p. 37.

not say one single word about these things?

Article 7 gives us the outline of the Encyclical's doctrine of Redemption which is developed in the following articles.

8.   The Redeemer of the world – the Redeemer of man.*

The Pope's introductory explanation (*RH* 7), to the effect that in the perspective of the new Advent and in the conciliar consciousness of the Church there is only one direction for the spirit: "Towards Christ, the Redeemer of man, towards Christ, the Redeemer of the world" (*RH* 7,2); that the Church as body of Christ, the Universal Redeemer, is the sacrament for the unity of all mankind (*RH* 7,2), and receives from him "the fundamental principle of her life and mission" (*RH* 7,4), provides the framework for the following development of his theology of the Redemption (*RH* 8-12).

Again and again, with numerous quotations from Scripture, the Pope turns to the central point of his Redemption doctrine, namely, *the revelation of the Redeemer to the world and to man* (*RH* 8).

Article 8 begins with: "The Redeemer of the world" (*RH* 8,1), and it finishes with: "He, the Redeemer of man!" (*RH* 8,2). That is not just a stylistic flourish,[6] it expresses also the theological line of thinking which reaches its high point with the latter exclamation. For indeed the relation of the Redeemer to man, who is the "most important point of the visible world" (*RH* 8,2), is the crystallization point of the Pope's Redemption doctrine.

Concerning the relation of the Redeemer to the world

---

[6] In the Latin original: *Mundi Redemptor!* (= Beginning of the article) ... *Ipse, hominis Redemptor!* (= End of the article). Evidently an intentional stylistic parallel, otherwise one would have expected the article to end with the Encyclical's title phrase: *Redemptor hominis!*

* Heading in the English translation="Redemption as a New Creation."

the Encyclical explains (*RH* 8,1):

> The Redeemer of the world! In him has been revealed
> in a new and more wonderful way the fundamental truth
> concerning creation to which the book of Genesis gives
> witness when it repeats several times: "God saw that it was
> good" (Gen. 1, passim). The good has its source in Wis-
> dom and Love. In Jesus Christ the visible world which
> God created for man (Gen. 1:26-30), the world that,
> when sin entered, "was subjected to futility" (Rom. 8:19-
> 22; *Gaudium et Spes* 2,13), recovers again its original link
> with the divine source of Wisdom and Love. Indeed,
> "God so loved the world that he gave his only Son" (Jn.
> 3:16). As this link was broken in the man Adam, so in the
> Man Christ it was reforged (Rom. 5:12-21).
>
> Are we of the twentieth century not convinced of the
> overpoweringly eloquent words of the Apostle of the Gen-
> tiles concerning the "creation (that) has been groaning in
> travail until now" (Rom. 8:22), and "waits with eager
> longing for the revelation of the sons of God" (Rom.
> 8:19), the creation that "was subjected to futility"?

At this point the Encyclical seems to interrupt the close
theological reasoning in order unexpectedly to turn in
more detail to "man of the twentieth century." As further
signs of the transitoriness of our time there are quoted one
after another: environmental pollution, armed conflicts,
possible self-destruction through atomic weapons, lack of
respect for unborn life. At first this interruption may seem
to be a break in style, but actually it fits in with the basic
writing of the Encyclical, the theme of which is the Redeemer's relationship to our era. That is why each of the
theological themes brought up is immediately connected
with and applied to the characteristic features of our era. In
the present case that means that the reflections on the
Redeemer of the world are confronted with the problems
of contemporary man. However the inner logic of the
theological reasoning is unbroken: the Pauline thought,
that creation waits for the revelation of the children of God

(Rom. 8:19), follows on the Redemptive work of Christ. So the description of the marks of the passingness of this world, such as modern man experiences them, comes to an end with the rhetorical question:

> The world of the new age, the world of space flights ... is it not also the world "groaning in travail" (Rom. 8:22) that "waits with eager longing for the revealing of the sons of God" (Rom. 8:19)?

The very important statements in this text concerning the Redeemer's relationship to the world may be summarized as follows:

The basic truth of the goodness of creation, arising from the divine source of Wisdom and Love, has, in the Redeemer of the world, been revealed afresh and in more splendid fashion. God created the visible world for man (*propter hominem*).[7] With the entry of sin into the world, it

---

[7] The Church teaches that the creation of the world is the work of the divine wisdom and goodness (D 1783). The purpose of creation (*finis operis*) is primarily to show forth God's perfections and thereby to give God the glory which is due Him (D 1805). The secondary purpose of creation is the bestowal of benefits on creatures, but especially the calling of rational creatures to the beatific vision (D 1783). Both ends of creation are inseparably linked to each other, for the glorification of God through the knowledge and the love of Him is the very beatitude of rational creatures. – Can one isolate the second end from the first, or so shift the emphasis, by simply saying that the visible world was created for man?

But the Encyclical treats primarily the relations between the Redeemer and the world. Cf. also the controversy between the Thomists and the Scotists over the conditioned or unconditioned predestination of the Incarnation. The question is whether the deciding factor in the Incarnation of the Son of God was the redemption of man, so that the Incarnation would not have taken place without the fall of our first parents into sin (conditioned predestination), or if the deciding factor was the glorification of God, so that the Son of God would have become man as the crowning of creation even without the fall of our first parents, only without assuming a body subject to suffering (unconditioned or absolute predestination of the Incarnation).

became subject to perishing. In Jesus the visible world recovers its original connection with the same divine source of Wisdom and Love. "For God so loved the world, that he sent his only-begotten Son" (Jn. 3:16). Just as in the man Adam that bond (*vinculum illud*) was broken, so in the Man Christ is it restored. Creation, which with sin became subject to perishing, lies in birth-pangs and waits with longing for the revelation of the sons of God.

The text can from start to finish be interpreted in the sense of classical theology. However, in the perspective of the new Advent and the new conciliar consciousness of the Church, it is rather to be understood in the sense of universal salvation. This becomes quite clear when the Encyclical next turns in quite specific fashion to "the most important point of the visible world," namely man (*RH* 8,2). Before that, however, a few remarks on the text laid out above.

Firstly, how far is precisely the goodness of creation revealed in a particularly splendid way in the *Redeemer* of the world? –

True, the Old Testament teaches that God created the world good (Gen. 1). But we find the world is not in accord with its being as creation. The same holds true for

---

The scriptural foundation for the Scotist position is Col. 1:15-19. The speculative foundation: The end cannot be less than the means. The Incarnation as the highest of all God's works could not be primarily relative to the purpose of redeeming sinful creatures.

The Scotists find it unfitting that sin, which God hates, be the occasion of the most sublime revelation and glorification of God, but the Thomists see therein an even greater demonstration of the love and mercy of God: *O felix culpa, quae talem ac tantum meruit habere Redemptorem* (*Exsultet*).

Furthermore, according to the Scotist position, all grace derives from the merits of the God-man, not only the grace of fallen mankind, but also the grace of our first parents and even the grace of the angels. – Cf. Ludwig Ott, *Fundamentals of Catholic Dogma* (St. Louis: Herder Book Company, 1954), pp. 175-177, 242. – It is interesting to note the close relation between the Pope's covenant theology and the Scotist position.

man. He is God's creature, so created in goodness. But he rose up against God and was cast out of paradise: he is a sinner! Here are the facts of the case in the language of classical theology: World and man are no longer in their condition of the original goodness of creation. Man is no longer in the state of original justice (*in statu iustitiae originalis*), which he himself destroyed by his first sin, rather he is in the state of original sin (*in statu naturae lapsae*). Through sin he has undergone an "ontological" change, a change of his very being; the supernatural likeness to God is gone, the natural image of God is wounded.[8] He stands in absolute need of redemption.

So the *specific* relationship of the Redeemer to world and man is not simply the goodness of creation, but the fall into sin and the absolute need of redemption on the part of the world created good by God. The text of the Encyclical should read: In the Redeemer is revealed the basic truth of creation's having been originally created good but having then fallen and so being in need of redemption. The text taken by the Pope out of the book of Genesis (1, *passim*) to prove his point refers to God's act of creation – before the Fall! Whereas the Encyclical is referring to the *Redeemer* of the world, i.e. the condition of fallen creation.

Yet the Pope says: In the *Redeemer* the basic truth of the goodness of creation has been revealed in a new and more splendid way. This statement can only be fully understood on the presupposition that all men are redeemed. If man from the outset, from the very act of his creation, possesses once and for all the supernatural likeness of God (*RH* 13,3) and his "being in Christ," then one can say, as the Encyclical says, that in the Redeemer of the world, the basic truth of creation's goodness is revealed in a new way. In fact the Encyclical's phrasing reflects the basic thesis of the Pope's theology of the Covenant (see above, 7.3, pp. 24-32), a

---

8 Cf. Part I, pp. 82-87.

thesis which has no foundation in Scripture. The real condition of the cosmos from the Fall onwards and the relationship of the Old to the New Age are seen differently in Scripture.[9]

– Is the whole visible world really "created by God for man" as the Encyclical so baldly states, and does Genesis 1:26-30 really suffice to prove the point? All that Genesis 1:26-30 talks about is how man should rule "over the whole earth and everything that moveth upon the earth." Yet the Encyclical's statements are set in the context of *Christ*, the Redeemer of the world! Should we not rather say of Christ, as Creator of the world, what the Epistle to the Colossians says: "All things were created by him and in him" (1:16)? The Encyclical's manner of expressing itself, occupying as it does a central place in the Pope's theology, means nothing less than the beginning of a shift of emphasis from Christ-centeredness to man-centeredness.

– The text of the Encyclical so far has not explained how we are to understand the bond between man and God having been broken in Adam and restored in Christ, but the explanation does come in the course of the further development of the theme (*RH* 8;9). We may anticipate by saying: the text is to be interpreted in the sense of the Pope's theology of the covenant, whereby creation and the making of the covenant took place in one and the same act (see above, 7.3, pp. 24-32).

In a theology of the redemption based on the axiom of universal salvation and worked out in the perspective of the new Advent and the Church's conciliar consciousness, the justifying faith as we know it in the New Testament ceases being necessary for salvation, even actually hinders it. The infinite wisdom and love of God are seen as the unique and

---

9 Hermann Sasse, Art. *kósmos*, in: *Theologisches Wörterbuch zum Neuen Testament* [*Theological Dictionary of the New Testament*] (Stuttgart 1949ff), III, pp. 867-898. By the same author, *Ibid.* Art. *aióon*, I, 197-209.

exclusive source of the objective and subjective universality of Redemption. Thus we read in the text above: "God so loved the world, that he gave his only-begotten Son." However we are missing – not unintentionally! – the completion of the Scripture quotation which is so important for the justification of the sinner: "... that whosoever believeth in him, may not perish, but may have life everlasting" (Jn. 3:16).

– Do the words of the Apostle of the Gentiles concerning the "expectation of the creature for the revelation of the sons of God" (Rom. 8:19) – taken in their authentic biblical sense! – really so simply convince "us, men of the twentieth century"? Including non-believers and non-Christians? Is "the world" really waiting with longing for the "revelation of the sons of God"? Is that not a quite specific expectation of the Church?

Be that as it may, we can now add to the Pope's portrait of our era another characteristic: our era, time of a new conciliar consciousness of the Church, of a new Advent of the Church and mankind, in expectation of the Jubilee Year 2000, of the messianic kingdom of world peace and of the new coming of the Lord, is now also a time "*of longing expectation by the world*" for the "revelation of the sons of God."

The still unanswered question, whether by "revelation of the sons of God" is really meant all men, because the Son of God in his Incarnation has formally united himself with every man and so all men are children of God in the state of grace (*RH* 11,4), is finally answered by the Encyclical itself, now turning to the special relationship of the Redeemer to man. The Encyclical continues (*RH* 8,2):

In its analysis of "today's world," says the Pope, the council revealed that "most important part of the visible world that is man by penetrating like Christ the depth of human consciousness and by making contact with the inward mystery of man, which ... is expressed by the word 'heart'." This "inward mystery of the human heart in the depth of human consciousness" is stated by the Encyclical in one pithy sentence (*RH* 8,2):

> Christ, the Redeemer of the world, is the one who penetrated in a unique unrepeatable way into the mystery of man and entered his "heart."

Again the question arises: Did Christ enter the heart of every man, and if so, in what way? The Encyclical answers the question with the text well known to us from the Pastoral Constitution *Gaudium et Spes* 22, which reads as follows (*RH* 8,2):

> Rightly therefore does the Second Vatican Council teach: "The truth is that only in the mystery of the Incarnate Word does the mystery of man take on light. For Adam, the first man, was a type of him who was to come (Rom. 5:14), Christ the Lord, Christ the new Adam, in the very revelation of the mystery of the Father and of His love, fully reveals man to himself and brings to light his most high calling." And the Council continues: "He who is the image of the invisible God (Col. 1:15), is Himself the perfect man who has restored in the children of Adam that likeness to God which has been disfigured ever since the first sin. Human nature, by the very fact that it was assumed, not absorbed, in Him has been raised in us also to a dignity beyond compare. For, by His Incarnation, He, the Son of God, in a certain way united Himself with each man. He worked with human hands, He thought with a human mind. He acted with a human will, and with a human heart He loved. Born of the Virgin Mary, He has truly been made one of us, like to us in all things except sin," He, the Redeemer of man.[10]

This quotation from *Gaudium et Spes* 22 is *for the Pope's*

---

10 Emphasis in the text of the Encyclical is only in the English translation, therefore they are omitted here. On the text itself, see Footnote 3.

*New Theology as a whole the fundamental key text, so it is the key text also for the doctrine of Redemption in **Redemptor Hominis**.* Out of this text of the Pastoral Constitution Cardinal Wojtyla evolved his man-centered concept of revelation which he put forward in *Sign of Contradiction*. This concept of revelation is also the Pope's, so that we are sure of how the Pope understands and interprets the Council text quoted above. All of this was laid out in detail in Part I of this work (pp. 78-123) and recapitulated in brief in the Introduction of this book (see above, 6 & 7, pp. 14-36). Hence from the Pope's concept of revelation we know exactly how to interpret the text quoted:

Accordingly revelation consists "in the Son of God's having through the Incarnation united himself with every man," and that in the sense of a formal union infusing grace.[11] This revelation which contains the axiom of universal salvation we named *a priori* revelation.[12]

A priori revelation includes the whole "mystery of man": through formal union with Christ in the Incarnation every man "has been raised to a dignity beyond compare," every man from the first moment of his conception possesses the supernatural likeness of God indestructibly within him (*RH* 13,3) and "being in Christ" as his own truest and deepest human being. Hence too the Redeemer by becoming man has entered into the "heart" of every man, hence too St. Paul's phrase of "the revelation of the sons of God" is in the Encyclical to be referred to all men. The phrasing of the *Council text*, whereby the Son of God through the Incarnation united himself "in a certain way" with every man, leaves room for the interpretation of a material union in the sense of the Church Fathers' theology.[13] But the Pope leaves no such room for a patristic interpretation with

---

11 Cf. Part I, pp. 61-98. Cf. also Footnote 3.
12 Part I, pp. 111-116. Cf. also Footnote 3.
13 Cf. Part I, pp. 60-73.

his thesis of a formal (supernatural) union, i.e. the thesis of
universal salvation.

To *a priori* revelation corresponds *a posteriori revelation*,
the revelation offered in history to men, through the life of
Christ.

The "mystery of man," so it says, is solved through the
"mystery of the Incarnate Word." "Christ reveals man fully
to himself, but does this through the revelation of the
Father and his love."[14]

Revelation as a whole "circles around man"; it has a
man-centered character (see above, 7, pp. 17-36). The historical revelation becomes a means of *interpretation*,
whereby man's deepest being as man is made known or
conscious to man. Christ himself becomes the *interpreter* of
man *a priori* redeemed and justified. Christ's work of Redemption, whose redeeming and justifying effect has already been imparted *a priori* to every man, becomes a
manifestation of the Father's mercy and love. The Pope's
constantly recurring comment thereon is the saying of Jesus: "Whosoever has seen me, has seen the Father." The
revelation of the Father's love and mercy in and through
Christ puts before man's eyes the *great motive* that should
move them to return love for love.

To this *a posteriori* revelation, revealing to man his deepest being as man, so that he may truly "find himself,"
"come to himself," corresponds "*faith*" as a mere process of
awareness. Such a "faith" is not the justifying faith of the
New Testament. Man is no longer, as the Council of Trent
teaches, through justifying faith and baptism transferred
from the state of the sinner far from God into the state of
sanctifying grace, because he is already *a priori* redeemed
and justified. The application of the fruits of the Redemption to the individual man through the process of justification lapses, because these fruits have already been imparted

14 Cf. Part I, pp. 112-116.

a priori to all men on the basis of God's unconditional love and mercy.

Revelation and Faith have thereby forfeited their truly *historical* character. The question as to how the Pope's theology of the covenant is presented as a whole on the basis of the man-centered "double revelation," was already answered in the Introduction (7.3, pp. 24-32). Cardinal Wojtyla's *covenant theology* has fully passed over into the Encyclical, and gives us the key to understanding Article 9, which follows.

9. The divine dimension of the mystery of the Redemption.

If the Son of God through his Incarnation has formally united himself with every man and has already entered into the "heart" of every single man (RH 8), how then does the Pope's theology present the "rest" of the Redeemer's work of salvation, in particular the sacrifice of the Cross?

In this Article 9 the Encyclical answers the question as to the Pope's concept of salvation history. After the above (*RH* 8,2) quoted text from *Gaudium et Spes* the Encyclical goes on (*RH* 9,1):

> As we reflect again on this stupendous text from the Council's teaching, we do not forget even for a moment that Jesus Christ, the Son of the living God, became our reconciliation with the Father (cf. Rom. 5:11; Col. 1:20). He it was, and He alone, who satisfied the Father's eternal love, that fatherhood that from the beginning found expression in creating the world, giving man all the riches of creation, and making him "little less than God" (Ps. 8:6), in that he was created "in the image and after the likeness of God" (Gen. 1:26). He and He alone also satisfied that fatherhood of God and that love which man in a way rejected by breaking the first Covenant (Gen. 3:6-13), and the later covenants that God "again and again offered to man" (Eucharistic Prayer No. 4).

The "stupendous text from the Council's teaching" taught, as the Pope understands it, the formal union of the Son of God with every man through the Incarnation (= *a posteriori* revelation), and it expressed the man-centered theory of "double revelation" (cf. previous section, pp. 108-118). What is there still left for the Redeemer of man to do, if the reunion of mankind with God in principle already took place with the Son of God's Incarnation?

What is "still left" for him to do, which we may not "forget even for a moment (!)," is "that Jesus Christ, the Son of the living God has become our reconciliation with the Father." "He it was, and he alone, who satisfied the Father's eternal love (*satisfecit*)."

The Pope uses the traditional terminology, but not in the traditional sense.

According to *the Church's traditional teaching*, any single deed of Christ was of sufficient value to work our salvation, and all of his deeds taken together make up the complete work of Redemption. However, in the sacrifice on the Cross his redeeming activity reached its highest point, so that the Cross is held to be the main but not exclusive efficient cause of our salvation.[15]

It is the Church's teaching that Christ by his sacrificial death on the Cross redeemed us, *reconciled us with God* (D 983; 790), and by his suffering and death *made vicarious atonement for the sins of men* (D 122; 799).[16]

Scripture teaches the universality of Christ's work of Redemption and so indirectly of his satisfaction. By satisfaction is meant the reparation or making good again of an offense. The universality of Christ's vicarious satisfaction refers however only to the objective Redemption: Christ made atonement sufficient for all men without exception. Christ so offered up to God the merits of his atonement,

---

15 Ludwig Ott, *op. cit.*, p. 184.
16 *Ibid.*, pp. 184-188.

that to it corresponds on the part of God a true and sincere will to make all men blessed, and by reason of that atonement all men may and should expect the remission of their sins.[17] Although Christ's *physical and historical activity* alone wrought salvation, redemption and atonement (*opus salutis seu redemptionis*) and was performed only *half-way through world history*, nevertheless the moral efficacy of Christ's meritorious work of Redemption includes the entire history of mankind, reaching back as far as sinful Adam and forwards to the end of the world.[18]

However this objectively universal salvation requires the *subjective application of the fruits of the Redemption to, and their appropriation by, every single man through the process of justification.* The subjective appropriation of the fruits of the Redemption is dependent on the fulfillment of certain conditions, on faith (Mk. 16:16) and on observance of the commandments (Heb. 5:9; II Pet. 1:10). In other words: in the sacrifice of the Cross, Christ's satisfaction is universal; as regards man's acceptance of the fruits of that sacrifice, it is particular (cf. *Summa contra Gentiles* IV,55).[19]

However, *underlying the Encyclical's theology of the Savior is the Pope's theology of the covenant* (see above, 7.3, pp. 24-32). The Church's old doctrine of Redemption thereby takes on a new form, and familiar theological concepts undergo a change of meaning.

The Pope speaks in the text quoted of a *double satisfaction*, which Jesus made to the Father's eternal love:

– Firstly, "to that fatherhood," "that from the beginning found expression in creating the world, giving men all the riches of creation, and making him 'little less than God,' in

---

[17] Matthias Joseph Scheeben, *Erlösungslehre, Handbuch der katholischen Dogmatik* [*Handbook of Catholic Dogma*] (Freiburg i. Br. 1954), Gesammelte Schriften [Complete Works], Vol. VI, 2, pp. 163ff, 203ff, 205ff.

[18] *Ibid.*

[19] Ludwig Ott, *op. cit.*, p. 189.

that he was created 'in the image and after the likeness of God.'"

– Secondly, "to that fatherhood," "which man in a way rejected by breaking the first covenant (cf. Gen. 3:6-13) and the later covenants that God 'again and again offered to man.'"

How are we to understand the first of these two statements? Did neither the bringing into existence of man's being nor his creation as image of God through the Father require Jesus Christ's satisfaction? ... Or did they? ...

As to the Pope's second statement here concerning the satisfaction made by Jesus Christ to God's fatherhood, at first sight it seems to be less difficult to understand. Obviously, the breaking of a covenant with God, or the refusal by man of offers of covenants made by God, offend the Father's love and demand satisfaction. However the phrasing which says that God's loving fatherhood was "in a way rejected" by man, is odd nonetheless.

Both statements and also the Encyclical's *doctrine on the Savior* become understandable when we take into account the Pope's covenant theology which we laid out alongside our presentation of the Church's traditional teaching (see above):

Although the physical activity of Christ in history is the saving, redeeming and atoning work of Redemption and only took place half-way through world history, nevertheless the "ontological" efficacy of Christ's meritorious work of Redemption includes the whole history of mankind, backwards not only to Adam having fallen into sin – as in the traditional teaching – but even *to the act of creation*, and forwards to the end of the world.

That makes the Redemption *not only objectively but also subjectively universal.* Any subjective application or appropriation of the fruits of Redemption thereby lapses. What remains is a mere process of awareness by way of revelation from without or self-discovery from within of what was *a priori* existent.

This view arises from the basic thesis of the Pope's covenant theology, according to which the creation of man and the making of the covenant with Adam took place simultaneously, and arose from one and the same redeeming love of God. Thus when the man Adam entered into a covenant with God in the act of creation, he was made in the image of God as redeemed "being in Christ" at the same moment. That is to say, Adam was created as the *redeemed* child of God, and entered into existence as "son in the Son of God" the Redeemer. Since "being in Christ" is the being of the *Redeemer,* then Jesus Christ also made satisfaction to "that fatherhood" which is expressed in the creation of man. So man's deepest being as man, his "being in Christ," also belongs to his nature as man.

The same thought process explains how the Pope views the break or destruction of the first covenant and its restoration "even more radically, in even greater measure, by the Redemption."[20] This restoration of the destroyed covenant with Adam through the historical work of Redemption by the second Adam halfway through time, reaches back with its effect of atonement and satisfaction as far as the cove-

---

[20] See above, pp. 27ff. – The Pope summarizes his thoughts on the "divine dimension of the Redemption" in *Dives in Misericordia* 7. The creation of man in the image of God carries the traits of the Redeemer "from the beginning." On the relationship between the creation of man, i.e. the first covenant with Adam, and the covenant made on Golgotha, we hear in *Dives in Misericordia* (7,5): "It is precisely beside the path of man's eternal election to the dignity of being an adopted child of God that there stands in history the cross of Christ, the only-begotten Son, who, as 'light from light,true God from true God,' came to give the final witness to the wonderful *covenant of God with humanity, of God with man* – every human being. This covenant, as old as man – it goes back to the very mystery of creation – and afterwards many times renewed with one single chosen people, is equally the new and definitive covenant, which was established there on Calvary, and is not limited to a single people, to Israel, but is open to each and every individual."

nant with Adam in the act of creation. What we have is so
to speak a *"sanatio in radice"* of the first broken covenant
on the even deeper basis of the Redemption in the moment
of Adam's creation, so that Adam entered into existence
quite "legitimately" as the supernaturally redeemed adop-
tive son of the Father "in Christ." So "being in Christ"
belongs indestructibly to man from the very beginning as
the deepest being of man's being. Man could lose it neither
by breaking the first covenant with God, nor by refusing
God's following offers of a covenant, for which "Jesus
Christ, Son of the living God, became our reconciliation
with the Father." From the first moment of his existence
every man carries *indestructibly* within him the image and
likeness of God (*RH* 13,3), and "all men from the beginning to the end of the world have been redeemed and
justified by Christ through his Cross," "independently of
whether man knows it or not, accepts it or not."[21]

This aspect of salvation history belongs for the Pope "to
the divine order of things, to the divine view of man and
the world." What we have here is "the divine dimension of
the mystery of the Redemption," which "corresponds to
the divine order of things and to the divine view of man
and the world."[22]

The other, human, aspect of salvation history arises from
the fact that the "being in Christ" imparted *a priori* to man
through Christ's work of Redemption has become "a historical fact rooted in time and space."[23] That by no means
denies that the Redeemer of mankind wrought his historical work of salvation halfway through time, that he made
satisfaction to the Father through his Passion, and that he
reconciled mankind with God. Accordingly, the *historical
work of salvation* is and remains the saving, redeeming and

---

21 Karol Wojtyla, [*Sign of Contradiction*], p. 103, 108.
22 *Ibid.*, p. 103. See above, pp. 30ff.
23 *Ibid.*, pp. 108ff. See above, pp. 30ff.

reconciling act of Redemption by Jesus Christ, only its "ontological," *redeeming and justifying* effect reaches further back, even to the act of man's creation, so that all men from the beginning to the end of the world are effectively redeemed and justified by the Cross.[24]

The question was raised at the outset: What is still left for the Redeemer to do if he has performed his work of Redemption and applied its saving fruits *a priori* to every man born alive? We can now answer it: "Ontologically," or in the order of being, nothing whatsoever! All that remains to be added is an awareness, in the order of knowing. The whole traditional view of salvation history and redemption acquires, if we keep the traditional theological vocabulary, a subtle, far-reaching change of meaning. Illuminating in this connection is what the Encyclical for instance does *not* mention. This change of meaning also shows up, now that the Pope turns to the central concept of Redemption.

After the explanations of "reconciliation" and "satisfaction," the Encyclical now gives its definition of *Redemption*. This goes (*RH* 9,1):

> The redemption of the world – this tremendous mystery of love in which creation is renewed (*Gaudium et Spes* 37; *Lumen Gentium* 48) – is, at its deepest root, the fullness of justice in a human heart – the Heart of the First-born Son – in order that it may become justice in the hearts of many human beings, predestined from eternity in the First-born Son to be children of God (Rom. 8:29,30; Eph. 1:8), and called to grace, called to love.
>
> The Cross on Calvary, through which Jesus Christ – a Man, the Son of the Virgin Mary, thought to be the son of Joseph of Nazareth – "leaves" this world, is also a fresh manifestation of the eternal fatherhood of God, who in him draws near again to humanity, to each human being, giving him the thrice holy "Spirit of truth" (Jn. 16:13).

---

24 *Ibid.*, p. 103.

As to the first part of this definition of the Redemption, let us note that it says that in the mystery of the Redemption creation is renewed. According to the Pope's theology, that already effectively took place in the very act of man's creation together with the simultaneous making of the covenant. The "broken covenant" was in principle already renewed in the act of creation "on a deeper basis and in a more comprehensive way."[25] Thus man exists from the beginning "in Christ." Adam is already an "anonymous Christian." Through Christ's work of Redemption, this "being in Christ" of Adam and so of mankind has become a historical fact out in the open.

As for the central part of the Encyclical's definition, it runs: the Redemption of the world is in its deepest root the fullness of justice in the human heart of the First-born Son, so that it can become justice in the hearts of many men. Here two things are being said: firstly, Redemption is the fullness of justice in the Son's human heart; secondly, the purpose of this justice is its communication to the hearts of men.

The fullness of justice is present in the heart of the First-born Son at the moment of the Incarnation of the Word. Since according to the Pope's basic thesis the Son of God has through the Incarnation formally united himself with every man, then through the Incarnation the fullness of justice in the Son's human heart has also become the fullness of justice in all men's hearts. So the purpose of God's becoming man, namely the Redemption, has already been attained and realized with the Incarnation. So also realized is what the Encyclical further says of men, namely that they "are predestined from eternity in the First-born Son to be children of God and called to grace, called to love."

The Encyclical's definition of Redemption is even more

---

25 See above, pp. 27ff.

clearly outlined when we set it before the background of
the New Testament and the Church's teaching: the Church
teaches that the "Redemption of the world" – precisely "in
its deepest root" – is the freeing of Adam's descendants
from the power of darkness or from the slavery to Satan, it
is their being rescued from the condition of sin and death,
in which the children of Adam are really to be found,
through Christ's sacrifice on the Cross. "Accordingly (justification) is the transfer from the state in which man as son
of Adam is born into the state of grace and of acceptance as
child of God through the second Adam, Jesus Christ, our
Savior" (D 796), but that is not possible without faith and
baptism (D 793-801).

The difference between this definition of Redemption
and the Encyclical's is obvious. Although according to
Church teaching the Redemption consists essentially in the
effacing of original sin through Christ's vicarious expiatory
sacrifice on the Cross, in the Encyclical's definition the
word sin is not even mentioned. Such an omission illuminates the Encyclical's definition. The thesis of Universal
salvation passes over in silence what is in historical reality
the condition of mankind's absolute need of redemption.

The second part of the definition of redemption in the
quoted text takes the thought process of the first part one
stage further and answers the question still hanging: What
does the Cross on Calvary mean, if the Redemption of the
world has already in principle taken place through the
communication to all men of the fullness of justice in the
human heart of the First-begotten Son? Here is the Encyclical's precise answer in the Latin text:

> The Cross on Calvary, through which the man Jesus
> Christ ... "leaves" this world, is also a fresh demonstration
> (*nova demonstratio*) of the eternal fatherhood of God, who
> in him again draws near to humanity, to every single
> human being (*unumquemque hominem*), giving him the
> thrice holy "Spirit of truth."

The sacrifice of the Cross on Calvary is obviously the deed of Redemption by which Jesus Christ made satisfaction to God's eternal fatherhood and wrought reconciliation with the Father. But why is the Cross on Calvary a *new demonstration* of God's eternal fatherhood, who in Christ *again* draws near to humanity? What do the new demonstration and the new love of the Father refer to? Surely to the first part of the definition, meaning the Incarnation of the Son of God, whereby the fullness of justice in his human heart was imparted to the hearts of all men. But why does the Encyclical speak precisely of a "demonstration"?

It would have been altogether possible for the Pope on the basis of his covenant theology to have characterized the Cross on Calvary directly as the saving deed, which wrought the Redemption of the world, had he here too in the Encyclical repeated his familiar phrase, "All men from beginning to end of the world have been redeemed and justified by Christ through his Cross."[26] Or had he recalled that other phrase drawing all men straight into the Church even more inclusively: "The birth of the Church at the moment of Christ's messianic death was basically also the birth of man, independently even of whether man knows it or not, accepts it or not. At this moment man's existence received a new dimension, which is briefly and tersely called by Paul 'being in Christ.'"[27] Christ's physical-historical work of Redemption is and remains in the Pope's theology too the deed of salvation, which underlies and works the Redemption. But the historical work of Redemption stretches in its "ontological" efficacy according to the Pope's covenant theology backwards as far as the act of creation and forwards to the end of the world, so that all

26 Karol Wojtyla, [*Sign of Contradiction*], p. 103.
27 *Ibid.*, p. 108.

men from beginning to end of the world are effectively redeemed and justified through the Cross (see quotation above). And that is the thesis of universal salvation.

There we have the answer to the question: What is the meaning of the Cross, if mankind is already redeemed and justified through the Incarnation? The fullness of justice in the human heart of the First-born Son, which is imparted by the Incarnation to all men's hearts, is the fruit *of the whole historical work of Redemption*, meaning the Incarnation, the Cross and the Resurrection, in other words the *whole* supernatural "being in Christ." That is why the Encyclical can perfectly aptly speak of the Cross on Calvary as a *demonstration*, even a *new demonstration* of the eternal fatherhood of God, who draws near to each man *again* and grants him the Holy Ghost.

This interpretation of the definition of Redemption, arising from the Pope's covenant theology and ultimately from his concept of Revelation, is confirmed by the following self-interpretation in the Encyclical (*RH* 9,2):

> This revelation of the Father (= new demonstration of God's eternal fatherhood) and outpouring of the Holy Spirit (= the thrice holy Spirit of truth), which stamp an indelible seal on the mystery of the Redemption, explain the meaning of the cross and death of Christ. The God of creation is revealed as the God of redemption, as the God who is "faithful to himself" (cf. I Thess. 5:24), and faithful to His love for man and the world, which He revealed on the day of creation. His is a love that does not draw back before anything that justice requires in Him. Therefore "for our sake (God) made him (the Son) to be sin who knew no sin" (II Cor. 5:21; cf. Gal. 3:13). If he "made to be sin" Him who was without any sin whatever, it was to reveal the love that is always greater than the whole of creation, the love that is He Himself, since "God is love" (I Jn. 4:8,16). Above all, love is greater than sin, than weakness, than the "futility of creation" (Rom. 8:20); it is stronger than death; it is a love always ready to raise up and forgive, always ready to go to meet the prodi-

gal son (Lk. 15:11-32), always looking for "the revealing
of the sons of God" (Rom. 8:19), who are called to the
glory that is to be revealed (Rom. 8:8). ... This revelation
of love is also described as mercy; and in man's history this
revelation of love and mercy has taken a form and a name:
that of Jesus Christ.

From the first sentence of this quotation we can draw a
threefold statement:
– Firstly, in the sentence concerning the *revelation of the
Father* appears the Pope's concept of revelation: the demonstration of God's eternal fatherhood on the Cross on Calvary is the *a posteriori*–historical revelation. The pouring
out of the Holy Ghost into the hearts of all men is in
content tantamount to the *a priori* revelation; the two ways
of revelation make together the *"double revelation,"* the
Pope's principle of theological knowledge which implies
universal salvation.
– Secondly, the new demonstration of the eternal fatherhood in the Son on the Cross on Calvary and the pouring
out of the Holy Ghost into the hearts of all men stamp on
the mystery of the Redemption an indelible sign (*indelibile
imprimunt signum*). Accordingly God's eternal fatherhood
embracing all men, the Son's Incarnation whereby all men
are sons of the Father, and the pouring out of the Holy
Ghost into all men's hearts present the inextinguishable seal
in the mystery of the Redemption.
Then Redemption means the self-communication of the
triune God in Christ, the Son of God, and the pouring out
of the Holy Ghost into the hearts of all men. *What is true
for the redeemed and justified Christian believer, holds true for
all without any conditions, whether they know it and want it,
or not. The indelible seal in the mystery of the Redemption is,
then, universal salvation.*
Therewith that text from the Pastoral Constitution has
found in the Encyclical its specific application. The text
runs (*Gaudium et Spes* 22,5):

What holds for Christian believers, holds also *"for all men* of good will, in whose hearts grace is active invisibly. For, since Christ died for all, and since all men are in fact called to one and the same destiny, which is divine, we must hold that the Holy Spirit offers to all the possibility of being made partners, in a way known to God, in the paschal mystery." The Vatican II text leaves room for an interpretation in the sense of the traditional teaching, but that is no longer the case with the Encyclical. What God alone knows becomes, through the criterion of "double revelation" in the Pope's covenant theology, the rationalist axiom of universal salvation.

– Thirdly, the *meaning* of Christ's Cross and death is explained by the revelation of the Father presented above and by the *pouring out* of the Holy Ghost (*Per hanc Patris revelationem effusionemque Spiritus Sancti ... explanatur significatio Crucis ac mortis Christi*). So what we have is the "explanation of the meaning" of Christ's Cross and death, then given according to the principle of "double Revelation." If man is already effectively redeemed and justified by Christ's Cross, then indeed all that remains is *"the explanation of the meaning"* of Christ's Cross and death!

This "explanation" is given by the Encyclical following on the first sentence. It follows amidst the quotation of numerous texts from Scripture, which must however be understood in the sense of the Pope's covenant theology and concept of revelation: "The God of creation" who reveals himself in Christ's death on the Cross as the "God of Redemption," is the God of the Covenant, who "on the very first day of creation" bestowed on man his entire redemptive love and called him into existence as a justified child of God. And to this creative and redemptive love from the day of creation he remains faithful! The "being in Christ" communicated *a priori* to every man in the act of creation and the Adam covenant as man's true being as man (= *a priori* revelation) is "made known" to him *a posteriori* (*a posteriori* revelation) through Christ's saving work in history. "Christ, the new Adam," as the Encyclical said above (*RH* 8,2), "in the very revelation of the mystery of the Father and of his love, *fully reveals man to himself* and brings to light his most high calling." This time the Encyclical says, "This revelation of love and mercy (the Father's) has *in man's history* taken a form and a name: that of Jesus Christ."

10. The human dimension in the mystery of the Redemption.

The divine dimension in the mystery of the Redemption is completed by the human dimension. Under Redemption's human aspect Church dogma brings fully into view the concrete man situated in history: man in the condition of creature fallen away from God, stripped of sanctifying grace and wounded in his human nature, in the state of original sin and absolutely in need of redemption. It brings also fully into view the human-historical character of the work of Redemption itself: the genuinely historical life and activity of the Redeemer for the salvation and rescue of mankind far from God and in absolute need of redemption. The presupposition of redeeming work is mankind in absolute need of redemption as being Adam's descendants in original sin, and mankind's rescue from this condition is that work's purpose. Also brought fully into view is the decision made between eternal salvation or eternal damnation, when sinful mankind far from God meets in history with its crucified Redeemer. Here we have demands being made by God and genuine decisions being made by man: to convert, to believe, to be baptized (Mk. 16:16). The Church clearly teaches that while the Redemption as work of the triune God's mercy and love may be objectively universal, nevertheless it requires the acceptance and subjective application of the Redemption's fruits to the individual man through the process of justification by faith in

Jesus Christ. And justification means the real transition from death to life: "The transfer from the state in which man is born as son of the first Adam into the state of grace and acceptance as children of God through the second Adam, Jesus Christ, our Redeemer," (Denzinger 796) as the Council of Trent defines.

None of this comes into view in the Encyclical. Nor can it possibly come into view, because it would fundamentally contradict the Pope's doctrine of the Redemption: a man who is on the basis of the infinite love, mercy and generosity of God's fatherhood is *a priori* redeemed and justified, is no more in need of justification or the application of the Redemption's fruits, but only of *self-knowledge and love*. This is exactly the point picked up by the Encyclical as it goes on (*RH* 10,1):

> Man cannot live without love. He remains a being that is incomprehensible for himself, his life is senseless, if love is not revealed to him, if he does not encounter love, if he does not experience it and make it his own, if he does not participate intimately in it. This, as has already been said, is why Christ the Redeemer "fully reveals man to himself." If we may use the expression, this is the human dimension of the mystery of the redemption. In this dimension man finds again the greatness, dignity and value that belong to his humanity. In the mystery of the redemption man becomes newly "expressed" and in a way, is newly created. He is newly created! "There is neither Jew nor Greek, there is neither slave nor free, there is neither male nor female; for you are all one in Christ Jesus" (Gal. 3:28).

The text is an authentic interpretation of the "human dimension of the mystery of the Redemption" by the author himself:

The argument follows inductively from the principle of "double Revelation": man is a riddle to himself.

To understand himself he needs to experience love. That is why (!) "Christ the Redeemer fully reveals man to himself." This happens by means of the Father's revelation and his love, whereby the Father's love is set before men's eyes as God's deepest motive in the work of creation and of Redemption. At the same time the deepest motive in man for gratitude and for loving God in return is touched on, insofar as Christ manifests to man his true being as man. This is shown in the "human dimension of the mystery of the Redemption." It includes: "the greatness, dignity and value man has that belongs to his humanity (!)." For man, every man, is, as the Encyclical establishes, *a new creature*, and so redeemed and justified. Hence what the Apostle Paul says of the *believer in Christ* (II Cor. 5:17; Gal. 6:15), and of the *Church of Christ*, holds true for *Christian and non-Christian*, for the *whole of mankind*: "You are all one in Christ Jesus" (Gal. 3:28). Accordingly the whole of mankind is in hidden fashion the body of Christ, the latent Church.[28] The old "ontological" wall of partition between Christian and non-Christian and the old distinction between nature and grace are removed by the axiom of universal salvation.

However, there remains the *barrier of consciousness*. How the *individual man* can break through it, the Encyclical goes on to describe in the following way (*RH* 10,1):

> The man who wishes to understand himself thoroughly – and not just in accordance with immediate, partial, often superficial, and even illusory standards and measures of his being – he must with his unrest, uncertainty and even his weakness and sinfulness, with his life and death, draw near to Christ. He must, so to speak, enter into Him with all his own self, he must "appropriate" and assimilate the whole of the reality of the Incarnation and Redemption in order to find himself.
>
> If this profound process takes place within him, he then bears fruit not only of adoration of God but also of deep wonder at himself. How precious must man be in the eyes of the Creator, if he "gained so great a Re-

---

28 Cf. Part I, pp. 67-73, and above, Footnote 3.

deemer," and if God "gave his only Son" in order that man "should not perish but have eternal life" (Jn. 3:16).

What we have here in the man "who wishes to understand himself thoroughly," is a subjective *process of awareness*: "Man must 'appropriate' and assimilate the whole of the reality of the Incarnation and Redemption in order to find himself." However, "the whole of the reality of the Incarnation and the Redemption" is in the Encyclical the formal union of the Son of God with all men, so that every man (cf. *RH* 13,3) from the first moment of his existence onwards possesses in an indestructible, inalienable fashion "being in Christ" (= *a priori* revelation). The historical revelation in Christ (= *a posteriori* revelation) becomes overall a means of making man aware of his dignity *as man*. As the Pope expresses it elsewhere, Revelation has overall a "man-centered character"; it "circles around man."[29] This version of Revelation is presented step by step in what follows, with implacable logic.

The first unusual highlighting of the *greatness of man* follows in the text in this way: the process of awareness of man's self-discovery leads not only to the adoration of God but also to man's "deep wonder at himself."[30]

The wonder at the marvelous works of God runs through the whole of Scripture. This wonder includes wonder at man as God's creature, especially those men in whom God shows forth in special fashion His marvelous power: His people, pious souls, saints, martyrs. This wonder is *God-centered.*[31] However there follows in the Encycli-

---

29 Karol Wojtyla, [*Sign of Contradiction*], p. 120.

30 Cf. the *Magnificat*, i.e. Mary's sense of wonder over the ineffable benefits which the Lord realized in her. The emphasis is clearly God-centered.

31 Georg Bertram, Art. "*thaumázein*," *ThWzNT* (Kittel), *op. cit.*, III, p. 34. – However in the Hellenistic versions of the Old Testament, there is also the danger of profanation through an excessive hero worship (p. 35).

cal a subtle displacement of emphasis from Christ and God to man being at the center: in the *"Exsultet"* of the Easter Vigil liturgy it says: *"O felix culpa, quae talem ac tantum meruit habere Redemptorem."* In the Encyclical it is the *"value of man,"* who "deserved to have such and so great a Redeemer." Whereas in the *Exsultet* the adoring wonder goes to the *Redeemer,* in the Encyclical the wonder goes to *man.* In the Creator's eyes the *value of man* is so great, that "God gave his Son, so that man might not be lost but have eternal life" (cf. Jn. 3:16). That evokes the question: how great then is the value of man who not only is not lost but once in existence cannot even be lost? As great as the value of the Son, or still greater?

What provokes the question is that the Encyclical gives an incomplete quotation of the text from Scripture and undertakes a double change of meaning. The text from St. John's Gospel runs complete as follows: "God so greatly loved the world, that He gave His only-begotten Son, so that whosoever believeth in him may not be lost, but may have eternal life" (Jn. 3:16). In context in St. John's Gospel the text is saying that through the sacrifice of His only Son even unto death, God gave visible proof of His love "for the world." But "world" here means, as emerges from what follows, *mankind in the darkness of sin turned away from God and so exposed to judgment and eternal death with no means of salvation.* To this world the way to eternal life is opened up through belief in the Son of God, who gives up his life for its redemption.[32]

The double change of meaning is obvious: in the Gospel what we have is *God's love for lost mankind,* in the Encyclical *it is the greatness, dignity, and worth of man,* that very man who *a priori* and inalterably, inalienably possesses "being in Christ" as his own being as man.

---

32 Eduard Schick, *Das Evangelium nach Johannes* [*The Gospel According to John*] (Würzburg 1956, Echter-Bibel), pp. 43ff.

In the Gospel *faith is the way to eternal life*. In the Encyclical faith gets – surely deliberately – left out of the Scriptural quotation. The reason is clear: in the Redemption theology based on the axiom of universal salvation, there is no room for belief in Jesus Christ as a condition for obtaining eternal life. Man is *a priori* redeemed and justified! But through belief in Jesus Christ man is and remains oriented on Christ. On removing faith from the Scriptural text as condition for obtaining eternal life there follows simultaneously the re-orientation of Scripture's centeredness on Christ to the Encyclical's centeredness on man. In the same way, whereas God's love for lost man remains precisely through the condition of faith in Christ, *centered on Christ and God*, when the condition of faith is removed, then the course is set for *an interpretation centered on man*. These are precisely the lines along which the Encyclical proceeds to unfold its thinking.

What the Encyclical with its man-centered re-interpretation of the "Exsultet" and of the Scriptural text of Jn. 3:16 introduced by way of "man's deep wonder at himself," it has no fear of taking to its logical conclusion. The Encyclical continues (*RH* 10,2):

> In reality, the name for that deep amazement at man's worth and dignity is the Gospel, that is to say, the Good News. It is also called Christianity. This amazement determines the Church's mission in the world and, perhaps even more so, "in the modern world." This amazement, which is also a conviction and a certitude – at its deepest root it is the certainty of faith, but in a hidden and mysterious way it vivifies every aspect of authentic humanism – is closely connected with Christ. It also fixes Christ's place – so to speak, His particular right of citizenship – in the history of man and mankind. Unceasingly contemplating the whole of Christ's mystery, the Church knows with all the certainty of faith that the Redemption that took place through the cross has definitively restored man's dignity and given back meaning to his life in the world, a mean-

ing that was lost to a considerable extent because of sin. And for that reason, the Redemption was accomplished in the paschal mystery, leading through the cross and death to resurrection.

To realize, blow by blow, the full force of what the Pope is here saying, as he says it, one must turn to the original text in Latin: *"Re quidem vera miratio maxima de pretio ac dignitate hominis nuncupatur Evangelium, id est Bonus Nuntius. Vocatur item Christianismus."* (The deep amazement of man at himself, at his value and dignity, is called the Gospel, it is the Good News. It is called Christianity.) *So man's amazement at himself is identical with the Gospel!*

– From the very same amazement of man at his own value and dignity proceeds the Church's function in this world! Does not the Church's function (or mission) in this world stem from Christ? Yet the original Latin text is unambiguous: *"Ex eadem ipsa admiratione proficiscitur Ecclesiae munus in hoc mundo."* Later in the Encyclical the Pope makes the same point in a formula just as expressive but looking in the reverse direction: "Man is the way of the Church" (*RH* 14,4).

– Man's amazement at his value and dignity determines also *Christ's place and particular right of citizenship in the history of man and mankind.* For the full force of this sentence too (provided by the Pope with a "so to speak"), one needs to turn to the Latin original which leaves no room for doubt: *"Ea (= miratio) etiam statuit locum Christi ac – si ita fas est dicere – peculiare eius ius civitatis in historia hominis hominumque generis."*

– Man's amazement at his value and dignity is both conviction and certainty. *This certainty is, according to its innermost nature, the certainty of faith.* Why? The Encyclical answers:

Because this amazement is "closely connected with Christ." That stands to reason. For in the Pope's Redemption doctrine every man is through the Incarnation closely connected with Christ. This indissoluble supernatural connection of Christ to every man is for the Pope, according to its innermost nature, "certainty of faith." But that is not all.

– This "certainty of faith" in a secret and hidden way also gives life to true *humanism* in every area. That too stands to reason, if all men, whether as conscious or anonymous Christians, are connected to Christ. True humanism is accordingly "anonymous Christianity."

– The theological basis of the astonishing statements which the Pope deduces from man's amazement at himself, is the thesis of universal salvation. He says: "The Church, unceasingly contemplating the whole of Christ's mystery, knows with all the certainty of faith that the Redemption that took place through the Cross has definitively restored his dignity to man and given back meaning to his life in the world, a meaning that was lost to a considerable extent because of sin. And for that reason, the Redemption was accomplished in the paschal mystery, leading through the Cross and death to Resurrection."

These statements are to be understood and interpreted in the sense of the Pope's theology:

Universal salvation is in the Encyclical the "more complete (awareness of the) mystery of Christ" (cf. *RH* 11,3), which the Church unceasingly contemplates "as a whole" – and now proclaims through the Pope. Only through Vatican II has the Church in her contemplation experienced a broadening of her awareness and gained a broader knowledge of Christ. For, as the Pope says, "The opening made by the Second Vatican Council has enabled the Church and all Christians to reach a more complete awareness of the mystery of Christ" (*RH* 11,3). On this reckoning Christianity which until Vatican II had possessed only an incomplete knowledge of the mystery of Christ, was granted only "in recent times" the "more complete knowledge" of the central mystery of its faith.

It is a matter of intense concern to us that the Pope emphasizes in the strictly dogmatic part of his Encyclical that the thesis of universal salvation is a "certain truth of Faith of the Church." The original Latin runs: *"Ecclesia novit ex certa sua fide."* Are we in the presence of an *ex cathedra* statement?[33]

Lastly there appears also in the text a subtle change of meaning of the *paschal mystery* on the basis of universal salvation: it says that the Redemption "has definitively restored man's dignity and given back meaning to his life in the world, a meaning that was lost to a considerable extent because of sin. And for that reason, the Redemption was accomplished in the paschal mystery." It does *not* say that man lost his (supernatural) dignity through Adam's sin (*propter peccatum*) – which on the basis of the Pope's covenant theology would in no way be possible – but that man lost to a considerable extent *the meaning of his existence.* So the relative clause speaks only of a *considerable loss of meaning,* with the result that the mention of the paschal mystery refers *exclusively to the loss of meaning!* Accordingly the Encyclical says: *Because* man lost the *meaning* of his existence in the world to a considerable extent (!) because of sin, "for that reason (*quocirca*) the Redemption was accomplished in the paschal mystery." The accomplishment of the Redemption in the paschal mystery is here no more than the disclosure of the meaning of man's existence, a presentation of his inalienable dignity. And that is a pure process of awareness!

Finally the Encyclical gives a brief outline of the Church's task, as it emerges from everything said heretofore (*RH* 10,3):

---

33 Cf. Matthias Joseph Scheeben, Theologische Erkenntnislehre, *Handbuch der katholischen Dogmatik* [*Handbook of Catholic Dogma*] (Freiburg i. Br. 1948), Gesammelte Schriften, Vol. III, pp. 231-242.

The Church's fundamental function in every age and particularly in ours is to direct man's gaze (*hominis mentem*), to point the awareness and experience of the whole of humanity towards the mystery of God, to help all men to be familiar with (*ut percipiant*) the profundity of the Redemption taking place in Christ Jesus. At the same time man's deepest sphere is involved – we mean the sphere of human hearts, consciences and events.

The first task of a Church whose function proceeds (see above) from man's wonder at his own dignity which he possesses *a priori* in the mystery of universal salvation in Christ, can only consist in directing men's attention and awareness to this mystery, and in helping them to perceive within themselves what was always ontologically present in hidden fashion in the deepest recesses of their heart and consciousness.

Accordingly the principal task of the Church consists in stirring up, guiding, supporting, and prompting from without the awareness process of self-discovery by the *individual* man, such as the Encyclical described it above (cf. *RH* 10,1).

This doctrine of Redemption proceeding from the Pope's man-centered concept of revelation and covenant theology is a new, self-contained, all-embracing idea, which as such takes the place of the Church's old teaching.

11. The mystery of Christ as the basis of the Church's mission and of Christianity.

The theology of the Redemption (*RH* 7-10) is the basis for the theology of the mission of the Church and of Christianity (*RH* 11-12).

The Pope takes up again the main ideas of the Council which he discussed in the first Chapter (*RH* 3-6), namely ecumenism and dialogue, in order to illustrate them on a broader basis (cf. *RH* 7-10) and once again in a greater and more universal perspective (*RH* 11-12). The thinking does not proceed as linear, systematic development, but rather in a circular, associative pattern.

The main objective of the new pontificate is the unity of Christianity and of all mankind, attained by means of ecumenism and dialogue (cf. *RH* 5-6). –

According to the Encyclical, the Second Vatican Council has provided the necessary means for the Church to fulfill her mission in today's world, by defining the Church as the sacrament for the unity of all mankind:

1. Vatican II has helped to bring about a new, "full and universal awareness of the Church" (*RH* 11,1).

2. Vatican II has given to Christianity a new, "more complete awareness of the mystery of Christ" (*RH* 11,3).

3. Vatican II has thereby laid the theological foundation, on which the Pope develops the principles of the mission of the Church and Christianity in today's world (*RH* 11,4-5).

11.1 A new, full and universal awareness of the Church.

On the new awareness of the Church, the Encyclical says the following (*RH* 11,1):

> The Second Vatican Council did immense work to form that full and universal awareness by the Church of which Pope Paul VI wrote in his first encyclical. This awareness – or rather self-awareness – by the Church is formed "in dialogue"; and before this dialogue becomes a conversation, attention must be directed to "the other," that is to say; the person with whom we wish to speak. The Ecumenical Council gave a fundamental impulse to forming the Church's self-awareness by so adequately and competently presenting to us a view of the terrestrial globe as a map of various religions. It showed furthermore that this map of the world's religions has superimposed on it, in previously unknown layers typical of our time, the phenomenon of atheism in its various forms ...

The text says three things: The Council did immense work in order to form the "full and universal awareness" of the Church. Furthermore: That awareness is formed through dialogue with "the other." The very nature of dialogue presupposes knowledge of the other. Finally: It was by its view of other religions that the Council gave a fundamental impulse for the formation of the Church's new self-awareness.

– The Church's new "full and universal awareness ... – or rather self-awareness," which was attained through the Council's painstaking efforts, is not unfamiliar to us. The above quoted text appeals to the Encyclical *Ecclesiam Suam*, where Pope Paul VI wrote about the awareness of the Church. We already discussed and analyzed this "present-day consciousness of the Church" at great length in Chapter I (3; 4). But to maintain that the Church's "awareness – or rather self-awareness ... is formed 'in dialogue'" is novel indeed. – Thus it is not formed by means of revelation, Holy Scripture or Church doctrine.

– Dialogue is by no means something new in the life of the Church. Dialogue means nothing other than "a conversation between two or more persons," even in New Testament times, in the ancient world, up to the present day.

Jesus' conversation with Nicodemus, with His disciples, with the Scribes and Pharisees are all "dialogues." Dialogue, which was long known to Egypt and the Ancient Orient, found its way to the Greeks. That is where it became a classical form of philosophical debate (Socrates, Plato), which was then taken up by early Christianity. The first Christian dialogues were written around 140 or 150, in a debate with Judaism, starting with the "Dialogue between Jason and Papiskos" and St. Justin's "Dialogue with the Jew Tryphon." These dialogues then attained literary status in Minucius Felix's "Octavius," and culminated in St. Augustine's dialogue-works from Cassiciacum.[34] Up to

---

[34] Cf. Ernst Günther Schmidt, Art. *"Dialogus," Der Kleine Pauli* (Munich 1979), II, p. 1575.

Vatican II, dialogue was an essential element in the Church's mission.[35] The theological basis of dialogue was the faith of the Church. Its goal was to convince non-Christians of their errors and of the truth of the Christian faith, thus to move them to conversion.

The dialogue to which John Paul II refers in *Redemptor Hominis*, however, means something entirely different. It has a new theological basis, which the Encyclical has already laid in its essentials in Chapter I (3-6): In this perspective, it was the broadening of the Church's dogma which led to the "worldwide broadening of the Church's consciousness," from which the Church's "missionary dynamism" breaks forth and also determines the nature of dialogue (*RH* 4). In Chapter II, the Encyclical through its Redemption doctrine has widened the theological basis for the "dialogue of salvation" and declared the thesis of universal salvation as a truth which "the Church knows with all the certainty of faith" (*RH* 10,2). *The dialogue, which the Encyclical teaches and demands, rests on the axiom of universal salvation. Therefore it represents an absolute novelty in the history of the Church.*

The buzz word "dialogue" is a key idea in the Pope's theology. Through the introduction of a new theological basis, the word dialogue undergoes an essential change in meaning. But the purpose of dialogue has essentially changed, just like the meaning. –

There is no doubt that Vatican II gave a fundamental impulse for the formation of the Church's new self-awareness. The question is: In which Council documents is this decisive impulse to be found? Which Council documents does the Pope acknowledge as a faithful expression of the Council's standpoint, which he then makes his own?

The Encyclical gives us the answer (*RH* 11,2):

---

35 Cf. Thomas Ohm, *Machet zu Jüngern alle Völker* [*Make Disciples of all Nations*] (Freiburg i. Br. 1962), pp. 562-566.

The Council document on non-Christian religions in particular is filled with deep esteem for the great spiritual values (*spiritualium bonorum*), indeed for the primacy of the spiritual (*quae spiritualia sunt*), which in the life of mankind finds expression in religion (*in ipsa religione*) and then in morality, with direct effects on the whole of culture.

The Fathers of the Church rightly saw in the various religions as it were so many reflections of the one truth, "seeds of the Word" (*diversis in religionibus totidem imagines unicae cuiusdam veritatis tamquam "semina Verbi"*), attesting that, though the routes taken may be different, there is but a single goal to which is directed the deepest aspiration of the human spirit as expressed in its quest for God and also in its quest, through its tending towards God, for the full dimension of its humanity (*plenae significationis generis humani*), or in other words for the full meaning (*sensus pleni*) of human life. The Council gave particular attention to the Jewish religion, recalling the great spiritual heritage common to Christians and Jews (*magnum illum thesaurum spiritualem commemorans, qui Christianis et Hebraeis est communis*). It also expressed its esteem for the believers of Islam, whose faith also looks to Abraham (*ad Abraham refertur*).

In support of his overwhelmingly positive view of non-Christian religions, the Pope appeals only to the Declaration *Nostra Aetate*, which is specifically dedicated to this theme. As a Council document, a declaration has an essentially weaker theological weight than a decree or a dogmatic constitution.

As a document which should further peace and harmony among men, the declaration *Nostra Aetate* emphasizes above all the positive aspect of non-Christian religions, while neglecting to stress the negative aspects with equal force. The document thus comes across as a one-sided, undiscerning appreciation for non-Christian religions.

The short summary of *Nostra Aetate* in the Encyclical appears still more one-sided, still more undiscerning in its high esteem for non-Christian religions than the Council document itself. Since the Pope in his summary, however, adopts and explains the Council's theological position authoritatively, the above quoted text must be viewed as an authentic interpretation of the supreme magisterium, which clearly states what the Council really meant and desired, as well as what the Pope intends to enforce in his new pontificate.[36]

All the same, the reader will allow some remarks on this Encyclical text:

In its first lines, the "Declaration on the Relation of the Church to non-Christian Religions," *Nostra Aetate*, defines the Church's task as follows: "Ever aware of her duty to foster unity and charity among individuals, and even among nations, she reflects at the outset on what men have in common and what tends to promote fellowship among them" (NA 1,1). According to this view, the Church's task is simply to further the unity of mankind. This definition of her task corresponds perfectly with the key phrase for the ecclesiology of Vatican II as a whole: The Church is the sacrament for the unity of all mankind (*Lumen Gentium* 1,1). The declaration *Nostra Aetate* lays the theological foundation for the path of interreligious of dialogue, which is the aim in view. The main idea is: That which is common to all men leads to unity among all men. In the area of religion, the motto runs: What is common to all religions leads to unity among all religions. Translated that means a one-world religion.[37]

If one can speak of such a thing in the history of religion, the common element in all religions – an idea in vogue since the enlightenment – could only be the least common denominator, after stripping off the overlay of all concrete-

---

[36] Cf. also *Redemptor Hominis* 6,3.

[37] See my analysis of *Nostra Aetate* in: "One Truth and Many Religions," *Respondeo* 8 (Abensberg 1988), pp. 53-61.

historical particularities, resulting in an irrational bewilderment in face of the divine, something in the vein of Rudolf Otto, founder of the modern science of religion, who also brought about the "religious society of mankind" for the purpose of "fostering peace and harmony among religions, conscious as we are of our religious responsibility."[38]

The Church's task according to Vatican II in *Nostra Aetate* is therefore: Start with the common element in all religions and use it in order to lead all men to religious unity and fellowship! This missionary duty is far removed from that which Christ enjoined to His Church (Matt. 28:18-20).

In the Council documents, we can find numerous texts which blatantly contradict the exuberant, one-sided and undiscerning high esteem for non-Christian religions in the Encyclical's summary. Here is a case in point: The following text from *Ad Gentes* (9,2), the *Decree on the Church's Missionary Activity*, offers a balanced judgment of the "values" of non-Christian religions:

> [The Church's missionary activity] purges of evil associations (*a contagiis malignis liberat*) those elements of truth and grace which are found among peoples, and which are, as it were, a secret presence of God; and it restores them to Christ their source who overthrows the rule of the devil and limits the manifold malice of evil. So whatever goodness is found in the minds and hearts of men, or in the particular customs and cultures of peoples (*quidquid boni ... seminatum invenitur*), far from being lost is purified, raised to a higher level and reaches its perfection (*sanatur, elevatur et consummatur*), for the glory of God, the confusion of the demon, and the happiness of men.[39]

---

38 *Ibid.*, pp. 134ff.
39 Christian Gnilka, *Satura tragica. Zu Juvenal und Prudentius*. Wiener Studien (Verlag der Österreichischen Akademie der Wissenschaften 1990), Vol. 103, p. 146.

In support of its oversimplified and high estimate of
non-Christian religions, the Encyclical makes a totally unfounded appeal to the Church Fathers. By maintaining that
the Church Fathers would have seen "in the various religions as it were so many reflections of the one truth, 'seeds
of the Word'" and various ways of union with God, the
Pope makes a contention more in line with the classical
form of heathen syncretism than with the teaching of the
Church Fathers. The Pope's contention is contradicted by
the facts of history. St. Justin, from whom the expression
"seeds of the Word" originates, was the very person who
brandmarks the heathen religions of his time as so many
manifestations of the demonic.[40] The rest of the Church
Fathers shared this view.[41] The theologians and Church
Fathers made a critical assessment of the ancient culture
associated with these heathen religions. It was a matter of
taking individual cultural monuments and customs, sifting,
purifying and aligning them on the Faith and thus assimilating them to the Church (e.g. philosophy, art). But the
reaction of the theologians and Church Fathers towards the
heathen religions as religions, along with their worship, was
an unqualified rejection of these religions as idolatry!
   The principles which guided the Church Fathers in dealing with the culture of the ancient world, however, are in
complete agreement with the points specified in the text
from *Ad Gentes* (9,2). These points of agreement were laid
out with amazing clarity and erudition by Christian
Gnilka:
   "The doctrine of the 'seeds' of goodness in pre-Christian

---

[40] Paul Hacker, *Theological Foundations of Evangelization* (St. Augustin
   1980), p. 36f. Ample proofs can be found there.

[41] *Ibid.*, pp. 40-60. – On the whole question, see also Christian
   Gnilka, *Die vielen Wege und der Eine* [*Many Ways and One Way*], in:
   Literaturwissenschaftliches Jahrbuch (Berlin 1990), Vol. 31, pp. 9-51.
   – Johannes Dörmann, "One Truth and Many Religions," *Respondeo*
   8 (Abensberg 1988). .

culture, which St. Justin made the first attempt to develop
with the help of Stoic philosophy; the synthesis of internal
and external, personal and cultural conversion, which is
found everywhere in the Church Fathers; the God-centered
aspect of any missionary effort to use the elements of goodness at hand for the glory of God; the firm principle of the
Fathers that all goodness belongs to the Creator and must
be referred to Him, so that the Christian, in the course of
adopting and assimilating elements of truth and goodness,
takes in nothing foreign or alien to the Faith, but only that
to which he has a right as a worshiper of the true God; the
conviction of Church authors, based on experience, that
the goods of pre-Christian culture can never be adopted
without due caution and filtering out, since partial aspects
of the good and beautiful among heathen peoples are in-
variably marred by unclean and even detrimental elements;
and finally the knowledge that, by collecting these elements
of goodness and directing them towards Christ, the
Church not only preserves them, but also 'purifies, elevates
and perfects' them or, as the Council says elsewhere (*Ad
Gentes* 11), 'illuminates' them: all the above stated principles served as central ideas in the early Christian *Chrêsis*
[correct usage of elements of heathen culture], and they are
all to be found in the above quoted text, implicitly or
explicitly."[42]

The high esteem of non-Christian religions in the Encyclical text, *allegedly supported by the Council and the
Church Fathers, has in reality no foundation, neither in Holy
Scripture, nor in the Church Fathers, nor in the entire body of
the Council documents.*

Finally: Does the Pope really believe Mohammed's claim
to teach and preserve intact the revelation first proclaimed

---

[42] Cf. Christian Gnilka, as in Footnote 39, p. 146f. See also Gnilka's
fundamental work: *Chrêsis. Die Methode der Kirchenväter im
Umgang mit der antiken Kultur* [*The Methods of the Church Fathers in
Their Contact with Antique Cultures*] (Basel 1984).

in Mecca to Abraham?[43] It is entirely inappropriate to include this historical untenable assertion on the part of Mohammed, and thus to declare Abraham respectfully as the common progenitor of Jews, Christians and Moslems. The real basis of the Encyclical's novel theological view of non-Christian religions is found in the various pre-conciliar versions of the thesis of "anonymous Christianity" and the Conciliar broadening of Church dogma, from which emerges the new "full and universal awareness of the Church." From this basis results the one-sided interpretation of the Council documents and the misinterpretation of the Church Fathers.

11.2 The new and fuller awareness of all Christians concerning the mystery of Christ.

The Encyclical locks into the statements of *Nostra Aetate* and moves on in the text (*RH* 11,3):

> The opening made by the Second Vatican Council has established the Church and all Christians to reach a more complete awareness of the mystery of Christ, "the mystery hidden for ages" (Col. 1:26) in God, to be revealed in time in the Man Jesus Christ, and to be revealed continually in every time. In Christ and through Christ God has revealed Himself fully to mankind and has definitively drawn close to it; at the same time, in Christ and through Christ man has acquired full awareness of his dignity, of the heights to which he is raised, of the surpassing worth of his own humanity, and of the meaning of his existence.

---

43 Cf. Gustav Mensching, *Allgemeine Religionsgeschichte* (Heidelberg 1949), p. 221. – H. L. Gottschalk, *Der Islâm, seine Entstehung, Entwicklung und Lehre.* In: Hg. Franz König, *Christus und die Religionen der Erde* [*Christ and the Religions of the World*] (Freiburg i. Br. 1956), III, p. 14. – W. Montgomery Watt and Alford T. Welch, *Der Islâm.* In: *Die Religionen der Menschheit* [*The Humanist Religion*], published by Christel Matthias Schröder (Stuttgart – Berlin – Cologne – Mainz 1980), Vol. 25,1, pp. 72-77; 118-130; 222ff.

The Encyclical text, which we will try to clarify with the help of the Latin original, makes the following statements:

– Because of the new outlook on non-Christian religions, which the Council introduced in *Nostra Aetate* (*Rebus sic a Concilio apertis*, and not simply "The opening made by the Second Vatican Council has established"), the Church and all Christians were able to reach a "more complete awareness of the mystery of Christ" (*potuerunt pleniorem assequi conscientiam mysterii Christi*).

Therefore the novel high esteem for non-Christian religions, as expressions of the one and only truth and as different ways of union with God, has bestowed on Christianity a more complete awareness of the mystery of Christ. The acknowledgement of the work of the Holy Ghost in all religions led accordingly to a more broad-minded knowledge of Christ as the Universal Savior. This recent mind-broadening of Christianity in reference to the central dogma of Christian faith requires an explanation, which is then given immediately:

– The mystery of Christ is the mystery which was hidden in God from all eternity, which was to be revealed in time: that means in the person of Jesus Christ, and was to be revealed throughout all ages(!), therefore not only preached (*ut in tempore recluderetur: hoc est in Homine Iesu Christo, et ut continenter singulis aetatibus revelaretur*).

The revelation of the mystery of Christ is here defined as a gradual *process of unfolding* of that which is at first hidden in God, then made known through Christ and then continuously down the centuries. Thus it becomes understandable why the Church and all Christians up to Vatican II had to wait in order to receive a new outlook on non-Christian religions and thereby achieve a "more complete awareness of the mystery of Christ." Revelation is then a *process of awareness*, and the more complete mystery of Christ includes all religions, all mankind! That is also explained in due course:

– In Christ and through Christ, God has fully manifested Himself to man and has definitively drawn close to him (*plene se ipsum Deus monstravit hominibus ad eosque modo stabili accessit*). At the same time, in and through Christ, man has acquired full awareness (*plenam conscientiam*) of his dignity and exaltation, thus full awareness of the sense of his existence, of the transcendental value of his own being as a person.

The process of revealing the more complete awareness of the mystery of Christ happens therefore in two ways: As *a posteriori* – historical revelation, in which God fully manifested Himself to man in and through Christ, and as *a priori* revelation, in which God has definitively drawn close to man in and through Christ, or has formally united Himself with each and every man. Through this "double revelation," Christ, through the manifestation of the Father and the Father's love, reveals man to himself by making him aware of his paramount dignity, of the meaning of his existence, and of the value of his transcendent nature as man.

The more complete awareness of the mystery of Christ, which was bestowed on Christianity through the Second Vatican Council, is the mystery of universal salvation.

11.3 The fuller awareness of all Christians concerning the mystery of Christ: foundation for the ecumenical unity and mission of Christianity.

The Church's new, full and universal self-image as well as the new, more complete awareness of the mystery of Christ, which all Christians could achieve through the Second Vatican Council, these both form the premise, from which the Encyclical now infers the need for the union of all Christians (*RH* 11,1) on which follows their common mission (*RH* 11,5) for the unity of all mankind (*RH* 11,4):

All of us who are Christ's followers must therefore [= a

mandate] meet and unite around Him [= Christ]. This unity in the various fields of the life, tradition, structures and discipline of the individual Christian Churches and ecclesial communities[44] (*consociatio – variis in partibus vitae*) cannot be brought about (*perfici*) without effective work aimed at getting to know each other and removing the obstacles blocking the way to perfect unity. However, we can and must immediately reach and display to the world our unity in proclaiming the mystery of Christ, in revealing the divine dimension and also the human dimension of the Redemption, and in struggling with unwearying perseverance for the dignity that each human being has reached and can continually reach (*attingere*) in Christ, namely the dignity of both the grace of divine adoption and the inner truth of humanity, a truth which – if in the common awareness of the modern world it has been given such fundamental importance – for us is still clearer in the light of the reality that is Jesus Christ.

The text enables us to outline the Pope's entire theological view of *Conciliar ecumenism*:

The "more complete awareness of the mystery of Christ," which all Christians could achieve through the new outlook on religions and the dogmatic broadening of Vatican II, is also the common theological basis for the unity of all Christian denominations. Since all Christians possess "being in Christ" *a priori* in virtue of this more broad-minded mystery of Christ, Christian ecumenism has an *"ontological" unity*, and since this Christian ecumenism shares the common belief in Jesus Christ, *the Universal Savior*, it forms a *unity in the faith*. Of course this ecumenical faith includes the conviction of the (conscious or unconscious) "ontological" unity of all mankind in Christ.

From this *basic dogmatic premise* of papal ecumenism, the Encyclical infers the obligation for *Christ's followers*, i.e. for

---

44 The Latin text runs: "*Haec vero consociatio – variis in partibus vitae, traditionis, structurarum ac disciplinarum apud singulas Ecclesias vel Communitates ecclesiales – perfici non potest sine assiduo opere, ...*"

all Christians, to meet and unite their efforts for the sake of Christ Himself (*circa illum ipsum congrediamur et coniungamur*). Since the ontological unity in Christ and the unity of belief in Christ the Universal Savior is assumed, the Pope is genuinely convinced that all Christian denominations form one Church, despite the numerous differences among them. The Encyclical says elsewhere that "each Christian in the community of the people of God builds up the Body of Christ" (*RH* 21.3). We will refer to this clearly defined unity of all Christians in brief as the *ecumenical Church*. That is precisely how the Protestant bishop Kruse described the Church at the ecumenical service with the Pope in Augsburg: Christ at the center is the sun; the Church or Church communities are the planets, which revolve around the sun according to their own paths; all Christian communities form the solar system (= the ecumenical Church).[45]

This union of all Christian confessions despite the diversity of their traditions, structures and disciplines, this union in and through Christ is a real, even fundamental unity of all Christians, which however remains an *imperfect unity* by reason of that diversity. Thus *perfect unity* is the aim of papal ecumenism. The Encyclical indicates the way there: First of all the ecumenical Church itself must be practiced in everyday life. It must deepen and live its belief in the "more complete mystery of Christ," that means it must make all of its members aware of this mystery. The practice of the common awareness of the faith will serve to overcome all obstacles on the way to perfect unity, and to solve the problems arising from the different and opposed traditions, structures and disciplines.

It is the ecumenical Church's responsibility and obligation not only to live its already existing (imperfect) unity,

---

[45] May 4, 1987 in the Basilica St. Ulrich and Afra during the ecumenical service officiated by the Pope, Bishop Kruse, Hanselmann, Stimpfle, Metropolitan Augoustinos and Cardinal Höffner.

but also to attest (*testificari*) it to the world. The content of this ecumenical testimony is of course identical with the ecumenical Church's belief and vital principle. According to the Encyclical, the ecumenical testimony includes: The (more complete) mystery of Christ, the divine and human dimension of the Redemption, the dignity of the grace of divine adoption, a dignity which each person has attained in Christ. At the same time, this dignity represents the dignity of the inner truth of mankind (*humani generis*), which illuminates the *Christian* in that truth, Who is the Truth Himself: Jesus Christ.

In one sentence, the content of the ecumenical proclamation is: The more complete mystery of Christ or the axiom of universal salvation. We must lead an untiring fight for the inner truth and dignity of the person and of mankind.

Finally, with a few strokes, the Encyclical outlines *the office and obligations of the ecumenical Church* as follows (*RH* 11,5):

> Jesus Christ is the stable principle and fixed center of the mission (*stabile principium est sempiternumque velut centrum istius officii ac muneris*) that God Himself has entrusted to man. We must all share in this mission and concentrate (*dirigere*) all our forces on it, since it is more necessary than ever for modern mankind. If this mission seems to encounter greater opposition nowadays than ever before, this shows that today it is more necessary than ever ... [We are very willing to] join in the great mission of revealing (*ostendendi*) Christ to the world, helping each person to find himself (*detegat*) in Christ, and helping the contemporary generations (*subveniendi temporis nostri hominibus*) of our brothers and sisters, the people, nations, states, mankind, developing countries and countries of opulence – in short, helping everyone to get to know "the unsearchable riches of Christ" (Eph. 3:8), since these riches are for every individual and are everybody's property (*quippe quae omni homini praesto sint omnisque hominis bonum efficiant*).

According to the text, there is a missionary order, which God Himself "has entrusted to man" and in which we all (= all Christians) "must share." Jesus Christ is the "stable principle and fixed center" of this mission.

Is this possible? Jesus Christ not the one who entrusted, but rather God Himself? But Christ is still the "fixed center" of the mission. – This mission was not entrusted to the Church of Christ, not even to the "ecumenical Church," but quite simply to "man." We all (= all Christians) "must share" in this mission entrusted to mankind. We are therefore dealing with an indirect participation of ecumenical Christianity in the mission entrusted to mankind. – The general ecumenical mission itself, in which we consciously unite, is clear. It runs: Reveal Christ to the world (= of course the more complete mystery of Christ); help each person to find himself in Christ (= the dignity of the partaking in God's life as His adopted children, the dignity of human nature as such); help the men of our time to recognize "the inscrutable riches of Christ," which are at each person's disposal!

The Pope's remarks yield the following picture:

The fixed center of mankind is the Universal Savior Jesus Christ, Who is already formally united with all mankind by the Incarnation. Thus all mankind is ontologically oriented towards Christ and is associated with Him in an organic, supernatural unity. Thus all mankind is involved in the mission entrusted by God to "man" purely and simply, by which he should discover himself in Christ. All of ecumenical Christianity must participate in this mission entrusted to mankind: Christians are aware of the more complete mystery of Christ and live by it. Thus the mission of Christianity is to proclaim this mystery and to make all mankind aware of its "anonymous Christianity."

The ecumenical mission is centered on consciousness. It is the practical application of the axiom of universal salvation and the principle of "double revelation" to the ecumenical Church and its missionary duty in today's world.

This standpoint differs radically from the pre-conciliar understanding of *ecumenism* and the Church's *mission*:

The Pope's Conciliar ecumenism has an entirely new dogmatic foundation and therefore also an entirely different dogmatic character and meaning. If a basic, though imperfect unity among Christians already exists in the ecumenical Church, then membership in a particular church or Christian denomination is not required for Church unity. The visible unity of the Church, as it was understood and taught up to Vatican II by the Catholic Church, no longer exists. Moreover, the age-old doctrine of the Catholic Church, which demanded unity in the Catholic faith (*unitas fidei*) and in the communion of the Catholic Church (*unitas communionis*) as necessary for the visible unity of the Church, has been completely abandoned. Of course the ecumenism of John Paul II is directed towards the "perfect unity" of all Christian denominations, but based on his idea of the ecumenical Church, this goal is sought after in an entirely different way than was the case with the efforts towards unification led by the Catholic Church before the Council, namely as the return of the separated brethren to the fold of the Roman Catholic Church.

It is likewise evident that the mission, which according to the Encyclical "God Himself has entrusted to man," and which "we must all share," is essentially different from the missionary mandate given by Christ to His Church (cf. Matt. 28:18-20; Mk. 16:15ff).

12. The ecumenical Church's missionary activity and the right to religious liberty.*

After the Pope has presented the nature, content and

---

* Heading in the English translation="The Church's Mission and Human Freedom."

purpose of the ecumenical mission, he proceeds to formulate the practical principles of missionary activity. Upon the "missionary theory" follows the "missionary method."

The theme of Article 12 is, in the language of missionary evangelism, the relationship between the "missionary subject," i.e. the ecumenical Church, and the "missionary object," i.e. non-Christian religions, people and cultures (*RH* 12,1). On this point the problem of religious liberty plays a crucial role (*RH* 12,1-4). The pillars of the Pope's theological position are the Council documents *Nostra Aetate* and *Dignitatis Humanae*. The theological horizon which overshadows the theme of the article is the main objective of the pontificate: The unity of all mankind according to the Council's definition: "The Church is, in Christ, the sacrament ... for the unity of all mankind" (*Lumen Gentium* 1,1).

12.1 The ecumenical Church's missionary outlook on the non-Christian world.

All disciples gathered around Christ in the ecumenical Church were already called upon to manifest their imperfect, but fundamental unity in Christ and the "more complete mystery of Christ," which unites them in the faith, and also to proclaim to the whole world particularly the "dignity of the grace of divine adoption" of all men, which at the same time represents "the dignity of the inner truth of humanity" (cf. *RH* 11,3).

The Encyclical now explains this *unity of mission* and formulates *the principles of the ecumenical Church's missionary outlook on the non-Christian world* (*RH* 12,1):

> In this unity in mission, which is decided principally by Christ Himself, all Christians must find what already unites them, even before their full communion is achieved. This is apostolic and missionary unity, missionary and apostolic unity.
> Thanks to this unity we can together come close to the

magnificent heritage of the human spirit that has been manifested in all religions, as the Second Vatican Council's Declaration *Nostra Aetate* (1-2) says.

It also enables us to approach all cultures, all ideological concepts, all people of good will. We approach them with the esteem, respect and discernment that since the time of the apostles has marked the missionary attitude, the attitude of the missionary. Suffice it to mention St. Paul and, for instance, his address in the Areopagus at Athens (Acts 17:22-31).

The missionary attitude always begins with a feeling of deep esteem for "what is in man" (Jn. 2:25), for what man has himself worked (*excogitavit*) out in the depths of his spirit concerning the most profound and important problems. It is a question of respecting everything that has been brought about in him by the Spirit, which "blows where it wills" (Jn. 3:8). The mission is never destruction, but instead is a taking up and fresh building, even if in practice there has not always been full correspondence with this high ideal. And we know well that the conversion that is begun by the mission is a work of grace, in which man must fully find himself again.

With a few strokes the Encyclical gives us an overview of the ecumenical Church's missionary outlook. No doubt this touches a rather delicate subject in the "modern world."

The "missionary subject" is the ecumenical Church in the sense defined above (see 11.3). The "apostolic and missionary unity" consists in proclaiming to mankind the "more complete mystery of Christ" and hence in proclaiming man's true dignity as man. The *ecumenical Church* is *a missionary and apostolic Church*. The familiar adjectives "apostolic and missionary" have undergone a complete change in meaning.

Whereas the preceding articles described the ecumenical mission as one "which God Himself has entrusted to man" (*RH* 11,5), now we are told that the mission was "decided principally by Christ Himself." That is no contradiction, no implication of a double mission. The sentence should rather be understood in the context of the Encyclical's missionary outlook, according to which "Jesus Christ is the stable principle and fixed center of the mission that God Himself has entrusted to man" (cf. *RH* 11,5). That means: It is "principally ... Christ himself" (= the Universal Savior), Who "decides" on the *content and form* of the mission, which is to say: Jesus Christ is the model and norm.

Thanks to the solidarity and unity of mission, the former missionary pluralism of opposing Christian denominations is replaced by the friendly and peace-making mission of the ecumenical Church. The Church begins by making religious peace within, among the evangelizing denominations themselves, then she continues without, in a united missionary effort, by striving for religious peace in the non-Christian world. This she does in accordance with "the Second Vatican Council's Declaration *Nostra Aetate*" (uti docet Concilii Vaticani II Declaratio *Nostra Aetate*).

The topic of the declaration *Nostra Aetate* is "the Church's relations with non-Christian religions."[46] The present topic of the Encyclical is "the *ecumenical Church's* relations with non-Christian religions." The principles established by *Nostra Aetate* for the Church's relations hold equally for the ecumenical Church.

Since the Pope has already explained the principles of the declaration *Nostra Aetate* more extensively in the preceding (cf. *RH* 11,2), he can afford to state them here more succinctly. The ecumenical Church's relations with the "missionary object" are of course determined by how she *evaluates* them (i.e. non-Christian religions). On the subject of that "missionary object," the Encyclical can only speak with the utmost esteem (cf. *RH* 11,2):

---

46 The Latin title runs: "*Declaratio de Ecclesiae habitudine ad religiones non-christianas.*" The issue is quite literally the Church's "attitude" towards non-Christian religions.

All religions are a "magnificent heritage of the human spirit." That is no *theological*, but rather a purely *human assessment*. All other forms of human culture, all world views and all men of good will are evaluated on that very basis (*cunctas humani cultus formas; omnes ideologicas opinationes; singulos homines bonae voluntatis*).

The evaluation of the "missionary object" follows from the high esteem for the "missionary subject," the ecumenical Church (*RH* 11,2).

Based on this attitude (with the spirit of "discernment"), the Pope claims that the Church's missionary outlook was realized in an exemplary fashion since apostolic times. He says: "We approach [the religions, cultures, world views and persons] with the esteem, respect and discernment that since the time of the apostles has marked the *missionary* attitude, the attitude of the *missionary*." As proof it suffices to quote the example of St. Paul's discourse at the Areopagus (Acts 17:22-31).

What holds in the general holds also for the individual case: "The missionary attitude always begins with a feeling of deep esteem for 'what is in man' (Jn. 2:25), ... [and especially for] everything that has been brought about in him by the Spirit, which 'blows where it wills' (Jn. 3:8)."

Therefore mission is never destruction, but rather taking up the existing values and building on them afresh. "Conversion" is also mentioned at the conclusion. It must originate from the mission. Conversion is the effect of grace. In and through it, "man must fully find himself again (*homo se ipsum plene reperiat oportet*).

The Pope's missionary ecumenism is a totally new *idea*, which as such replaces the Catholic Church's pre-conciliar position. Some remarks on this point are in order:

It is obvious that the "more complete awareness of the mystery of Christ" (which includes unity of being, of belief and of mission in the ecumenical Church) has no basis in the New Testament nor in the Tradition of the Catholic

Church. The mission of an ecumenical Church, which is founded on the axiom of universal salvation as its content and purpose, is plainly *an absolute novelty in the history of the Church.*

It is obvious that the mission of the ecumenical Church, "which God Himself has entrusted to man," in which all Christians "must participate" (cf. *RH* 11,5), and "which is decided principally by Christ Himself," has very little to do with the missionary mandate which Christ gave to His Church (cf. Matt. 28:18-20; Mk. 16:15f). In the Encyclical text on the topic of mission, there is no mention of the requirement to believe and to be baptized! The reason for that omission is of course the axiom of universal salvation.

The concept of an "ecumenical Church," which is gathered around Christ in a fuzzy pluralism of "Churches and Church communities" who find in Christ their fundamental, though imperfect unity, solemnly pleads ignorance of the dogma of the visibility of Christ's Church, which is a historical reality in virtue of the unity of the Catholic faith (*unitas fidei*) and in the unity of the communion of the Catholic Church (*unitas communitatis*, i.e. hierarchical and liturgical unity). For the ecumenical Church and her "apostolic and missionary unity," the "four marks" of the true Church of Christ are unimportant. By the very concept of the ecumenical Church, the Encyclical renounces *per se* any former claims of the Catholic Church to be the one true Church instituted by Christ.

The declaration *Nostra Aetate* is not the Council's only statement on the relationship of the Church towards non-Christian religions. Nevertheless, according to the Encylical, it is the only admitted standard for judging the relations of the ecumenical Church towards non-Christian religions, people and cultures. Suprisingly enough, the Encyclical does not quote the Council's decree on missions *Ad Gentes* when treating the question of missions.

The attitude demanded by the ecumenical Church towards non-Christian religions, people and cultures can be summed up in one word: Respect. But the very nature of mission involves not only the question of a purely human, cultural, anthropological or missionary evangelical view and appraisal, but rather first and foremost the question of eternal salvation, and hence mission must be judged from the point of view of the New Testament and of Catholic dogma.

Even the most nonpartisan student, who considers the history of religion and civilization solely from the point of view of science and who ventures an evaluation, would not dare make such brazen and sweeping statements as the Encyclical does when it speaks of the "magnificent heritage of the human spirit" which merit the greatest esteem, but the objective student would also acknowledge the darker aspects of these religions, which often reach significant proportions. Or should only Christianity and Christian culture be laid bare for criticism?

The Encyclical, however, also considers the theological point of view. In support of its high esteem for all religions, cultures and world views, albeit with "discernment," it appeals to Holy Scripture and to the Church's missionary tradition since apostolic times. The Encyclical merely refers to the Apostle St. Paul. Such a pretention as invoking the Apostle of the Gentiles and the Church's entire missionary history in support of its own thesis is fully unwarranted. What is more, the reference to St. Paul's discourse at the Areopagus lends no support to the high esteem, which the ecumenical Church demands of its missionaries in their dealings with non-Christian religions and cultures. There is not even a trace of the spirit of "discernment" in the Encyclical. One should at least give due consideration to the context of the passage from the Acts of the Apostles, which is given as a paradigm (i.e. model and exemplar). Did St. Paul really "approach" the heathen religions "with respect?" We hear in the Acts of the Apostles (17:16):

Now whilst Paul waited for them [his companions] at Athens, his spirit was stirred within him, seeing the city was wholly given to idolatry.

On that passage, a Biblical commentary says the following:[47]

Paul's indignation flares up on account of that very element which was the Athenians' greatest claim to glory and the touchstone of their piety, namely that nowhere else in the world could one see as many different representations of the divinity as in their city. But this piety, in Paul's eyes, was total confusion; his anger is the biblical anger in the face of heathenism, the same anger as expressed by the prophets, reflecting the anger of God (cf. Rom. 1:18ff).

St. Paul's judgment on the heathen religions in his Epistle to the Romans (cf. 1:18ff) is simply devastating. One might object that the judgment of Scripture and Tradition is erroneous or relative to the mentality of its time, but in that case one cannot appeal to it in support of the novel high esteem for all religions. Holy Scripture would not have us bow down before every idol that comes our way.

It is the Church's traditional doctrine that God desires all men to be saved, that He gives each person a chance to save his soul, that His grace precedes and aids the work of missions and conversions (*gratia praeveniens*). Therefore the pre-conciliar Catholic Church's missionary work also posed the question of what the Holy Ghost could have already worked in the hearts of person and their cultures, to prepare them for the reception of the Faith. But this outlook was not founded, as in the Encyclical, on the thesis of universal salvation and the presence of the Holy Ghost in

---

47 Gustav Stählin, *Die Apostelgeschichte. Das Neue Testament Deutsch* [*Acts of the Apostles. The German New Testament*] (Göttingen 1966), V, p. 228.

the hearts of all men, but on the central dogma of Christianity concerning man's absolute need for Redemption from original sin, in virtue of the Catholic Church's faith by which she judges all things. Once again, there is no trace of this spirit of "discernment" in the Encyclical. Nor is there any mention of the depths of misery and sin of mankind without redemption (cf. Rom. 3:9-18).

The bald statement: "Mission is never destruction, but rather taking up the existing values and building on them afresh," could be interpreted according to the traditional concept of mission. But in the Encyclical it can only be understood in the sense of universal salvation, which also forms the wide-scale basis for the post-conciliar missionary activity. According to the Prefect of the Congregation for the Evangelization of Nations, Cardinal Tomko, the consequences for the missions have been "devastating."[48] Moreover, the traditional view is still faithfully set forth in the decree *Ad Gentes* and confirmed by the Council for our times (see above AG 9,2). But the decree on missions is completely ignored in the Encyclical.

The Pope concludes his remarks on the mission of the ecumenical Church with the mention of "conversion." Of course it was a bit hard to leave that word out altogether.

The biblical key word "conversion" marks the goal of Christian missions from the beginning. In the New Testament, conversion means: Doing penance, changing one's evil ways, turning away from sin, giving oneself over to the God of biblical revelation.[49] Conversion is a prerequisite for belief in the gospel. St. Mark the Evangelist sums up the whole Gospel in one sentence (1,15): "The kingdom of God is at hand: Repent and believe the Gospel!" St. Paul

---

48 Cardinal Tomko in the essay: "The rising influence of sects and the preaching of Christ as the one and only Savior" (*OR*, dt. Apr. 26, 1991).

49 Cf. Johannes Behm and Ernst Würthwein, Art. *metanoéoo*, ThWzNT (Kittel), IV, pp. 972-1004.

praises the Thessalonians because they "turned to God from idols, to serve the living and true God" (I Thess. 1:9).

For St. Paul, the Apostle of the Gentiles, conversion means being liberated from idols through Christ crucified, and turning with one's whole heart to God and the Father of Jesus Christ. In the Encyclical, "conversion" is fully compatible with respect for the gods of non-Christian religions; conversion means simply turning towards man: so that man can "fully find himself again." In the Bible, the prophets' call to penance was: "shubu," return to God! The Pope's call to penance is: Man, discover your greatness! In Holy Scripture, conversion is God-centered; in the Encyclical, it is man-centered: that is the consequence of the man-centered character of "double revelation," of the Pope's principles of theological knowledge.

12.2 The ecumenical Church's missionary mandate and the right to religious liberty.

In our day and age, a mission for the purpose of conversion, be it in the sense of Tradition or of the Encyclical, must face the problem of religious liberty which is generally acknowledged as a human right.

The rapid expansion of Christianity in the first centuries came about by acts of conversion, faith, baptism, reception into the Church. Conversion to Christianity (not self-discovery) was often associated with persecution and martyrdom. The same holds today above all in the more stringent Islamic countries. The Church, which up until Constantine was not a religion officially approved in the Roman empire, also demanded for herself the right to the free exercise of her religion. Later there developed an intricate and involved fusion of the state, politics, the Church and missions which led to well-known conflicts in the course of history. Even the history of Christian missions traversed periods of the unholy alliance of the sword and the Cross, of political conquest, forced conversions, while at the same

time more noble heroes fought for the rights of the op-
pressed and for the freedom of the act of conversion.
Therefore, after discussing the general principles of the
ecumenical Church's mission, the Encyclical comes to the
point by facing the problem: Conversion and religious liberty. The paragraph closed with the definition of "conversion": "Man must fully find himself again" (*RH* 12,1).
Later on in the text, we read (*RH* 12,2):

> For this reason the Church in our time attaches great
> importance (*pondus maximum*) to all that is stated by the
> Second Vatican Council in its *Declaration on Religious
> Liberty* ... We perceive immediately that the truth revealed
> to us by God imposes on us an obligation. We have, in
> particular, a great sense of responsibility for this truth. By
> Christ's institution the Church is its guardian and teacher,
> having been endowed with a unique assistance of the
> Holy Spirit in order to guard and teach it in its most exact
> integrity (cf. Jn. 14:26). In fulfilling this mission, we look
> towards Christ Himself, the first evangelizer (*Evangelii
> Nuntiandi* 6), and also towards His apostles, martyrs and
> confessors.

One could hardly be more explicit about the obligation
to proclaim revealed truth. It is likewise strongly emphasized that missionary relations with the non-Christian
world should be guided by revealed truth without any re-
ductions or omissions. But for the Encyclical, the "integ-
rity" or fullness of revealed truth is the "fuller awareness of
the mystery of Christ," which ecumenical Christianity has
been enabled to reach thanks to the opening of Vatican II
(cf. *RH* 11,3).

In the fulfillment of her mission, the ecumenical Church
looks towards Christ. Christ Himself is the first one to
preach the Gospel; Christ Himself, together with the apostles, martyrs and confessors, is *the* exemplar and model for
the fulfillment of the ecumenical Church's mission. But the
Christ of universal salvation in the Encyclical is not the

Christ of the Gospel!

One would expect the Encyclical to present the problem in question: conversion and religious liberty, in light of the New Testament. But that does not happen. Rather the Pope appeals to the *Declaration on Religious Liberty* to prove his point. For the moment, we will not follow his line of reasoning, but will retain the undisputed fact that Christ Himself and the apostles are the exemplar and model for the missionary evangelization, for our analysis of the problem: conversion and religious liberty, in the context of the New Testament.

The Gospel is the only basis on which we can hold a theological discussion on conversion and religious liberty. From beginning to end, the Gospel is a call to conversion (cf. Mk. 1:15). Thus conversion plays a crucial role in the New Testament. But the Gospel is also a continual "dialogue" between Jesus Christ and the various representatives and groups of His people. The way in which Jesus and His apostles first preached the Gospel, as outlined in the New Testament, also sets the norm for the Church's later missionary activity until the end of time. Thus the question is : How is the relationship between conversion and religious liberty presented in the context of the Bible?

In the "dialogue" of Jesus and the apostles with their "dialogue partners," man is directly confronted with the person of his God, Who has become man, and Who calls upon man to convert. At the same time, all the consequences of his decision, whether for or against, are placed before his eyes. The faith required in the Gospel is and remains a free, personal act of each man. He can refuse it. It is up to each man whether he converts or not. The preaching of Jesus and the apostles is addressed to man's freedom to choose. It is thus primarily a question of man's free will, which is required for any human act of the moral or religious order. Hence, in his attitude towards God and Christ, man has the possibility to accept or refuse the Gospel, even God Himself and his commandments. Hence, for the free act of conversion, this freedom is essential, which the Gospel leaves intact. But does man have also the *moral right* to refuse God's Will, especially since he has the obligation to follow God's commandments? The first three commandments are also included in the Decalogue. As man has the freedom, but not the right, to steal, to murder, to lie or to commit adultery, so also he has the freedom, but not the right, to do away with the commandments which concern his duties to God. If he had such a right, there would be no such thing as judgment day. Such a right is not "part" of divine revelation. Thus it cannot be founded on that revelation.

The New Testament's perspective should serve as the basis for the Encyclical's presentation. In presenting the way Christ and the apostles first proclaimed the truth, the Pope does not appeal to Holy Scripture, but rather to the Council's *Declaration on Religious Liberty*. He thus continues as follows (*RH* 12,2):

> The *Declaration on Religious Liberty* shows us convincingly that, when Christ and, after Him, His apostles proclaimed the truth that comes not from men but from God, ... a deep esteem for man, for his intellect, his will, his conscience and his freedom. Thus the human person's dignity itself becomes part of the content of that proclamation, being included not necessarily in words but by an attitude towards it. This attitude seems to fit the special needs of our times. Since man's true freedom is not found in everything that the various systems and individuals see and propagate as freedom, the Church, because of her divine mission, becomes all the more guardian of this freedom, which is the condition and basis for the human person's true dignity.

Unquestionably, the way in which Christ and the apostles proclaimed the Gospel is "part of the content of that proclamation" – and also the norm of the Church's mis-

sionary activity for all times. Thus the founding of the
Congregation for Missions (1622) was directed towards the
evangelization of the heathens in the spirit of the apostles
and the early Church.[50] The continued reform of the
Church's missions from Benedict XV down to John XXIII
was nothing fundamentally novel, but it was the realization
of the original objectives of the Congregation for the
Propagation of the Faith: the renewal of the Church's missions in the spirit of the apostles and the early Church.

But did the Council's *Declaration on Religious Liberty*
really "show us convincingly" the way in which Christ and
the apostles preached? The Encyclical offers us the bleak
phrase: The preaching of Christ and the apostles shows "a
deep esteem for man, for his intellect, his will, his conscience and his freedom." Should we simply swallow it?
This formula, which neglects altogether the religious aspect
of Holy Scripture, remains on the level of the purely human, and hence follows in the footsteps of the declaration
Nostra Aetate, which also mentions the esteem and respect
for all religions, cultures, and world views, which allegedly
has marked the Church's missionary attitude since the time
of the apostles (cf. *RH* 12,1). The Encyclical stoops from
the Gospel down to a modern and purely human perspective, which becomes clear at the latest with the following
statement: "This attitude (= of Christ and the apostles)
seems to fit the special needs of our times."

In this way, thus in accordance with the declaration *Dignitatis Humanae* and its description of the attitude of
Christ and the apostles, by which they always showed the
utmost respect for the intellect, will, conscience and freedom of those persons to whom they preached the Gospel,
"the human person's dignity itself becomes part of the con-

---

50 Johannes Dörmann, *Die universale Mission der Kirche vor der
Herausforderung der einheimischen Kulturen. Das Problem der Indi-
genisation.* In: *Weltmission in der Weltkrise* (St. Augustin 1979), p.
13f.

tent of that proclamation." Why this detour through the declaration *Dignitatis Humanae*, when dealing with the attitude of Christ and His esteem for man and his freedom? Man himself, the things he loves and the way he lives, is surely a key element in the Gospel, indeed in the entire biblical perspective. But the Gospel is mainly concerned with man's relations to God His Lord and Savior, man's sinfulness and need of redemption, man's faith or rejection of the faith, his salvation or damnation, therefore his dignity as a child of God, which he can and should attain through participation in the glory (*doxa*) of God the Son through faith. In this biblical context, the "attitude" of Christ and the apostles, as well as their "deep esteem" for man, is directed towards the proclamation of the Gospel. Indeed, one cannot separate these elements from their biblical context. But that is just what happens in the Encyclical when it appeals to *Dignitatis Humanae*: The attitude of Christ and the apostles is lifted from the biblical context, and thereby isolated, re-interpreted and christened as an element of the Gospel. Thus the modern notion of religious liberty is given definitive status as an element of the Gospel, and the Church is declared the divinely commissioned "guardian of this freedom."

If one bears in mind that, in the Encyclical, the dignity of the human person already includes the grace of divine adoption, which in turn constitutes the very nature of man (cf. *RH* 11,4), then through the phrase maintaining that, in virtue of the attitude of Christ and the apostles, "the human person's dignity itself becomes part of the content of that proclamation," the thesis of universal salvation has surreptitiously been introduced as "part of the content" of the Gospel.

Finally a philosophical question: Is freedom really "the condition and basis (*condicio ac fundamentum*) for the human person's true dignity?" Is not the ontological basis of freedom rather the spiritual nature of man and the dignity ensuing therefrom? When Christ was in chains and deprived of His freedom, did He thereby lose His dignity?

According to the Encyclical, Jesus Christ is not only the one Who through His attitude proclaims human freedom, the condition and basis for the human person's true dignity, as an element of the Gospel, but also the one Who teaches and imparts true freedom to man. Thus the text of the Encyclical continues (*RH* 12,3):

> Jesus Christ meets the man of every age, including our own, with the same words: "You will know the truth, and the truth will make you free" (Jn. 8:32). These words contain both a fundamental requirement and a warning: the requirement of an honest relationship with regard to truth as a condition for authentic freedom, and the warning to avoid every kind of illusory freedom, every superficial unilateral freedom, every freedom that fails to enter into the whole truth about man and the world. Today also, even after 2,000 years, we see Christ as the one who brings man freedom based on truth, frees man from what curtails, diminishes and as it were breaks off this freedom at its root, in man's soul, his heart and his conscience.
>
> What a stupendous confirmation of this has been given ... by those who, thanks to Christ and in Christ, have reached true freedom and have manifested it even in situations of external constraint!

In his presentation, the Pope argues from Jn. 8:32. The true meaning of the passage is seen by the context, which runs as follows (Jn. 8:31f):

> Then Jesus said to those Jews who believed in Him: If you continue in my word, you shall be my disciples indeed. And you shall know the truth; and the truth shall make you free.

Jesus therefore turns especially to the believing Jews. To these He explains the true nature of being a disciple:) namely the acceptance and faithful observance of His word. In those true disciples who believe in Christ and

follow His word, it is this living faith which brings forth
the knowledge of the truth. In St. John, the word truth
assumes not a philosophical, but rather a religious meaning. It means always the reality of the divine, made known
to man through divine revelation. Jesus claims not only to
communicate divine truth, but also to be that very truth in
person (Jn. 12:45;14:6,9f). *The knowledge of the truth is
therefore the knowledge of Jesus Christ.* A second fruit of
living faith promised by Christ is Redemption through the
truth, which He Himself is. *Freedom* is not merely a natural, ethical endowment, but a supernatural, religious gift,
which the Evangelist then declares as *Redemption from the
slavery of sin.*[51]

The comparison of the biblical text with the above
quoted Encyclical text clearly reveals the following differences:

The text in Jn. 8:32 is meant to be neither a "fundamental requirement," nor a "warning." It is rather *Jesus' own
promise* to the Jews, "who believed in Him." *This promise is
based on the condition of belief in Christ.* To be a true disciple of Christ means not only the readiness to believe, but
also the actual acceptance of Christ's word and the faithful
observance of it in everyday life. That means therefore exactly what Jesus said to His disciples in Jn. 15:14: "You are
my friends if you do the things that I command you."

None of this is mentioned in the Encyclical. The Pope is
surely not preaching unbridled liberty. But the Encyclical
shifts the emphasis from fidelity in Christ's service to the
"condition for authentic freedom" of each person. Faith in
Christ is by no means required for this freedom, but "an
honest relationship with regard to the truth" is enough,
provided one avoids any false freedom, "that fails to enter

---

51 For the interpretation of Jn. 8:32, see Eduard Schick, *Das Evangelium nach Johannes* [*The Gospel According to John*] (Würzburg
1956, Echter-Bibel), pp. 86ff.

into the whole truth about man." Anyone can accept and satisfy this condition. It has nothing to do with the Joannine condition for being a disciple of Christ, which is based on the faith. The word faith is not even mentioned.

In the Encyclical text, what is meant by freedom, "authentic freedom," which for St. John is freedom from the slavery of sin? Answer: It is marked by "the whole truth about man" and is therefore already in man *a priori*. For, as the Encyclical states, Christ is the one Who "frees man from what curtails, diminishes and as it were breaks off this freedom at its root, in man's soul, his heart and his conscience." Of course that means the man's hidden dignity which he already possesses *a priori* thanks to universal salvation.

The scriptural passage Jn. 8:32 is therefore lifted from its context, sanitized and re-interpreted in a merely human perspective. In the Encyclical, the very meaning of Christ's words is altered in virtue of the principle of man-centered "double revelation."

The Pope's line of reasoning can be traced as follows: The conversion sought after by ecumenical missionary work is essentially *man's self-discovery*, which leads to man's full knowledge of the truth about himself, his true dignity and authentic freedom. It is Christ who reveals to man the full truth about human nature: "Christ reveals man to himself." He also makes man aware of his "authentic freedom," which is the "fundamental requirement" for man's true being as man. That is how Christ frees man from everything that stifles freedom in the human soul, and breaks off freedom at its roots (*ipsis in eius radicibus*). Consequently the Encyclical has bridged the gap between conversion and universal salvation, and thus laid the theological foundation for the requirement of religious liberty as a right of all men. All this is eloquently confirmed by those who have attained this freedom.

Finally the Encyclical appeals to Christ as witness and

guarantor of its interpretation of Jn. 8:32 (*RH* 12,4):

> When Jesus Christ Himself appeared as a prisoner be-
> fore Pilate's tribunal and was interrogated by him about
> the accusation made against Him ... , did He not answer:
> "For this I was born, and for this I have come into the
> world, to bear witness to the truth" (Jn. 18:37)? It was as
> if with these words spoken before the judge at the decisive
> moment He was once more confirming what He had said
> earlier: "You will know the truth, and the truth will make
> you free."

Later on it becomes clear that the Evangelist's idea of
truth differs considerably from the Encyclical's idea, which
is centered on man (*RH* 12,4):

> In the course of so many centuries, of so many genera-
> tions, from the time of the apostles on, is it not often
> Jesus Christ Himself that has made an appearance at the
> side of people judged for the sake of the truth? And has
> He not gone to death with people condemned for the
> sake of the truth? Does He ever cease to be the continuous
> spokesman and advocate for the person who lives "in
> spirit and truth" (Jn. 4:23)? Just as He does not cease to
> be it before the Father, He is it also with regard to the
> history of man. And in her turn the Church, in spite of all
> the weaknesses that are part of her human history, does
> not cease to follow Him who said: "The hour is coming,
> and now is, when the true worshipers will worship the
> Father in spirit and truth, for such the Father seeks to
> worship him. God is spirit, and those who worship him
> must worship in spirit and truth" (Jn. 4:23-24).

These pressing words would be rather convincing, if understood from the biblical standpoint of Jn. 8:32 and the
whole of St. John's Gospel, and not from the theological
principles of the Encyclical. In the Encyclical, Christ is said
to be the advocate "for the person who lives in spirit and in
truth." Of course Christ is always present "with regard to
the history of man," but He has promised this abiding

presence only to His Church: "Behold I am with you always even unto the consummation of the world" (Matt. 28:20). Article 12 of the Encyclical closes with the scriptural passage Jn. 4:23-24. The article comes to a triumphal conclusion with this passage mentioning the true adorers "in spirit and in truth." It joyfully announces the first stages of a "new, universal religion based on freedom in the Holy Spirit, who is given to all men, and who reveals to all men the full truth of their greatness. For this hour has now arrived! Assisi *is* the beginning of this new age!"[52]

The prayer meeting of all religions is not only the main objective of the pontificate, which the Pope proclaims in his inaugural Encyclical (*RH* 6,3), but also the public manifestation of the core of his Redemption doctrine.

12.3 Digression: The mission of the ecumenical Church and natural right to religious liberty.

The new outlook on the ecumenical Church's missionary relations to non-Christian religions, people and cultures (cf. *RH* 11,2;12,1) leads the Pope to raise the problem of religious liberty and to consider it in the perspective of the Conciliar declaration *Dignitatis Humanae* (cf. *RH* 12,2). The question at hand is not the *theological basis* for the right to religious liberty in the context of the Encyclical's Redemption doctrine, therefore the Pope is not concerned with the realization of this right in the domain of state affairs. He goes into that point later in more detail (cf. *RH* 17).

The *traditional doctrine* founded the right to religious liberty on the nature of the one true revealed religion: Since God has revealed Himself and has accomplished the work of the Redemption for the salvation of the world through

52 Johannes Dörmann, "Assisi: Beginning of a New Age," (Abensberg 1988), *Respondeo* 8, pp. 126-182.

His Son, it followed that only the religion which God founded had the right to free and public exercise of its worship. The grave issues involved in divine revelation therefore resulted in dogmatic intolerance, which however was always tempered by tolerance in the practical order.[53] The Catholic Church always taught that conversion to the true religion could not be obtained by force, but had to be a free decision, no matter if the biblical expression "compel them to come in" (Lk. 14:23) gave rise to misinterpretations in ages gone by. In the Gospel itself, nobody is ever forced to convert or to believe. But the does not mean that man has a right to religious liberty before God (*ius ad libertatem religiosam*). The basic tenet held sway: The right to freedom is founded on the rights of objective truth. Traditional teaching upheld the primacy of the truth over freedom, as well as the principle that error could have no rights against the truth.

The declaration *Dignitatis Humanae* is not an insignificant, but rather a substantial deviation from the traditional teaching.[54] The Council document acknowledges the public right of each person to religious liberty, which it defines as an inalienable right of the human person. It touches the private and public exercise of religion according to the demands of one's conscience. This right to freedom is not founded on any determined subjective dispositions of the person, for instance on his belief in the true faith, but rather on his objective being and nature. Thus the critical step is made from the "rights of the truth" to the "rights of the person." The declaration clearly states that the right to religious liberty exists regardless of the objective truth of the individual's religious conviction and irrespective of his personal effort to attain this truth. The right remains even

---

[53] Cf. Part I, pp. 1ff and Footnote 2.

[54] Ernst-Wolfgang Böckenförde, "Der Abschied vom Gottesstaat," Article (*Deutsche Tagespost*, Apr. 18, 1987), pp. 21ff. – The contrary position is there defended by Arthur F. Utz (pp. 23ff).

for him who does not fulfill his duty to search for the truth and to adhere to it. The Council's declaration has thereby acknowledged the modern, liberal principle of freedom of thought – and that in the name of the Gospel!

The *Encyclical* firmly adheres to the Council's declaration *Dignitatis Humanae* without any misgivings (cf. *RH* 12). However, in the context of the Encyclical, the Pope's doctrine has a structure and theological foundation all its own. John Paul II founds the right to religious liberty on the only true revealed religion, as well as on the dignity of the human person. *The "rights of the truth" are at the same time the "rights of the person."*

In the Encyclical, the problem of religious liberty is raised in light of the ecumenical Church's missionary outlook on non-Christian religions, people and cultures (cf. *RH* 12). The theological evaluation of the ecumenical Church's relationship to other religions reflects the standpoint of the declaration *Nostra Aetate.* Accordingly, the missionary outlook is marked by a high esteem for other religions, in which the Holy Ghost also operates (cf. also *RH* 6,3). In the context of missions, "conversion" is an important factor. In the Encyclical, conversion, towards which the first step is made by missionary work, is defined as man's complete self-discovery. Thus it is clear that this whole conception is based on the Pope's idea of revelation, which therefore is also the basis for the right to religious liberty.

Nevertheless for the theological basis of the right to religious liberty, the Encyclical also appeals to the Council's declaration *Dignitatis Humanae* (cf. *RH* 12,2). On that subject, it emphasizes three points: Firstly, the right to religious liberty is a truth which is indirectly revealed. For on account of the missionary outlook of Christ and the apostles in the proclamation of the Gospel, which shows "a deep esteem for man, for his intellect, his will, his conscience and his freedom," the dignity of the human person "becomes part of the content of that proclamation." On which follows, secondly, that freedom is "the condition and basis for the human person's true dignity" (*condicio ac fundamentum*), and thus also an inalienable element of the dignity of the human person. Therefore the right of each person to religious liberty (*ius ad libertatem religiosam*) is an inalienable right of the human person, a right which is also confirmed by revealed truth. Thirdly, in virtue of her divine mission, the Church is the teacher and guardian of this freedom.

The Pope's theology of religious liberty, presented here in light of *Nostra Aetate* and *Dignitatis Humanae*, is based on a totally self-contained conception of revelation, from which the right of religious liberty can be rigorously proven:

For John Paul II, revelation consists in the fact that the Son of God has formally united Himself with each man through His Incarnation.[55] Thus each man, from the beginning of his existence, possesses "being in Christ" which belongs to his very nature as man (cf. *RH* 13,3).[56] "Being in Christ," as the core of human nature, is equivalent to the dignity of "the grace of divine adoption," as well as the dignity of "the inner truth of humanity" (cf. *RH* 11,3). This revelation *a priori* involves the subjective universality of revelation as well as that of salvation.

If the right to religious liberty is based on universal revelation and salvation *a priori*, so also the right to religious liberty is per se a universal human right, rooted in the nature and dignity of each person as such. One can then also say: The right to religious liberty is founded on both the one true revelation (*a priori*) and the dignity of the human person. Or: The "rights of the truth" are at the same time the "rights of the person" (see above). The indisputably free act of conversion is merely that of self-discov-

---

55 Cf. Part I, pp. 78ff.
56 *Ibid.*

ery.

From the idea of revelation *a priori* follows the hidden presence and operation of Christ and the Holy Ghost in the hearts of all men. Therefore all other religions must have legitimate standing as divine revelation.

The (historical) revelation *a posteriori* in and through Christ reveals to man his true being, the dignity of the inner truth of his being as man, and hence also his right to religious liberty which flows from that dignity. The historical revelation *a posteriori* is therefore not only the Christian interpretation of the revelation *a priori*, but also of the universal human right to religious liberty. Thus, in the Encyclical, Christ appears as the bearer, guarantor and interpreter of this human right. In the Encyclical, religious liberty, in virtue of the attitude of Christ and the apostles, becomes a truth revealed *a posteriori* and the Church, "because of her divine mission," becomes the teacher and guardian of this truth (cf. *RH* 12,2-3). Thus religious liberty belongs to the substance of "double revelation" and the ecumenical Church's "divine mission."

We can conclude: Thanks to the principle of universal salvation, all persons and religions have a fundamental right to religious liberty.

On this universal basis, we are authorized in promoting interreligious dialogue among equals, in the spirit of dogmatic tolerance and mutual respect; a person's self-discovery can pass for his conversion, which is begun by the mission of the ecumenical Church (cf. *RH* 12,1). The paradigm is Assisi!

CHAPTER III

REDEEMED MAN AND HIS SITUATION IN THE MODERN WORLD

Chapter 3 goes into the Encyclical theme and main points for the third time: Jesus Christ, the Redeemer of man, and the uniqueness of our era.

The *Redemptor Hominis* is indeed the Savior of each man, since the Son of God has formally united Himself with each man through His Incarnation: "This man is the way of the Church" (*RH* 13-14). Then the Pope confronts this man with the circumstances and demands of our era (*RH* 15-17).

13. Christ united Himself with each man.

The Pope speaks of the many ways in which the Conciliar Church must move forward in our era, one of which is the way which has stood the test of centuries and is the basis for all the others (*RH* 13,1):

> When we penetrate by means of the continually and rapidly increasing experience of the human family into the mystery of Jesus Christ, we understand with greater clarity that there is at the basis of all these ways that the Church of our time must follow, in accordance with the wisdom of Pope Paul VI (*Ecclesiam Suam*), one single way (*quasi fundamentum*): it is the way that has stood the test of centuries and it is also the way of the future.

Accordingly it is through the "rapidly increasing experience of the human family"–and not through divine revelation–that we penetrate more profoundly into the mystery

of Christ and understand with greater clarity the one single
way of the Church which has stood the test of centuries.
This way is then further specified (*RH* 13,1):

> Christ the Lord indicated this way especially, when, as
> the Council teaches, "by His Incarnation, He the Son of
> God, in a certain way united Himself with each man"
> (*Gaudium et Spes* 22). The Church therefore sees its fun-
> damental task in enabling that union to be brought about
> and renewed continually. The Church wishes to serve this
> single end: that each person may be able to find Christ, in
> order that Christ may walk with each person the path of
> this life, with the power of the truth about man and the
> world that is contained in the mystery of the Incarnation
> and the Redemption and with the power of the love that
> is radiated by that truth.

The way that has stood the test of centuries, and which
Christ Himself indicated, is accordingly that unity (*unitas*)
which comes about in virtue of the formal union of the
Son of God with each man through the Incarnation. *The
axiom of universal salvation is therefore the foundation of all
the Conciliar Church's activities.*

The wording of the above quoted text confirms this interpretation: The Encyclical does not say that the fundamental task of the Church is "to do all in its power to bring
about" the (formal) union of the Son of God with all men
through conversion, faith and baptism, but rather "to en-
able that union to be brought about and renewed continually." This unity is therefore assumed *a priori*. The Church
sees her fundamental task as one of bringing about and
renewing this unity: "The Church wishes to serve this single end!"

The means referred to in the text, by which the Church
works towards this end, are all found in the area of consciousness and in light of revelation *a posteriori*, in which
Christ "reveals man to himself" and makes him aware of
"the power of the truth about man," and of course "by

revealing the Father and His love."

The way of the Conciliar Church spoken of in the Encyclical is by no means the way that has stood the test of centuries, which Christ Himself has indicated to His Church. If the latter were the case, then the text would have to read: Guided by *revelation*, the Church constantly penetrates deeper into the mystery of Christ. All her ways are founded on only one way, which the Son of God indicated to His Church by the Incarnation. And this way is Jesus Christ Himself. *That* is the Church's way which has stood the test of centuries, which is also the "one single way" of Christianity. The way which the Encyclical declares as having stood the test of centuries is in reality a startling innovation!

If *the unity of the Son of God with each man* (= the axiom of universal salvation) is the way of the Church and foundation for all other ways, or more clearly expressed, if that unity is "at the basis" of all the Church's activities, what remains of Our Lord's words: "I am the way" (Jn. 14:6)? The Encyclical is quick to address this inescapable question (*RH* 13,2):

> Jesus Christ is the chief way for the Church. He Himself is our way "to the Father's house" (cf. Jn. 14:1ff) and is the way to each man. On this way (*in hac via*) leading from Christ to man, on this way on which Christ unites Himself with each man, nobody can halt the Church.

Based on the foregoing, there are two fundamental ways of the Church: On the one hand, the "one single way," based on Christ's unity with each man, thus on the axiom of universal salvation; on the other hand, the "chief way," who is Christ Himself: He is the way to the Father's house and, at the same time, the way to each man. The "chief way" therefore goes in two directions, namely to the Father's house and to man. But in the above quoted text's further explanation of the "chief way," the direction to the

Father is no longer mentioned. There remains just the pithy phrase: The way leads "from Christ to man," and Christ assists every man (!) on this way. We are left on a one-way street! That is already an indication of the subtle *man-centered twist!* This becomes entirely clear, when the Encyclical describes the "chief way" more precisely as follows (*RH* 13,2):

> Out of regard for Christ and in view of the mystery that constitutes the Church's own life, the Church cannot remain insensible to whatever serves man's true welfare, any more than she can remain indifferent to what threatens it. In various passages in its documents the Second Vatican Council has expressed the Church's fundamental solicitude that life in "the world should conform more to man's surpassing dignity" (*GS* 91) in all its aspects, so as to make that life "ever more human" (*GS* 38). This is the solicitude of Christ Himself, the good Shepherd of all men.

Thus *the Church's fundamental concern* is to make life in this world more and more human, so that in all its aspects it conforms "more to man's surpassing dignity." In this increasingly more human formation of the world, man is declared as the measure of all things. *That is a purely man-centered view, limited to this world!* And this solicitude of the Church for the welfare of man in this world is allegedly Christ's own concern, the concern of the "good Shepherd of all men!"

It is clear that the "chief way for the Church," which leads "from Christ to man," is a distortion of the God-centered character of the Gospel, which is watered down to a merely temporal, man-centered search for prosperity in which Christianity plays no part.

It is clear that the Good Shepherd of the Gospel, Who knows His own, calls and leads them, and by laying down His life for them, gives to those who believe in Him a participation in His own inner life of communion with the

Father (cf. Jn. 10:1-21), is not the Encyclical's "good Shepherd of *all* men," whose fold includes *all* men without distinction.

It is clear that the Christ's pastoral concern for the eternal life of souls is not the pastoral concern of the Encyclical's good Shepherd, which is directed towards the increasingly more human formation the "life in this world" according to the measure of man. It is also clear that the fundamental solicitude of the true Church of Christ, which faithfully reflects the concern of the Good Shepherd of the Gospel for the eternal life of souls and for the supernatural, is not the fundamental solicitude of the Church of the Encyclical, which is concerned about "life in this world," thus about the merely natural life. With an appeal to the pastoral care of its good Shepherd, the Encyclical text goes on (*RH* 13,2):

> In the name of this solicitude, as we read in the Council's Pastoral Constitution, "the Church must in no way be confused with the political community, nor bound to any political system. She is at once a sign and a safeguard of the transcendence of the human person" (*GS* 76).

Of course the Conciliar Church of the Encyclical, despite its alignment on the ever more human formation of "life in this world," does not want to "be confused" with political communities and systems, whose task is also the formation of the temporal sphere, and this distinction is in accordance with the Church's fundamental solicitude for the temporal sphere. Characteristically enough, the Encyclical, in the name of the good Shepherd's pastoral care, can invoke no higher basis for the Church's mission than the humanistic claim to be "at once a sign and a safeguard of the transcendence of the human person." However, in the name of the good Shepherd's pastoral care, the Church can define and promote her mission on a much higher basis, namely that of Christianity.

In the Pope's theology, the Church's claim to be "at once
a sign and a safeguard of the transcendence of the human
person" has a very special meaning. This was already formulated by Cardinal Wojtyla in *"Sign of Contradiction"*
(pp. 27ff) as follows:

> The Church of the living God gathers together all men
> who in one way or another share this marvelous transcen-
> dence of the human spirit ... This transcendence of the
> human person ... is a special manifestation (in prayer and
> silence) of the vital bond linking God and the human
> spirit. The Church of our day has become particularly
> conscious of this truth; and it was in light of this truth
> that the Church succeeded, during the Second Vatican
> Council, in redefining her own nature.

The Encyclical's statement: the Church is "at once a sign
and a safeguard of the transcendence of the human person," therefore expresses the thesis of universal salvation,
which has its place in the context of a "good Shepherd of
all men" and a Church which includes all men, since all
men participate in the transcendence of the human person.

We learn, however, from the Encyclical itself what exactly is meant by the "transcendence of the human person"
mentioned above, and why the Conciliar Church, in the
name of the pastoral care of the Universal Savior, lays claim
to being "a sign and a safeguard of the transcendence of the
human person." The important text puts it as follows (*RH*
13,3):

> Accordingly, what is in question here is man in all his
> truth, in his full magnitude. We are not dealing with the
> "abstract" man, but the real, "concrete," "historical" man.
> We are dealing with "each" man, for each one is included
> in the mystery of the Redemption and with each one
> Christ has united Himself for ever through this mystery.
> Every man comes into the world through being conceived
> in his mother's womb and being born of his mother, and
> precisely on account of the mystery of the Redemption is

entrusted to the solicitude of the Church. Her solicitude is about the whole man and is focused on Him in an altogether special manner. The object of her care is man in his unique unrepeatable human reality, which keeps intact the image and likeness of God Himself (cf. Gen. 1:27). The Council points out this very fact when, speaking of that likeness, it recalls that "man is the only creature on earth that God willed for itself" (GS 24). Man as "willed" by God, as "chosen" by Him from eternity and called, destined for grace and glory – this is "each" man, "the most concrete" man, "the most real"; this is man in all the fullness of the mystery in which he has become a sharer in Jesus Christ, the mystery in which each one of the four thousand million human beings living on our planet has become a sharer from the moment he is conceived beneath the heart of his mother.

The text formulates the axiom of universal salvation with surprising clarity.[1] At long last we have the answer to the question: For the Pope, in what specifically does the "transcendence of the human person" consist, why is Christ the "good Shepherd of all men," and why, in virtue of the mystery of the Redemption, the Conciliar Church includes all mankind in a hidden manner?

We can conclude: The Encyclical teaches that "Jesus Christ is the chief way for the Church." This way leads "from Christ to man," to man who is redeemed *a priori*. The solicitude of the "good Shepherd of all men," and therefore also the "fundamental solicitude of the Church," focuses on precisely this man. The solicitude common to both Shepherd and Church seeks to establish a life which is ever more human, which should conform to man's surpassing dignity in all its aspects.

14. For the Church all ways lead to man.

The focus on man continues adamantly in the next arti-

---

[1] See my analysis of the text in Part I, pp. 85ff.

cle (*RH* 14,1):

> The Church cannot abandon man, for his "destiny,"
> that is to say his election, calling, birth and death, salva-
> tion or perdition, is so closely and unbreakably linked
> with Christ. We are speaking precisely of each man on
> this planet, this earth that the Creator gave to the first
> man, saying to the man and the woman: "subdue it and
> have domination" (Gen. 1:28). Each man in all the unre-
> peatable reality of what he does, of his intellect and will,
> of his conscience and heart.

We are sufficiently informed as to the Encyclical's dogmatic outlook on man (cf. *RH* 13). The Encyclical offers
no further explanation for this outlook. The text from the
creation account quoted above, which for the Pope plays a
key role, is important for further analysis. From quotation
of Genesis 1:28 ensues the definitive alignment of all the
Church's activities on man, as well as the one-sided program for the human formation of the life of mankind in
temporal affairs.

On the subject of man, who is redeemed and is charged
to subdue the earth, the Encyclical goes on (*RH* 14,1):

> Man in the full truth of his existence, of his personal
> being and also of his community and social being ... this
> man is the primary route that the Church must travel in
> fulfilling her mission: he is the primary and fundamental
> way for the Church, the way traced out by Christ Him-
> self, the way that leads invariably through the mystery of
> the Incarnation and the Redemption.

It was "this man in all the truth of his life," which
Vatican II was bearing in mind, when it described his situation in today's world (*RH* 14,2). The Encyclical summarizes the Council's description in *Gaudium et Spes* (10) as
follows (*RH* 14,3):

> This man is the way for the Church – a way that, in a

sense, is the basis of all the other ways that the Church must walk – because man – every man without any exception whatever – has been redeemed by Christ, and because with man – with each man without any exception whatever – Christ is in a way united, even when man is unaware of it: "Christ, who died and was raised up for all, provides man" – each man and every man – "with the light and the strength to measure up to his supreme calling" (GS 10).

With these kinds of texts, which recur in varying forms and, in the Encyclical, should be understood according to the thesis of universal salvation, the foundation (= "the way of the Church") is laid, on which the Church's entire activity rests. The foundation for the Church's entire activity is redeemed man in all his relations, which include both "his personal being" and at the same time "his community and social being" (RH 14,1). Or, as the Encyclical puts it: "This man is the way for the Church." Inasmuch as man appears in light of his task assigned by the Creator in Genesis 1:28, the Church's activity is likewise oriented on the formation of man's life in this world. Thus human dignity is the standard by which "all areas of life" must be judged. Therefore the last paragraph of the Encyclical's present article summarizes the matter as follows (RH 14,4):

> Since this man is the way for the Church, the way for her daily life and experience, for her mission and toil, the Church of today must be aware in an always new manner of man's "situation." That means that she must be aware of his possibilities, which keep returning to their proper bearings and thus revealing themselves. She must likewise be aware of the threats to man and of all that seems to oppose the endeavor "to make human life ever more human" (GS 38) and make every element of this life correspond to man's true dignity – in a word, she must be aware of all that is opposed to that process.

Why does the text not at least say: The Church must

strive to make the life of man "ever more Christian"?

14.1 Digression: Who is the way of the Church, Christ or man?

The Encyclical enumerates three fundamental ways, which are the basis for all other ways of the Church: Firstly, the "one single way," which rests on the unity of the Son of God with each man, since the Son of God, through His Incarnation, has united Himself with each man. Then secondly, we hear: "Jesus Christ is the chief way for the Church." – Finally: "Man in the full truth of his existence is the primary and fundamental way of the Church."

Since each of these various ways is referred to as the basis of all the Church's activities, it is important to clear up the confusion at hand:

In the first of these ways, called the "one single way," which rests on *the unity of the Son of God with each man* and involves both partners, and which relationship is not further specified, we have the dogmatic axiom of universal salvation, only without explanation. That explanation is provided by the other two ways, which are nothing else than an elaboration on that unity possessed by all men at their birth.

Thus, in the Encyclical, there are not three fundamentally different ways, but only one, the "one single way," which represents the radical unity, from which the other two ways emerge as two impulses.

The concept of the various ways clearly follows on the Pope's idea of revelation.[2]

For the Pope, revelation primarily consists in the fact that the Son of God, through His Incarnation, has formally united Himself with each man. The "one single way" corresponds to, and is founded on this unity by definition.

---

2 On the Pope's idea of revelation, see Part I, pp. 111-123, and above, 7.1-7.3, pp. 18-32.

Since the Pope refers to this union as revelation, revelation *a priori* means that each man also possesses "being in Christ" *a priori* as his innermost being. Hence man who is already redeemed is also "the primary and fundamental way of the Church" and the basis of all her activity.

To revelation *a priori* corresponds the historical revelation *a posteriori in Christ. The latter is characterized by the fact that Christ "fully reveals man to himself," and hence makes man aware of his true and innermost being as man. "He does this by revealing the Father and His Love." Revelation a posteriori* becomes therefore the means by which all men come to know their salvation *a priori*, while Christ Himself is the interpreter and visible image of each man. That is how "Jesus Christ is the chief way for the Church."

To "double revelation" corresponds therefore the "double way of the Church": On the one hand, man who is already redeemed is "the primary and fundamental way for the Church," on the other hand, "Jesus Christ is the chief way for the Church." Both ways relate to each other just like revelation *a priori* to revelation *a posteriori*.

Just as "double revelation" inevitably bears a "man-centered character," so also the double way of the Church. Just as "double revelation" revolves "around man," so also the way of the Church founded on this revelation leads to the man-centered orientation of all her activity.

What remains for the Church to do, if the *Redemptor Hominis* has already imparted His supernatural work of Redemption to each man fundamentally and ontologically?

15. Mankind's risk of self-destruction and the mission of the Church.*

After the Encyclical sketches the "picture" of man in light of the last Council (*RH* 13-14), it proceeds, in the next three articles (*RH* 15-17), to adapt that picture to the

---

* Heading in the English Translation="What Modern Man Is Afraid Of"

demands of the present situation which is constantly changing, especially considering the "signs of the time" (cf. *RH* 15,1).

Since concrete man in all his aspects is the "way for the church," the description of his situation includes also the whole panorama of major contemporary problems. As the Pope's remarks in this paragraph are not the main topic of our research, we content ourselves with a brief summary of the most important statements.

The Pope places his general outlook at the beginning: Man has produced a culture which constantly turns against him, leads to alienation, and becomes even a threat for him. On that point we hear (*RH* 15,1):

> This seems to make up the main chapter of the drama of present-day human existence in its broadest and universal dimension.

Thus the Pope asks (*RH* 15,1):

> Why is it that the power given to man from the beginning by which he was to subdue the earth turns against himself, producing and understandable state of disquiet, of conscious or unconscious fear of menace, which in various ways is being communicated to the whole of the present-day human family and is manifesting itself under various aspects?

The Pope gives no deeper theological answer to the question at hand, but outlines first of all the various manifestations of the threat, each of which he criticizes in turn and presses his demands for a solution.[3]

---

3 Faced with the question of why man's power, given to him by God from the beginning (Gen. 1:28), turned against him, the way to the Bible's answer was suggested, namely: Adam's revolt against God, mankind's fall into original and personal sin. Hence follows man's absolute need of Redemption, mankind's need for a Redeemer. From Redemption in Christ (in the sense of the Church's traditional

The first manifestation of the threat from "what he produces" concerns *man's relationship to nature*. The Pope reprimands the uncontrolled exploitation of the earth for purposes of immediate use and consumption. In the Encyclical's own words, it is the will of the Creator (*RH* 15,2):

> that man should communicate with nature as an intelligent and noble "master" and "guardian," and not as a heedless "exploiter" and "destroyer."

Therefore the Pope demands a "long-range authentically humanistic plan" which spares man's natural environment and does not lead to his alienation from nature (*RH* 15,3-6).

The second manifestation of the threat from human production concerns *man's relationship to the progress of a civilization* (*RH* 3-6) *marked by technology*. The amazing progress in this area is on the one hand among the "authentic signs of man's greatness," as already revealed in Genesis 1-2, while on the other hand it is cause for concern, since the ethical and moral development is left behind.

Therefore the Pope demands a "proportional development of morals and ethics" to match the progress in technology (*RH* 15,3). This brings us to the "essential and fundamental question" (*RH* 15,3):

> Does this progress, which has man for its author and promoter, make human life on earth "more human" in every aspect of that life? Does it make it more "worthy of man"? ... [Is man,] in the context of this progress, ... becoming truly better, that is to say more mature spiritu-

---

doctrine), the line of reasoning leads necessarily to a (Christian) social order and world peace, in accordance with the Father's eternal decree: "to restore all things in Christ" (Eph. 1:10). – The Encyclical's presentation, however, rests on the Pope's *New Theology*, from which he develops the principles for a humanist social order and world peace, with man as the measure of all things.

ally, more aware of the dignity of his humanity, more
responsible, more open to others, especially the neediest
and the weakest, and readier to give and to aid all.

This is the question which the Christians should be the
first to ask, "because Jesus Christ has made them so universally sensitive about the problem of man."

Finally, all past achievements or projects for the future
must be examined with the following criterion: Do they
"accord with man's moral and spiritual progress?"

But why must the Church deal with all these problems?
The Pope's answers on three counts: Firstly, because the
subject of "development and progress" is on everybody's
mind. Secondly, because human nature has a fundamental
need for "solicitude by man for man, for his humanity, and
for the future of people on earth." Thirdly, because this
solicitude is an essential element of her mission. The Encyclical develops this last point as follows (*RH* 15,6):

> Inspired by eschatological faith, the Church considers
> an essential, unbreakably united element of her mission
> this solicitude for man, for his humanity, for the future of
> men on earth and therefore also for the course set for the
> whole of development and progress. She finds the princi-
> ple of this solicitude in Jesus Christ Himself, as the Gos-
> pels witness. This is why she wishes to make it grow
> continually through her relationship with Christ, reading
> man's situation in the modern world in accordance with
> the most important signs of our time.

On this analysis, Jesus Christ cares essentially about
man's humanity, his future on earth, and the course which
development and progress are taking; hence these are also
essential elements of the Church's mission, marked by her
eschatological faith.

The reader will allow some remarks on this point. The
Church cannot trace her solicitude for man's temporal future and for technological progress back to Jesus Christ, as

the Gospels attest. The Christ of the Gospels oriented the entire human person of His disciples on the kingdom of God which is not of this world, and on the supernatural, on life everlasting. He left the anxious worry about man's temporal welfare to those of little faith and to the heathens (cf. Matt. 6:25-34; Lk. 12:22-31).

Like the kingdom of God, so also the Church has an eschatological dimension. The Church, the bride of Christ, has her gaze entirely fixed on her Lord and waits with longing expectation for the arrival of her Bridegroom.

The purpose of the Church founded by Christ is purely religious: the sanctification and the eternal salvation of souls. She has *per se* no political, economic, social or purely cultural goals to achieve.[4] Nor are such programs found in the Gospel. Nevertheless, she is no enemy of culture or of progress. The particular character of her relationship to culture flows from the eschatological nature of her mission, which is: "Make disciples of all nations!" (Matt. 28:19). From the religious heart of her mission followed the "christianization" of cultures.[5]

The eschatological faith of the Church was never the solicitude "for the future of people on earth," but rather the expectation of Our Lord's Second Coming for the Last Judgment at the end of history. Ever since the Ascension, the Church's gaze is constantly fixed on Christ, on those things "that are above" (Col. 3:1). This fundamentally supernatural attitude is an essential element of Christian existence. In countless parables, Jesus Christ clearly emphasized the constant watch for the coming of the Lord at the

---

4 Cf. Ludwig Ott, *Fundamentals of Catholic Dogma* (St. Louis, MO: B. Herder Book Co., 1954), p. 273.

5 Cf. Thomas Ohm, *Machet zu Jüngern alle Völker* [*Make Disciples of All Nations*] (Freiburg i. Br. 1961), p. 56; 311; 413. – Johannes Dörmann, Series of Articles in the Pastoral Bulletin for the dioceses of Aachen, Berlin, Essen, Cologne, Osnabrück (Cologne), 9/1984-3/1985.

hour we least expect it. This attitude is plainly the heart of Our Lord's solicitude for man. In virtue of her union with Him and of *this* eschatological faith, the Church has furnished all the details for the living of a Christian life in this world.

By observing the contrast between the Church's traditional eschatological faith and the Encyclical's new outlook, which reflects the Pastoral Constitution's turning towards the world,[6] we come to discover the profound change in meaning from what the Gospel says. The New Testament's eschatology is transformed into a mere temporal hope for good things to come. The Encyclical's "eschatological faith" is situated in the perspective of salvation history, that means the "new Advent of the Church and of mankind," and the "Second Coming of the Lord." This is the faith of the "Church of the new Advent" (see above, 1.2b, pp. 49-57).

16. Our era: a time of great progress and of threats in many forms – Outline of a humane world order.*

Article 16 re-introduces and sheds more light on the problems raised in the previous article (15). This time the theme is: The present era as "a time of great progress," but also as "a time of threat in many forms for man" (*RH* 16,1). The Pope lays out his theological perspective, by which he assesses the problem, as follows (*RH* 16,1):

> We are dealing here only with that which found expression in the Creator's first message to man at the moment in which He was giving him the earth, to "subdue" it (Gen. 1:28). This first message was confirmed by Christ the Lord in the mystery of the Redemption. This is ex-

---

6 Regarding the reception and assessment of *Gaudium et Spes*, see Joseph Ratzinger, *Theologische Prinzipienlehre* [*Theological Principles*] (Munich 1982), pp. 395-411.

* Heading in the English Translation="Progress or Threat."

pressed by the Second Vatican Council in these beautiful chapters of its teaching that concern man's "kingship," that is to say his call to share in the kingly function – the *munus regale* – of Christ Himself (*LG* 10; 36). The essential meaning of this "kingship" and "dominion" of man over the visible world, which the Creator Himself gave man for his task, consists in the priority of ethics over technology, in the primacy of the person over things, and in the superiority of spirit over matter.

On this analysis, the Creator's injunction (Gen. 1:28), newly confirmed by the mystery of the Redemption, means the participation of mankind in the kingly function of Christ. The "essential meaning" of this kingship and this dominion of man over the visible world, according to the Encyclical, consists in the priority of ethics over technology, in the primacy of the person over things, in the transcendence of the spirit over matter. The Pope has thereby laid out his theological perspective, by which he considers and "x-rays" the global turn of events (*RH* 16,2). We will now sketch the most important points as follows:

– At each stage of progress, the nature of *man as a person* cannot be overlooked. For it is a question of the "advancement of persons," not of things; what matters is not "having more," but "being more" (*RH* 16,2).[7]

– There is a danger *that man lose his dominion over the world of things, and let his humanity become subject to them.* Therefore the motto (*RH* 16,2):

Man "cannot become the slave of things, the slave of economic systems, the slave of production, the slave of his own

---

7 From the philosophical standpoint, it must here be asked: Can one speak of "becoming" with respect to the person? Already in his main work, *Person und Tat* [*The Acting Person*], Karol Wojtyla speaks of a "*fieri* [becoming] of the person" – (especially pp. 120ff.). But can the person as such undergo a process of "fieri"? The person is an ontic reality, either *it is* or *it isn't*, though there is a development of the personal character.

products."

– In caring for present-day man, the following problem is at stake (*RH* 16,2):

> It is not a matter here merely of giving an abstract answer to the question: Who is man? It is a matter of the whole of the dynamism of life and civilization. It is a matter of the meaningfulness of the various initiatives of everyday life and also of the premises for many civilization programs, political programs, economic ones, social ones, state ones, and many others.

This text makes even more clear what the Pope means by the axiom: Man is the way for the Church. Since the Church cares about each individual person in the various aspects of his life, she must strive constantly to grasp the "meaningfulness" of the whole dynamism of life and civilization, and also of the premises for the many civilization programs in their relationship to man. The Church is thus the universal interpreter of the world's entire development, and at the same time the highest court in the humanistic, ethical sphere.

– The Pope makes a broad statement on the status of global development in the area of ethics and human dignity in the following words (*RH* 16,3):

> Man's situation is still "far removed from the objective demands of the moral order, from the exigencies of justice, and still more from social love."

This is demonstrated by the contrast between rich and poor, "consumer civilization" and third world, abuse of the freedom on the one hand and oppression of freedom on the other. The world's present-day status represents "the gigantic development of the parable in the Bible of the rich banqueter and the poor man Lazarus" (*RH* 16,5).

Hence the status and extent of the problem call into question "the financial, monetary, production and commercial mechanisms that, resting on various political pressures, support the world economy," and which are incapable "either of remedying the unjust social situations inherited from the past or of dealing with the urgent challenges and ethical demands of the present" (*RH* 16,6).

The Encyclical enumerates still further symptoms of this world-wide "moral disorder," such as "the fever of inflation and the plague of unemployment": All this "requires daring creative resolves in keeping with man's authentic dignity" (*RH* 16,7).

The realization of this task is not impossible. But the global reorganization of all the structures and mechanisms mentioned above, in accordance with the dignity of the human person, means nothing less than the creation of a new world order. On this point, the Pope formulates a number of basic principles. Here are the most important ones:

1) "The principle of solidarity, in a wide sense, must inspire the effective search for appropriate institutions and mechanisms, whether in the sector of trade, where the laws of healthy competition must be allowed to lead the way, or on the level of a wider and more immediate redistribution of riches and of control over them, in order that the economically developing peoples may be able not only to satisfy their essential needs but also to advance gradually and effectively" (*RH* 16,8).

2) This indispensable transformation of the structures of economic life requires "the intervention of a true conversion of mind, will and heart. The task requires resolute commitment by individuals and peoples that are free and linked in solidarity" (*RH* 16,9).

3) "But no truly human economy will be possible unless they are taken up, directed and dominated by the deepest powers in man, which decide the true culture of peoples. These are the very sources for the effort which will express man's true freedom and which will be capable of ensuring it in the economic field also. Economic development, with every factor in its adequate functioning,

must be constantly programmed and realized within a perspective of universal joint development of each individual and people" (*RH* 16,8).

It is therefore the "the deepest powers in man," and not the efforts of Christians as such, upon which "man's true freedom" and the reorganization of the world economy both depend.

> 4) "However, one thing is certain: at the basis of this gigantic sector it is necessary to establish, accept and deepen the sense of moral responsibility, which man must undertake. Again, and always man. This responsibility becomes especially evident for us Christians when we recall ... the scene of the last judgment according to the words of Christ related in Matthew's Gospel (cf. Matt. 25:31-46)" (*RH* 16,9).

The subject of this reorganization is thus again and always "man," without further specification. Such a responsibility becomes only "especially evident" for the Christian in virtue of the words of Matt. 25:31ff.

On Matt. 25:31ff, the Encyclical continues (*RH* 16,10):

> 5) "This eschatological scene must always be 'applied' to man's history; it must always be made the 'measure' for human acts as an essential outline for an examination of conscience by each and every one."

In this examination of conscience, we could even include the problem of tensions between North and South. And, of course, we must never forget that "the areas of misery and hunger on our globe could have been made fertile in a short time, if the gigantic investments for armaments at the service of war and destruction had been changed into investments for food at the service of life" (*RH* 16,10).

Surely the acknowledgement of Christ's Second Coming at the Last Judgment marks the way Christians live. Are Buddhists, Hindus or Animists also moved by this truth?

Does it suffice to reduce the serious reality of the Last Judgment to a mere "eschatological symbol," in order to make it a norm for human acts on the whole, and thereby to create a rough draft for an examination of conscience acceptable to all?

> 6) The Pope concludes by observing that the Church has only spiritual weapons at her disposal. He then reaches for the most powerful weapon, Holy Scripture, and supports his previous statements with a quote from St. Paul: "Preach the word! Be instant, in season, out of season (II Tim. 4:2). In context, "the word" means the Gospel.

The article ends with the appeal "in the name of God and in the name of man": "Respect each one's dignity and freedom!" (*RH* 16,11). This is the only time in the article that God is even mentioned.

The Pope's remarks are brief, and therefore remain somewhat up in the clouds (cf. *RH* 16,10). They appear at first glance like a scattered collection of isolated statements. Upon closer analysis, however, we come to see the grand, self-contained vision of a humanistic new world order, which is centered on each man in his numerous cultural relationships. It is the world of man, fashioned on the principles of the priority of ethics over technology, in the primacy of the person over things, in the transcendence of the spirit over matter (cf. *RH* 16,1).

It is obvious, however, that these undeniably noble humanistic principles by no means represent the "essential meaning" of man's kingship and domination over the visible world which he derives from Christ's own royal office. The "essential meaning" of Christ's offices as King and as Shepherd is to save man from the sinful state into which he has fallen, and to lead him on the straight path towards his supernatural goal.[8] The purposes of Christ's royal office (*munus regale*) are the establishment, growth and completion of the kingdom of God on earth.[9] It is the Church's common teaching that visible creation culminates in man (Gen. 1). That is why man in the state of original justice is made king over the visible world. However, the essential meaning of this kingship is for man to serve God through the enjoyment and right use of the goods of this world, and thus to glorify God through the whole of creation.[10] This God-centered character of man's kingship is not diminished "in the mystery of the Redemption," but rather is confirmed and elevated.

Through the Encyclical's definition of the "essential meaning" of man's kingship, derived from Christ's own kingly office, a central article of faith is stripped of its specifically Christian meaning, reduced to a purely human level, and established as the norm for all areas of life. The priority of ethics over technology, the primacy of the person over things and the transcendence of the spirit over matter are so many buzz words of humanistic ethics which anyone can accept and which are open to any interpretation.

The definition of that "essential meaning" is tantamount to the rejection of the supernatural, and includes the transformation of the Christian, God-centered religion into a humanistic, man-centered religion, directed towards life in this world. Through the Encyclical's description of the various destructive factors accompanying the global trend of "progress," we should be exhorted to go to the root cause of all disorder, namely sin in the world, to emphasize man's absolute need for Redemption, and hence to preach the Savior of the world and demand faith in Him, in order to

---

8   Cf. Ludwig Ott, *op. cit.*, p. 179

9   Cf. Matthias Joseph Scheeben, Erlösungslehre, *Handbuch der katholischen Dogmatik* [*Handbook of Catholic Dogma*] (Freiburg i. Br. 1954), Complete Works VI /2, p. 305.

10 Matthias Joseph Scheeben, trans. Cyril Vollert, S.J., *The Mysteries of Christianity* (St. Louis, MO: B. Herder Book Co., 1946), p. 237.

restore all things in Christ, and not in man. The world should even expect that from a Pope.

The Encyclical's presentation opens (Gen. 1:28) and closes (II Tim. 4:2) with Holy Scripture. It begins with the kingship of Christ and concludes with an appeal to the text of St. Paul, which concerns the preaching of the "word," therefore of the Gospel. We have here a breathtaking demonstration of the use of Scripture for promoting a new world order, based on the principles of the Pope's *New Theology*, and centered on man. Thus the Pope explains to mankind how his motto is to be understood: "Man is the way for the Church."

17. Human rights: the guiding principle of all endeavors for man's welfare.*

This article also re-introduces the same basic theme: Man in the midst of the great calamities, of the material and moral devastations of our century, and also whether this fateful development can be stopped (*RH* 17,1).

Therefore the Pope searches for collaborators and finds a powerful ally in the United Nations Organization, which has already laid the cornerstone for peace and the new world order by its declaration of human rights. Now it is only a matter of putting the spirit of this Charter into action. On the efforts of the UN, the Encyclical says point blank (*RH* 17,1):

> In any case, we cannot fail to recall at this point, with esteem and profound hope for the future, the magnificent effort made to give life to the United Nations Organization, an effort conducive to the definition and establishment of man's objective and inviolable rights, with the member states obliging each other to observe them rigorously. This commitment has been accepted and ratified by almost all present-day states, and this should constitute a

---

* Heading in the English Translation= "Human Rights: 'Letter' or 'Spirit'"

guarantee that human rights will become throughout the world a fundamental principle of work for man's welfare.

On the relationship between the Church and the UN in the area of human rights, the Encyclical states (17,2):

> There is no need for the Church to confirm how closely this problem [of the rights of man] is linked with her mission in the modern world. ... After all, peace comes down to respect for man's inviolable rights.

In addition to the UN, the Pope finds a second ally in the trend of our era: John Paul II thinks that, in today's world, no social, economic or political program can do without the "humanistic" dimension and spirit. The Pope is

> firmly convinced that there is no program in today's world in which man is not invariably brought to the fore, even when the platforms of the programs are made up of conflicting ideologies concerning the way of conceiving the world (*RH* 17,2).

Nevertheless human rights are still violated (concentration camps, violence and torture, terrorism and widespread discrimination), evidently as a consequence of the very elements which hinder the effectiveness of humanistic programs and systems. Therefore it is our duty to revise these programs constantly on the basis of objective and inviolable human rights (*RH* 17,2).

The Pope is therefore convinced that the UN's Declaration of Human Rights is a suitable basis "for continual revision of programs, systems and regimes." He further emphasizes that this revision be accomplished "precisely from this single point of view, namely the welfare of man." That is why the Encyclical demands (*RH* 17,3):

> [Human welfare] must, as a fundamental factor in the common good, constitute the essential criterion for all

programs, systems and regimes. If the opposite happens, human life is, even in time of peace, condemned to various sufferings ... *(The Encyclical then mentions explicitly the various forms of domination, totalitarianism, neocolonialism and imperialism).*

The Pope declares the Church as the "guardian of human rights." Her task is to check constantly "whether the Declaration of Human Rights and the acceptance of their 'letter' mean everywhere also the actualization of their 'spirit'." If human rights are violated, the transgressors bear "special responsibility towards [their] societies and the history of man" (*RH* 17,4).[11]

The realization of human rights occurs on the state level. Therefore the Pope defines the nature of the state and the relationship between citizens' rights and those of the state.

On the essence of the state, the Encyclical says (*RH* 17,5):

The essential sense of the state, as a political community, consists in that the society and people composing it are master and sovereign of their own destiny.

That is a profession of democracy.

On the relationship between citizens' rights, human rights and the state, the Encyclical goes on (*RH* 17,6):

The Church has always taught the duty to act for the common good and, in so doing, has likewise educated good citizens for each state. Furthermore, she always taught that the fundamental duty of power is solicitude for the common good of society, this is what gives power its fundamental rights. Precisely in the name of these

---

11 The Pope's mention of man's responsibility towards "societies" and the "history of man" is an eloquent demonstration of the reduction of Christianity to the level of the merely human and temporal sphere. Even the Preamble of the German Constitution speaks of responsibility before God.

premises of the objective ethical order, the rights of power can only be understood on the basis of respect for the objective and inviolable rights of man. The common good that authority in the state serves is brought to full realization only when all the citizens are sure of their rights. ... Thus the principle of human rights is of profound concern to the area of social justice and is the measure by which it can be tested in the life of political bodies.

The Encyclical's remarks end on the question of the religious liberty and freedom of conscience, for which the Pope claims special competence. In the UN Charter, religious liberty and freedom of conscience belong to the catalog of human rights. The Pope agrees with this, as he explicitly states (*RH* 17,7):

> These rights are rightly reckoned to include the right to religious freedom together with the right to freedom of conscience. The Second Vatican Council considered especially necessary the preparation of a fairly long declaration (=*Dignitatis Humanae*) on this subject. ... Certainly the curtailment of the religious freedom of individuals and communities is not only a painful experience but it is above all an attack on man's very dignity, independently of the religion professed or of the concept of the world which these individuals and communities have. The curtailment and violation of religious freedom are in contrast with man's dignity and his objective rights. ... In this case we are undoubtedly confronted with a radical injustice with regard to what is particularly deep within man, what is authentically human.

The violation of the human right to religious liberty is a general phenomenon in today's world. This time, however, the Pope spares us the details and concludes the article with a solemn appeal for the respect of the right to religious liberty (*RH* 17,9):

> Even if briefly, this subject must also be dealt with, because it too enters into the complex of man's situations

in the present-day world and because it too gives evidence of the degree to which this situation is overburdened by prejudices and injustices of various kinds. If we refrain from entering into details in this field in which we would have a special right and duty to do so, it is above all because, together with all those who are suffering the torments of discrimination and persecution for the name of God, we are guided by faith in the redeeming power of the cross of Christ. However, because of my office, I appeal in the name of all believers throughout the world to those on whom the organization of social and public life in some way depends, earnestly requesting them to respect the rights of religion and of the Church's activity. No privilege is asked for, but only respect for an elementary right. Actuation of this right is one of the fundamental tests of man's authentic progress in any regime, in any society, system or milieu.

Article 17 shows us for the third time how the Pope understands his motto: "Man is the way for the Church."

According to that principle, in striving for peace and the new world order, man must always be brought to the fore (cf. *RH* 17,2). Throughout the world, the fundamental principles of all work for man's welfare are human rights as contained in the Charter of the United Nations Organization (cf. *RH* 17,1). That means: By human rights are meant those rights which exist prior to the state and transcend the state. Therefore the state does not grant them, but these rights are in force independently of state constitutions, though they can be recognized by the ordinance of the state. By human rights are meant primarily the political rights to freedom or the fundamental rights (right to equality, protection, property, freedom of expression and of worship, right to resist oppression). We are therefore dealing with the idea of rights which exist prior to the state and transcend the state, of fundamental rights which are granted to man in virtue of his nature.[12]

The Church's agreement with the spirit of the UN Charter, the harmony between the Church's mission and the

efforts of the UN (cf. 17,2) means that the right to religious liberty and freedom of conscience are also to be understood in light of the UN's Declaration of Human Rights.
But the Encyclical also points to the Vatican II declaration
Dignitatis Humanae. That is meant to show that these human rights are not only inherent in the nature of man, but
are also found in revelation (cf. *RH* 17,8).[13] Therefore the
violation of the religious freedom of individuals and communities is an attack on man's nature, his dignity and his
inviolable human rights, independently of the religion professed or of the concept of the world which these individuals and communities have (cf. *RH* 17,8). This realization
should put an end to all arguments in the Church on the
meaning of religious liberty and freedom of conscience:
They are to be understood in light of the UN's Declaration
of Human Rights.

At first glance, it may come as a surprise that, in Pope's
concept of peace and the new world order, the question of
the various religions does not come up. But this question is
already answered by the UN's declaration of the human
right to religious liberty. Thus the universal right to religious liberty and freedom of conscience contains the principle of religious tolerance in the liberal sense, and lays the
cornerstone for universal religious peace.

The Pope demands respect for the rights of religion and
the Church's activity. He demands no privileges, but simply
respect for an elementary right, possessed by "believers" of
all religions alike, and which the Pope sees as a fundamental test of man's authentic progress (cf. *RH* 17,9).

It is a question of a social order conducive to world
peace, in which "the fundamental principles of all work for
man's welfare are human rights" as contained in the Charter of the UN (cf. *RH* 17,1), an order which is concen-

---

12 See Digression, 12.3, pp. 175-179.
13 *Ibid.*

trated entirely on man and on life in this world. The Pope's remarks on the humanist peace and the new world order, founded on the UN's Declaration of Human Rights, could just as easily have come from the UN General Secretary, with the exception of the last paragraph.

In the whole of Article 17, the name of "God" is only mentioned once, in the last paragraph (see above, *RH* 17,9). Here the Pope appeals, in virtue of his office, "in the name of all believers throughout the world to those on whom the organization of social and public life in some way depends." In the Pope's vocabulary, the God of "all believers" is the God of all religions: the God of Assisi!

CHAPTER IV

THE CHURCH'S MISSION AND MAN'S DESTINY

In Chapter 4, from yet another aspect, the Pope develops the Encyclical theme for the fourth time. Man's union with Christ determines the nature and mission of the Church in our era (*RH* 18). The Church's mission is her participation in "Christ's triple mission, His triple office": as prophet (*RH* 19), as priest (*RH* 20) and as king (*RH* 21). The last article is dedicated to Mary, the "mother of the Church" (*RH* 22).

18. The Church's nature and mission is centered on man.*

Article 18 forms the dogmatic basis for all of Chapter 4. The introductory text, which we reproduce here completely with a few unimportant omissions, runs as follows (*RH* 18,1):

> If Christ "united Himself with each man (*GS* 22)," the Church lives more profoundly her own nature and missions by penetrating into the depths of this mystery ... It was not without reason that the Apostle speaks of Christ's Body, the Church (cf. I Cor. 6:15; 11:3; 12:12-13; Eph. 1:22; 2:15-16; 4:4-5; Col. 1:18; 3:15; Rom. 12:4-5; Gal. 3:28). If this Mystical Body of Christ is God's People ... this means that in it each man receives within himself that breath of life that comes from Christ. In this way, turning to man and his real problems, his hopes and sufferings,

* Heading in the English Translation="The Church as Concerned for Man's Vocation in Christ"

his achievements and falls – this too also makes the Church as a body, an organism, a social unity perceive the same divine influences, the light and strength of the Spirit that come from the crucified and risen Christ, and it is for this very reason that she lives her life. The Church has only one life: that which is given her by her Spouse and Lord. Indeed, precisely because Christ united Himself with her in His mystery of The Redemption, the Church must be strongly united with each man.[1]

In the Pope's theology, Christ's union with each man (through the Incarnation) is the definition of revelation (*a priori*). In the text above, the mystery of this union is the source from which the Church also draws the deeper knowledge of her own nature and mission. This has notable consequences for the Encyclical's idea of the Church:

If Christ is united with each person, then all mankind is "anonymous Christianity" or the hidden Church.[2]

The hidden Church, which includes all mankind in an unknown fashion, is distinct from the visible Church "as a body, an organism, a social unity."[3] (Why is the visible Church not simply referred to as the Catholic Church?)

Thus in the Encyclical there is a twofold idea of the Church: the invisible and the visible Church. The invisible Church is ontologically not only more broad-minded, since it includes all mankind, but also more fundamental, since it emerges *a priori* from the union of Christ with each man and therefore embraces all mankind from the beginning to the end of the world.[4]

In a manner similar to the above quoted text, Cardinal

---

[1] The last sentence was made clearer based on the Latin text (*Nam, quia Christus in mysterio Redemptionis eam sibi iunxit, ob id ipsum oportet Ecclesia cum quolibet homine arcte coniungatur*).

[2] Cf. Karol Wojtyla, [*Sign of Contradiction*], p. 27ff.; see also Part I, pp. 80-98.

[3] Cf. *RH* 6; 11; 12.

[4] Karol Wojtyla, *op. cit.*, p. 103; 108.

Wojtyla already portrayed the Church under the images of the Body of Christ and the Bride of Christ, in order to illustrate the mystery of the Redemption. The twofold idea of the Church is conveyed by the Cardinal's usage of these two images, Body and Bride of Christ, not only for Christ's relationship to the visible Church, but also for His relationship to the invisible Church, to all mankind.[5]

From the unity of head and members follows the union of interior life and of mind. This is outlined above by the Encyclical: All members of the Body of Christ are also imbued with the breath of life that comes from Christ. The same holds for the image of Bride and Bridegroom: "The Church has only one life: that which is given her by her Spouse and Lord."

From the deeper knowledge of the Church's nature, the character of her mission is derived. The Church's mission is paraphrased as a turning towards the concrete man with his problems in today's world. That is how the Church follows the inspirations and powers of the Spirit of Christ, the Crucified and the Risen One. Hence this mission receives its divine authorization: The Church's mission in the Encyclical appears identical with that of given by Christ Resurrected – as in the Gospel (Matt. 28:18-20). But is it really the same in content?

In the following text, the Encyclical deepens and develops its thoughts from the first paragraph (*RH* 18,2):

> This union of Christ with man is in itself a mystery. From the mystery is born (*unde nascitur*) "the new man," called to become a partaker of God's life (II Pet. 1:4), and newly created in Christ (*denuo in Christo natus*) for the fullness of grace and truth (Eph. 2:10; Jn. 1:14,16). Christ's union with man is power and the source of power, as St. John stated so incisively in the prologue of his Gospel: "(The Word) gave power to become children

5 See Part I, pp. 67-78.

of God" (Jn. 1:12).

The text clearly states: From the union of Christ with man, which extends to every man through the Incarnation, the "new man" is born. What St. Paul says of the Christian believer: "He who is in Christ is a new creature" (II Cor. 5:17; cf. also Gal. 6:15), holds in the Encyclical for each man. What St. John says in the Prologue of the Christian believer's supernatural birth from God holds in the Encyclical for all persons. From the union of Christ with each man, emerges man redeemed and justified *a priori*. There are no conditions attached, neither that of faith nor that of baptism. Thus the striking words of St. John: "The Word gave power to become children of God," appear in the Encyclical – for a good reason – with characteristic omissions. The complete text from the Prologue runs: "But to them that received Him, to them He gave power to become children of God, to them that believe in His name." Logically, the Pope leaves out the subjective element of the Redemption: the reception of the Logos and faith in Jesus Christ. Why this omission? Because he teaches universal salvation.

If the unity of Christ with each man, if the birth from God which follows from that, is proper to all men, this must also be expressed in the life of everyone, whether Christian or non-Christian. But just how is this grace expressed in the life of each man, the grace of being a child of God which is given to all *a priori*? How does it work out in practice? The Encyclical answers this question immediately as follows (*RH* 18,2):

> Man is transformed inwardly (*Haec est illa vis*) by this power (Christ's union with each man) as the source of a new life that does not disappear and pass away but lasts to eternal life (Jn. 4:14). This life, which the Father has promised and offered to each man in Jesus Christ, His eternal and only Son ... is the final fulfillment of man's vocation. It is in a way the fulfillment of the "destiny"

(*sortis*) that God has prepared for him (man) from eternity. This "divine destiny" is advancing (*Ea "sors" divina efficitur*), in spite of all the enigmas, the unsolved riddles, the twists and turns of "human destiny" in the world of time. Indeed, while all this (earthly existence) ... necessarily and inevitably leads to the frontier of death and the goal of the destruction of the human body, beyond that goal we see Christ. "I am the resurrection and the life, he who believes in me ... shall never die" (Jn. 11:25f) In Jesus Christ, who was crucified and laid in the tomb and then rose again, "our hope of resurrection dawned (*spes beatae resurrectionis*) ... the bright promise of immortality" (Jn. 6:23), on the way to which man, through the death of the body, shares with the whole of visible creation the necessity to which matter is subject. We intend and are trying to fathom (*perscrutari*) ever more deeply the language of the truth that man's Redeemer enshrined in the phrase "It is the spirit that gives life, the flesh is of no avail" (Jn. 6:63). In spite of appearances, these words express the highest affirmation of man – the affirmation of the body given life by the Spirit."[6]

What the Encyclical says here of the divine principle of life for "man" in general, that is also the teaching of the New Testament regarding the Christian believer, but with two major differences: The New Testament also speaks of man's share in God's grace, but only with man's free cooperation, and faith is required above all. The Encyclical text is silent on this point. The second major difference becomes apparent in the application of Our Lord's words to Martha (Jn. 11:25). In the Gospel, the eternal salvation of each man depends on his faith in the resurrection of Christ here and now, in this life. In the Encyclical text, however, we hear: When a soul has overstepped "the frontier of death, ... beyond that goal we see Christ." He speaks to us the words: "I am the resurrection and the life, he who

---

6 The English translation should here be compared with the official Latin Text.

believes in me ... shall never die" (Jn. 11:25f). But that
means that the man, as portrayed in the Encyclical, can
wait until death before having to face the issue of Christ
and the need for faith in His resurrection. Such a theory
may dispense the "anonymous Christian" from the fundamental requirement of faith in the resurrection of Christ in
this life, but the issue is raised personally after death by
Christ Resurrected. After death, however, the Christian
does not expect an encounter with the Christ of faith in the
next life, but rather the vision of the divinity "face to face"
(I Cor. 13:9-12).

The Encyclical deals just as loosely with Our Lord's
words from the Eucharistic discourse: "It is the spirit that
gives life, the flesh is of no avail" (Jn. 6:63). This scriptural
passage refers to the Eucharist, not to "the highest affirmation of man." In the context of the Encyclical, should we
take these words of Our Lord, whose more profound import the Pope announces, to mean that the body of each
man is a temple of the Holy Ghost thanks to universal
redemption (cf. I Cor. 3:16f.; 6:19), just as each man from
the first moment of his existence already possesses the image (*imago*) and the likeness (the supernatural *similitudo*) of
God once and for all (cf. *RH* 13,3)?

The Pope penetrates still deeper into the inner life of
man who has been universally redeemed, in order to discover in the heart of each man the divine life of grace and
to lay bare for everyone the spiritual basis of the Church's
mission. The text runs (*RH* 18,3):

> The Church lives these realities; she lives by this truth
> about man, which enables him to go beyond the bounds
> of temporariness and at the same time to think with par-
> ticular love and solicitude of everything within the di-
> mensions of this temporariness that affect man's life and
> the life of the human spirit, in which is expressed that
> never-ending restlessness referred to in the words of St.
> Augustine: "You made us for Yourself, Lord, and our heart
> is restless until it rests in You." In this creative restlessness

beats and pulsates what is most deeply human (*quod potis-simum in homine est*)–the search for truth, the insatiable need for the good, hunger for freedom, nostalgia for the beautiful, and the voice of conscience. Seeking to see man as it were with "the eyes of Christ Himself," the Church becomes more and more aware that she is the guardian of a great treasure, which she may not waste but must continually increase. Indeed (*nam*), the Lord Jesus said: "He who does not gather with me scatters" (Matt. 12:30). This treasure of humanity enriched by the inexpressible mystery of divine filiation (Jn. 1:12) and by the grace of "adoption as sons" (Gal. 4:5) in the only Son of God, through whom we call God "Abba, Father" (Gal. 4:6; Rom. 8:15), is also a powerful force unifying the Church above all inwardly and giving meaning to all her activity. Through this force the Church is united with the Spirit of Christ, that Holy Spirit promised and continually communicated (*quem continenter impertit*) by the Redeemer and whose descent, which was revealed on the day of Pentecost, endures for ever (*semper descendit*). Thus the powers of the Spirit (cf. Rom. 15:13; I Cor. 1:24), the gifts of the Spirit (cf. Is. 11:2; Acts 2:38), and the fruits of the Holy Spirit (cf. Gal. 5:22-23) are revealed in men. The present-day Church seems to repeat with ever greater fervor and with holy insistence: "Come, Holy Spirit! Come! Come! Wash the stains of guilt away! ..."[7]

According to the text, the Church, who lives from the supposed reality and truth of universal salvation, recognizes in the hearts of men the Augustinian restlessness for God, for Whom this creative restlessness beats and pulsates. With Christ's own eyes, she looks still further and sees in the deepest recesses of the human heart even the life of grace in every man, a life which befits a child of God.

In this supposed reality and truth of man, which includes not only the noblest in the human heart but also the grace of divine adoption (Jn. 1:12), therefore grace as well as nature, the Church recognizes the most precious treasure

---

7 As in Footnote 6.

of humanity. This treasure belongs to humanity, since it represents its deepest nature. The Church understands herself as the guardian of this treasure. Why only as the guardian? Because the most precious fruits of Christ's redemptive work do not belong to the Church, and are not entrusted to her as the sole custodian – as previously believed – but because they are to be found already in the treasure of humanity.

But why is this treasure of humanity such a powerful force unifying the Church above all inwardly and giving meaning to all her activity? Because the Church possesses a most profound unity and solidarity with humanity. Because the Church herself is an integral part of redeemed mankind, and as such lives from the supposed reality and truth of this treasure, and derives her meaning therefrom.

Through the powerful force of this treasure (Jn. 1:12), which belongs in common to all mankind, the Church unites herself with the Spirit of Christ, with the Holy Spirit, Whom the Redeemer constantly bestows, and Who continually descends, of course not only on the Church, but also on all mankind. Therefore the power, gifts and fruits of the Holy Ghost are found quite simply "in man." What Holy Scripture says about the gifts and fruits of the Holy Ghost in the Christian believer and in the Church, the Encyclical applies with amazing consistency to all men, to all humanity.

The Pope understands revelation in the same way as he understands the descent of the Holy Ghost: as a continuing process. That concrete, historical event in God's plan of salvation, the descent of the Holy Ghost on the Church at Pentecost, becomes an outward sign of the perpetual descent of the Holy Ghost on all mankind. –

The Pope's vision of man and of mankind is certainly grand and impressively consistent from the standpoint of universal salvation. However, it is simply inadmissible when a Pope, in an Encyclical on the Redeemer, so grossly

ignores mankind's abysmal fall into sin and his absolute
need of Redemption, let alone when he completely disre-
gards the necessity of faith in the Redeemer, which is demanded on each page of the Gospel. Compared with the
authentic view of Holy Scripture, the Pope's vision is sheer
poetry. –

After the Encyclical's remarks on the operation of the
Holy Spirit upon all mankind, the question arises: does the
Church's prayer to the Holy Ghost also take place outside
her visible boundaries? The Pope asks the question anyway,
in order to examine the Church's nature and the mission
more profoundly from the spiritual nucleus of prayer. In
Assisi it was also a question of the prayer of all religions, as
we already saw in the first chapter, such that the firm
religious beliefs of the followers of non-Christian religions
is "an effect of the Spirit of truth operating outside the
visible confines of the Mystical Body" (*RH* 6,3; see above
6.1).

The Church's intense prayer to the Holy Ghost is therefore the occasion for the question (*RH* 18,4):

> Can it be said that the Church is not alone in making
> this appeal? Yes it can, because the "need" for what is
> spiritual is expressed also by people (*non pauci*) who are
> outside the visible confines of the Church. Is not this
> confirmed by the truth concerning the Church that the
> recent Council so acutely emphasized at the point in the
> Dogmatic Constitution *Lumen Gentium* where it teaches
> that the Church is a "sacrament or sign and means of
> intimate union with God, and of the unity of all man-
> kind?" – This invocation addressed to the Spirit to obtain
> the Spirit is really a constant self-insertion into the full
> magnitude of the mystery of the Redemption, in which
> (*quo*) Christ, united with the Father and with each man,
> continually communicates to us the Spirit who places
> within us the sentiments of the Son (*qui sensus Filii infun-
> dit*) and directs us towards the Father (cf. Rom. 8:15; Gal.
> 4:6).

In support of the thesis that the invocation "addressed to the Spirit to obtain the Spirit" is also expressed in the spiritual yearnings of the non-Christian world, the Pope appeals to the Council's key ecclesiological text on the Church as sacrament of the unity of all mankind. It is thereby affirmed that this sentence is to be applied to mankind, all of which is redeemed. Thus the Church is the sign of mankind's universal salvation, and also the instrument which should announce and make known this "reality."

Finally and in summary fashion, the Pope reveals "the full dimension of the whole mystery of the Redemption" (*totius mysterii Redemptionis*). It is its trinitary mystery: "Christ, united with the Father and with each man, continually communicates to us the Spirit who places within us the sentiments of the Son and directs us towards the Father." This formula is stated with reference to Rom. 8:15 and Gal. 4:6, where St. Paul proclaims the working of divine grace, bestowed by the three persons of the Trinity on the Christian believer. The Pope applies it to each man without distinction.

After the Pope has presented the full dimension of the mystery of the Redemption, he infers the Church's mission from that mystery once again. The text says (*RH* 18,4):

> This is why the Church of our time ... must concentrate and gather around that Mystery (*circa mysterium illud quasi se colligat et congreget*), finding in it the light and the strength that are indispensable for her mission (*ut inde lumen viresque necessarias hauriat ad munus suum implendum*). For if ... man is the way for the Church's daily life, the Church (*Ecclesia*) must be always aware of the dignity of the divine adoption received by man in Christ through the grace of the Holy Spirit and of his destination to grace and glory (Rom. 8:15,30). By reflecting ever anew on all this, and by accepting it with a faith that is more and more aware and a love that is more and more firm, the Church also makes herself better fitted for the service to man to which Christ the Lord calls her when

He says: "The Son of man came not to be served but to serve" (Matt. 20:28).

Hence the mystery of universal salvation is the basis for the Church's mission. The professed motto: Man is the way for the Church, is tantamount to saying that it is in reference to man, universally redeemed and possessing the dignity of divine sonship, that the Church's activity is defined, namely as "service to man." In the Encyclical, "man" always refers to universally redeemed man; for there is no other.

The visible Church performs the office of service to man by "sharing in the 'triple office' belonging to her Master and Redeemer," Christ's office as prophet, priest and king (cf. *RH* 18,4). The themes of the following three articles are thereby announced (19-21).

We can outline the Pope's dogmatic position briefly as follows: What holds in the Trinitary mystery of the Redemption for the Christian believer, the same holds for every man. What is true for the visible Church as a social unity, as Body and Bride of Christ, the same is also "ontologically" true for the invisible Church in the unity of all mankind, as Body and Bride of Christ in the wider sense.[8] The difference consists only in the diversity of dimensions: the "historical-human" and the invisible "divine dimension." Between the Christian believer and the anonymous Christian, between the institutional and the hidden Church exists only a difference of consciousness. The Trini-

---

8   See Part I, 67-78. – On the "mystery of unity in the Trinity," the Pope expressed the following characteristic view on May 25, 1986: "The Church bears this ineffable mystery of God in herself: God – Trinity. And every believer bears it within himself, since the Apostle asks the question: 'Know you not that you are the temple of God, and that the Spirit of God dwells in you?' In this Spirit, who is love and self-giving, God One and Triune offers Himself to His creatures." (*OR*, dt., May 30, 1986, S.3). Evidently, the expression "every believer" here refers to members of any religion.

tary mystery of the Redemption, present in all humanity, is either conscious or unconscious. This mystery is also the basis for the Church's mission as sacrament of the unity of all mankind.

The Pope's Redemption theology is nothing other than the unconditional application of the Council's thesis that everything relating to the paschal mystery "holds true ... for all men of good will" (cf. *Gaudium et Spes* 22,5). The Pope's presentation of this thesis, however, flows from his theological principle of knowledge, namely "double revelation." The invisible Church, which encompasses the Trinitary mystery or grace, of universal salvation, follows on revelation *a priori*, the historical reality of the visible Church on revelation *a posteriori*.

19. The prophetic office.*

By conceiving his doctrine on the triple office of Christ and the Church from the deeper insight of Vatican II into the mystery of the Redemption and the nature of the Church (cf. *RH* 18), John Paul II also arrives at a new theological standpoint. *We intend to focus on the Encyclical's new conception of the triple office of Christ and the Church in our following investigation.* Since the Encyclical is no theological treatise on the triple office, the Pope's thinking must be deduced from the texts. We can only single out a few sample texts for analysis, while leaving aside the Encyclical's extensive comments on the Church's discipline, morals, piety and motivation.

For the sake of an overview, we begin with a few remarks:

In classical theology, the triple office of Christ means the authorization and commission, by which the purpose of the Redemption is fulfilled. Thus Christ accomplished the

---

* Heading in the English Translation="The Church as Responsible for Truth" – Cardinal Wojtyla also delivered his main thoughts on the triple office in *Sign of Contradiction*, pp. 137-167.

work of the Redemption through His triple office as prophet, priest and king. This triple office is suggested by Christ's own words (Jn. 14,6): "I am the way (kingship–jurisdiction), the truth (prophet–magisterium) and the life (priesthood–ministerium)."[9]

To continue this work of Redemption for all time, Christ founded the Church (cf. D 1821). Therefore the triple office which He committed to His Church is the same office and mission which He received from His Father. The crucial difference regarding the office of Christ consists in this: Christ Himself accomplished the work of the Redemption and acquired the fruits of the Redemption through His own power, whereas the Church's task is to apply the fruits of the Redemption to men, through the exercise of the offices of magisterium, ministerium and jurisdiction which she received from Christ. Thus the Church is the continuation and prolongation of Christ on earth.[10]

The Encyclical begins with the *prophetic office of Christ and the Church*. As the Second Vatican Council affirmed, the Church is the society responsible for revealed divine truth, which has also been committed to her (*RH* 19,1).

For the understanding of the Church's prophetic office, faith and divine revelation are indispensable.

On revelation, the Encyclical says:

> Revealed truth is "the 'property' of God Himself." Furthermore it is the revelation of the Father in and through His Son Jesus Christ. The Father reveals Himself through the Son's human nature and actions: "He who sees me, sees the Father." The same is true of Christ's preaching: "The word which you hear is not mine, but the Father's who sent me" (Jn. 14:24). Christ is acting "in full fidelity"

---

[9] Cf. Ludwig Ott, *Fundamentals of Catholic Dogma* (St. Louis: Herder Book Company, 1954), pp. 179-189.

[10] *Ibid.*, pp. 274ff.

to the divine source of truth, by "transmitting that truth as a prophet and as a teacher" (*RH* 19,1).

The Church is held to that same fidelity towards revealed truth. Therefore this fidelity must be an essential part of her *faith*, when Christ teaches or proclaims it.

On faith, it is said (*RH* 19,1):

> Faith as a specific supernatural virtue infused into the human spirit makes us sharers in knowledge of God as a response to His revealed Word.

Is it precise enough to say that faith is infused into the "human spirit"? Can we therefore refer to the followers of all religions as "believers," as the Pope does constantly?

In any case, says the text, all members of the people of God, though in different ways "have their own part to play in Christ's prophetic mission and service of divine truth" (*RH* 19,6). This sharing "shapes the life of the whole of the Church in her fundamental dimension" (*RH* 19,5). In a summary statement on how the whole people of God share in the prophetic office of Christ, the Encyclical says (*RH* 19,2):

> Consequently, we have become sharers in this mission of the prophet Christ, and in virtue of that mission we together with Him are serving divine truth in the Church. Being responsible for that truth also means loving it and seeking the most exact understanding of it, in order to bring it closer to ourselves and others in all its saying power, its splendor and its profundity joined with simplicity.

Thus Christ, just like us, is a "servant" of divine truth *in the Church*. An unusual statement on the part of the Pope.

In the Encyclical's perspective, revelation occurs only in and through Christ. The Old Testament is not even considered. The problem of revelation in the non-Christian religions is not raised either. The logical thing would have been to address the question of Christian revelation in all religions from the standpoint of the universal principle of revelation *a priori*, as has long since been done in the theology of religions.[11] However, in the Encyclical that is not the case. For the Pope, this question has been adequately answered, both theoretically and practically by the Second Vatican Council: Theoretically by the axiom of universal salvation, through the positive outlook on other religions in *Nostra Aetate* (cf. *RH* 11,1) and through the declaration on religious liberty *Dignitatis Humanae* (cf. *RH* 12;17). The practical consequences of that are dialogue, contacts, prayer in common, and investigation of the treasures of human spirituality (cf. *RH* 6). The Pope's position is distinguished by its great clarity and simplicity: On the theological basis of the allegedly revealed right of all men to religious liberty, which in the UN's perspective implies dogmatic tolerance (cf. *RH* 17), the prayer meeting at Assisi appears as the visible manifestation and practical consequence of that theological principle. Thus the foundation for universal religious peace among men is firmly established.

The Pope's remarks concern primarily the Church's inner life, such as theology and magisterium, theology and philosophy, catechesis and modern science. But the crisis of the Church, which goes back to a collapse of the revealed faith, is totally overlooked. On the crucial problem in our century of the relations between theology and philosophy, we are merely told that philosophy "as the Second Vatican Council recalled, is closely linked with theology" (*RH* 19,3).

Nevertheless the Encyclical's presentation of the prophetic office of Christ and the Church has a recognizable basis in the Pope's specific understanding of revelation. The

---

11 On that point, see Johannes Dörmann, "Theology of Religions," in: *Christliches ABC* (Bad Homburg 1987), Gr. 4, pp. 131-146.

prophet office belongs to historical revelation *a posteriori* as a complement of revelation *a priori*.

In the above quoted texts, divine revelation proceeds from the Father; still more, it is the revelation of the Father and his love in Christ, in his humanity, life and teachings. And this revelation, according to the Pope's oft repeated phrase, "is centered on man": "Christ fully reveals man to himself, but he does so by revealing the Father and the Father's love (cf. Jn. 17:6)." The definition of Christ's prophetic office as the "office of service in the Church" makes sense only in light of this idea of revelation. Christ's prophetic office of service, and therefore that of the Church, are directed towards "revealing man to himself," making man more aware of himself, and that by means of the revelation of the Father.

The Encyclical's Article 19 closes with an appeal, which sounds traditional but means something novel (*RH* 19,6):

> The present-day Church, guided by a sense of responsibility for truth (*officii conscientia circa veritatem ducta*), must persevere in fidelity to her own nature, which involves the prophetic mission (*munus*) that comes from Christ Himself (*manans*): "As the Father has sent me, even so I send you ... Receive the Holy Spirit" (Jn. 20:21f).

The novel element in the Encyclical's presentation of the prophetic office of Christ and of the Church comes to light when compared with the Church's traditional doctrine: The Christ of the Encyclical is not portrayed as the absolute teacher of all mankind in such a way that, invested with divine authority, He demands of all mankind faith in Himself, and punishes the refusal of that faith with damnation (Mk. 16:16f). His teaching authority rests not only on His authorization by the Father, but also in the fact that He is God Himself and announces His word with full divine authority as the Son. He does not merely serve the revelation of the Father in the Church just as we do, but He is the sovereign Lord and God of His Church and over His Church. Through His humanity, He was not simply the human manifestation of the Father, but the actual revelation of the Second Divine Person. For only the Son, the eternal image of the Father, became man. Our Lord's words to Philip (Jn. 14:9) are to be understood in the very sense in which Jesus Himself interpreted them by means of His question to the Apostles: "Do you not believe that I am in the Father and the Father is in me?" (Jn. 14:10). The soteriological meaning of Christ's prophetic office consists in dispelling religious ignorance, into which mankind has fallen through sin, and bringing him to the light of true knowledge. Christ attests the saving power of the truth with His words: "The truth will make you free" (Jn. 8:32).[12] But man partakes of this liberating and saving truth only by his *free decision* to embrace the faith, thus only by faith in Christ. The Encyclical ignores this point. The character of the prophetic office of Christ and the Church is briefly and tersely expressed in the missionary mandate of the Risen Lord (Matt. 28:18ff). But this is the very character which the Encyclical text neglects and omits. The reason is simple: The Pope's idea of revelation implies universal salvation. In the Encyclical's conception of the prophetic office of Christ and the Church, which flows from the principle of "double revelation," Christ's only function is to reveal man to himself by means of the revelation of the Father and His love. Christ Himself is the great prophet of universal salvation and the revealer of the deepest truth of man. Hence the prophetic office of the Church is the participation in *this* mission of Christ.

---

12 Cf. Ludwig Ott, *op. cit.*, p. 180.

* Heading in the English Translation= "Eucharist and Penance."

20. The priestly office.*

Under this heading one would expect the Encyclical to offer a detailed presentation of the priesthood of Christ and the Church. That does not happen. Instead, more in the pastoral sphere, it furnishes an extensive treatment only of the sacraments of the Eucharist and of Penance, and attempts to correct certain post-Conciliar abuses. But the article begins with some basic principles which lay the dogmatic foundation for its subsequent remarks. Our question is: Does the Pope also understand the priestly office of Christ and the Church in the sense of universal salvation?

For an immediate focus on the essential point, we give a brief summary of the traditional teaching: This teaching holds that Christ brought to mankind not only a new knowledge of God and of His commandments (prophetic office), but through the work of the Redemption He has also restored the friendship between God and mankind, which was broken by sin.[13]

The central act of Christ's priestly office is the sacrifice of the Cross, which is the high point of the work of the Redemption in all of salvation history. But Christ's office as eternal High Priest includes not only the historical redemptive act, but also the continuing efficacy of Christ in heaven and on earth, therefore the application of the fruits of the Redemption to individual men throughout history. That is what makes up the whole economy of Christ's activity which is ordered to the sanctification and perfection of mankind, which He accomplished above all by the foundation of the Church.[14]

The most essential difference between the priesthood of Christ and that of the Church consists in this: The work of Redemption is Christ's own work, whereas the priesthood in the Church is a participation in the priesthood of Christ,

---

[13] *Ibid.*, p. 182.
[14] *Ibid.*, pp. 188ff, 274ff.

which comprises *the sacramental application of the fruits of the Redemption to individual men, fruits which Christ acquired for all men objectively.*

Therefore, in its presentation of the priesthood, the Encyclical must decide, at least indirectly, whether the Redemption is objectively or also subjectively universal, which touches the central question of universal salvation.

The article (20) begins with some general reflections on the Eucharist (*RH* 20,1):

> In the mystery of the Redemption, that is to say in Jesus Christ's saving work, the Church not only shares in the Gospel of her Master through fidelity to the word and service of truth, but she also shares, through a submission filled with hope and love, in the power of His redeeming action expressed and enshrined by Him in a sacramental form, especially in the Eucharist. The Eucharist is the center and summit of the whole of sacramental life, through which each Christian (*unusquisque Christianus*) receives the saving power of the Redemption, beginning with the mystery of Baptism, in which we are buried into the death of Christ, in order to become sharers in His resurrection, as the Apostle teaches (Rom. 6:3ff).
>
> In the light of this teaching, we see still more clearly the reason why the entire sacramental life of the Church and of each Christian reaches its summit and fullness in the Eucharist. For by Christ's will there is in this sacrament a continual renewing of the mystery of the sacrifice of Himself that Christ offered to the Father on the altar of the cross, a sacrifice that the Father accepted, giving, in return for this total self-giving by His Son, who "became obedient unto death" (Phil. 2:8), His own paternal gift, that is to say the grant of new immortal life in the resurrection, since the Father is the first source and the giver of life from the beginning. That new life, which involves the bodily glorification of the crucified Christ, became an efficacious sign of the new gift granted to humanity, the gift that is the Holy Spirit, through whom the divine life that the Father has in Himself and gives to His Son (cf. Jn. 5:26; I Jn. 5:11) is communicated to all men who are united with Christ.[15]

united with Christ.[15]

The phrase: "The mystery of the Redemption is the saving work of Jesus Christ," says nothing about the objective
or the subjective universality of the Redemption.

But can one say with the Encyclical that the Church
shares, through her submission "filled with hope and love,"
in the power of Christ's sacramental redeeming action,
therefore in the priesthood of Christ? The Church shares
Christ's powers because of her nature as a Church, not
because of subjective acts like fidelity and commitment.
The Church possesses her powers by virtue of divine institution, establishment and authorization. She can exercise
her offices carelessly and faithlessly, but by the same token,
she can also do it with zeal, devotion and total commitment.

Thus the Encyclical's expression leaves no place for the
objective fact of the founding of the Church by Christ as
an "institution" with definite powers, with divine authorization and orders, rights and duties. But that was the very
reason for the Catholic Church's claim to be the one true
Church. That was her claim to legitimacy by virtue of
divine right; that gave her the right to the lawful exercise of
her office, both before the state and before other Christian
denominations. Does the Encyclical's expression perhaps
betray a new understanding of the Church?

That is clearly the case. If it is so baldly stated that *each*
Christian (*unusquisque Christianus*), through the sacramental life, receives the saving power of the Redemption, then
we are in the presence of a new "ecumenical" understanding of the sacraments and of the Church, then have
Christians of all denominations – regardless of their understanding of the sacraments or of the question their apos-

---

15 The English translation should here be compared with the official
Latin Text.

tolic succession – are made to share in the priesthood of Christ, then each Christian receives (*redemptricis eius actionis*) through the sacramental life in his respective denomination.

The sacramental life of the Christian begins with baptism. In the Pope's conception, Baptism might represent the sacramental basis of the ecumenical Church. But, as the Pope states, the reception of the saving power of Christ's redemptive act through the sacramental life in all denominations is realized in *all* of their sacraments. The Encyclical says this explicitly of the Eucharist, which is defined as the center and fullness of the sacramental life, from which each Christian draws the saving power of the Redemption. Thus it is only logical if the ecumenical efforts are directed towards the formulation of Eucharistic liturgies which all Christians can pray together. Then the rejection of the Mass of St. Pius V is fully understandable, since the rite was so decidedly Catholic!

But the Pope by no means leaves the Eucharist open to any arbitrary interpretation, neither inside nor outside of his Church. Therefore he describes the nature of the Eucharist above in the text as follows: "For by Christ's will there is in this sacrament a continual renewing of the mystery of the sacrifice of Himself that Christ offered to the Father on the altar of the cross." That is not necessarily the Catholic Church's pre-Conciliar doctrine on the Holy Mass. Quite the contrary, the formulation remains open to many different interpretations. That becomes abundantly clear upon comparison with the declarations of the Council of Trent, where it is emphatically stated that the Mass repeats Christ's sacrifice of the Cross, and does not merely commemorate it. What is more, the Mass, like the sacrifice of the Cross, is a sacrifice of propitiation, i.e. for the forgiveness of sins; it is "a real sacrifice, which Christ offers to God through the ministry of the priest" (D 940; 948-950). Furthermore, the Council of Trent describes the relationship of the Sacrifice of the Mass to the Sacrifice of the Cross as follows: "It is one and the same victim, and the one who now offers Himself [Christ] through the ministry of the priest is the very same person as the one who offered Himself then on the Cross. Only the manner of offering is different" (D 940). The Church's participation in the priesthood of Christ is nowhere more clearly expressed than in the Sacrifice of the Mass.

But the Encyclical's definition omits all the controversial points defined by the Council of Trent in opposition to the views of the Reformers: It remains an open question whether the Eucharist is a simple commemoration of the Sacrifice of the Cross, or whether it is a true sacrifice in itself. The sacrifice of propitiation is not even mentioned, nor is the nature and purpose of the priesthood. For the ecumenical distribution of the sacraments, they are apparently unimportant. The Encyclical's formulation remains open to an "ecumenical" understanding of the Eucharist.

If, according to the above quoted Encyclical text, the Father gave the Son the gift of "new immortal life in the resurrection" in return for His Son's total self-giving, then this Resurrection is no longer a Resurrection which takes place by Christ's own divine power, but rather a "raising up" by which the Father grants a "new immortal life in the resurrection." This presentation is not so much a reflection of the words of Holy Scripture as it is the expression of the Pope's theology, in which the idea of everything coming from the Father as from "the first source and the giver of life from the beginning," is coherently developed.

Finally the Encyclical says: "That new life, which involves the bodily glorification of the crucified Christ," hence of the Risen Christ, is at the same time an "efficacious sign of the new gift granted to humanity (*doni hominibus traditi*), the gift that is the Holy Spirit, through whom the divine life that the Father has in Himself and gives to His Son is communicated to all men who are united with Christ."

The Pope's constantly recurring thesis maintains that all men are united with Christ *a priori* through the Incarnation. That means that all men possess the gift of the Risen One, the Holy Spirit.

As we know, post-Conciliar theologians since Karl Rahner uphold the thesis of "anonymous Christianity," according to which the *Church* is the sign of the saving presence of God's grace in all men and in all religions. The Encyclical goes even further, and is fully consistent, by declaring not only the Church, but also the Risen One as the "efficacious sign" of universal salvation! The theological principle of "double revelation" comes out once again: The Holy Ghost's inner gift of grace is given to all men (= revelation *a priori*), and is proclaimed to all men by the Risen Christ (= revelation *a posteriori*).[16]

That gives us the answer to the question which we posed at the outset: The Encyclical teaches the objective and subjective universality of the Redemption.

On the royal priesthood of the children of God, the Encyclical makes the following noteworthy statement (*RH* 20,2):

> For by becoming "children of God" (Jn. 1:12), adopted sons (Rom. 8:23), we also become in His likeness "a kingdom and priests" and obtain "a royal priesthood" (Apoc. 5:10; I Pet. 2:9), that is to say we share in that unique and irreversible restoration of man and the world to the Father that was carried out once for all by Him, who is both the eternal Son (cf. Jn. 1:1-4; et al.) and also true Man.

---

16 Many times and on important occasions, John Paul II has expressed his conviction that the Holy Ghost "is present in the hearts of all men in a mysterious way" (e.g. Address to the Cardinals, Dec. 22,1986, AAS 79 (1987), 1089; *Redemptoris Missio* 28). The Pope gave his shortest and clearest summary of the theology of Assisi in the address of Dec. 22, 1986.

In this text, the "royal priesthood" follows directly from the status as an adopted child of God. But as stated on numerous occasions, this privilege is a treasure of all mankind. That has noticeable consequences for the understanding of the offices of the Church, as will become clearer in the next article. Up until now we can say: On the basis of universal salvation, the sacramental life of Christians of all denominations is the very heart of Christianity, which however remains open for all mankind. – Unfortunately, the idea which the Encyclical text expresses, namely the restoration of the world to the Father, hardly bears upon the Encyclical's presentation as a whole.

We can conclude: In the Pope's remarks, one can discern a parallel in the structure of the prophetic and priestly offices. Just as Christ, as *Prophet*, receives divine revelation from the Father and, by revealing the Father and His love, reveals man to himself, so also Christ, as *Priest*, in return for His total self-giving on the Cross, receives the gift of a new immortal life in the resurrection, namely the Holy Ghost, who is granted to all mankind. The Risen Christ is the "efficacious sign" of this gift. Just as *the Church's participation in the prophetic office of Christ* consists in the fact that, in virtue of Christ's prophetic mission, she serves divine truth in the Church together with Him, so the Church also receives *a share in Christ's royal priesthood* on account of her devotion, and is thus in Christ a sign and instrument for the unity of all mankind.

St. Paul's words: "Let each man examine himself, and so eat of the bread and drink of the cup" (I Cor. 11:28), announce the shift of the Pope's attention to the sacrament of Penance. Both sacraments must ultimately be considered in the perspective of the "new Advent," as the conclusion of the chapter strongly emphasizes (*RH* 20,7):

> In the Church, gathering particularly today in a special way around the Eucharist and desiring that the authentic Eucharistic community should become a sign of the

gradually maturing unity of all Christians, there must be a lively-felt need for penance ... Nevertheless, it is certain that the Church of the new advent, the Church that is continually preparing for the new coming of the Lord, must be the Church of the Eucharist and of Penance. Only when viewed in this spiritual aspect of her life and activity is she seen to be the Church of the divine mission, the Church *in statu missionis*, as the Second Vatican Council has shown her to be.

21. The kingly office.*

The Second Vatican Council, so begins the article, built up the picture of the Church as people of God. The Council thereby began with the very foundations of the Church itself (*ab ipsis fundamentis propriis*) and also highlighted the particularly royal character of the Christian vocation. The exact words are (*RH* 21,1):

> In building up from the very foundations the picture of the Church as the People of God – by showing the three-fold mission (*munere*) of Christ Himself, through participation in which we become (*constituimur*) truly God's People – the Second Vatican Council highlighted (*qualitatem istam peculiarem*), among other characteristics of the Christian vocation, the one that can be described as "kingly." ... [That means] the sharing in Christ's kingly mission (*munere*), that is to say the fact of rediscovering in oneself and others the special dignity of our vocation that can be described as "kingship." This dignity is expressed in readiness to serve, in keeping with the example of Christ, who "came not to be served but to serve" (Matt. 20:38) ... Our sharing in Christ's kingly mission – His "kingly function" (*munus*) – is closely linked with every sphere of both Christian and human morality (*cum omni regione doctrinae moralis, tam christianae quam etiam humanae*).

---

* Heading in the English Translation="The Christian Vocation to Service and Kingship."

The text says the most important thing in parentheses, and casually drops a definition of the "people of God." This runs: We "become" the people of God by our participation in the triple office of Christ. Is that really correct? Yes, from the standpoint of the Encyclical and its double idea of the Church. No, from the standpoint of Catholic dogma:

– From the standpoint of Catholic dogma, we can say the following about the expression "people of God," which is necessarily the same as the Church: A Church which "becomes" or is founded by means of participation in the offices of Christ is not the Church of Christ. A Church which is constituted by participation in offices, that is to say in "functions," can itself only be a mere "function" and have only a "sense of identity" concerning its mission.[17] The Encyclical's definition is clearly marked by existentialist, nominalist thinking, which dissolves all being into existence, all substance into acts and functions. In contrast, from the standpoint of Catholic doctrine, it must be said: The Church *was founded by Christ Himself,* and that is the main point. She is a visible institution, the Catholic Church founded by Christ. To this Church, which is an already existing natural and supernatural entity, Christ then "handed over the same powers and duties, which He had Himself received from the Father, that the Church might continue His mission."[18] Just as there are no powers of Christ without Christ, so also there are no powers of the Church without the Church. But the Encyclical says something entirely different with its definition: the "people of God" is constituted, or "becomes" by means of participa-

---

17 Cf. Ludwig Rütti, *Zur Theologie der Mission* [*To a Theology of Mission*] (Munich 1972), pp. 257-345. – See further my rescension: *Theologie der Mission?* [*Theology of Mission?*], in: *Theologie und Glaube* [*Theology and Faith*] (1973), pp. 342-361.

18 Thus Leo XIII in the Encyclical *Satis Cognitum* (1896); see Ludwig Ott, *op. cit.*, p. 317.

tion in the offices of Christ. The idea "people of God" is a slogan which serves as the vehicle for introducing a novel idea of the Church.

– From the standpoint of the Encyclical, that is to say of "double revelation" and the "double idea of the Church" (cf. Article 18), the definition is correct. According to this understanding of the Church, the invisible Church includes all mankind in Christ. Thus the "people of God," which "becomes" by means of participation in *the offices* (=the functions) of Christ, can only be a mere function and can only possess a "sense of identity" concerning its mission. This works out as follows:

If all men possess the grace of adopted children of God or "being in Christ" *a priori* as the very core of human nature, and that through the Incarnation of the Son of God, then all men are also radically equal as persons, then the royal dignity of the human person belongs to all men, then all men form an "ontological" organic unity in the one invisible Church which is mankind.

But that means that the visible "ecumenical Church" has her "ontological" foundation in the invisible Church, that the Church of mankind is basically the same nature as the ecumenical Church. Thus the ecumenical Church can possess only a "sense of identity" concerning her "function," which she fulfills in the invisible Church of mankind. And this consists in being a sign and instrument for the visible unity of all mankind in Christ. Her duty is to bring to light the treasures of grace which lie hidden in the desires and aspirations of mankind, to proclaim universally, to make all aware of the ontological unity of all mankind, and to bring out the hidden unity of mankind into a historical unity.

On the basis of "double idea of revelation," the other formulations in the above quoted text become clearly understandable: From the "sharing in Christ's kingly mission," the following postulate is derived in particular, that is "the fact of rediscovering in oneself and others the special dignity of our vocation," our "kingship." In the preceding articles (18-20), we already noticed that all men are children of God (Jn. 1:12) and as such have attained (constituimur) the dignity of kingship (cf. 20,2). Thus one need only discover "in oneself and others" the royal dignity which all men possess. Whereas the "new man" is "constituted," or receives a *new being* through the gift of divine sonship (Jn. 1:12), the "people of God" are "constituted" by means of participation in the offices and tasks of Christ, hence through participation in Christ's functions. This is a logical application of the Pope's "double idea of revelation and of the Church."

Finally, man's royal dignity is expressed (*monstratur*) above in the text by the Christ's example of serving, and with that we are on the level of "both Christian and human morality," which is again consistent, if all men possess the treasure of divine sonship.

The Encyclical now sketches the picture of the (visible) Church and answers the question: who belongs to her. As a human society, the Church can of course be scientifically studied and defined according to the criteria which are applicable to any human society. However these criteria do not suffice in the case of the Church (*RH* 21,2).

The Encyclical develops the criteria in the particular case of the Church (*RH* 21,2):

> For the whole of the community of the People of God and for each member of it what is in question is not just a specific "social membership" (*vinculo sociali*); rather, for each and every one what is essential is a particular "vocation" (*sed potius requiritur, tamquam res unicuique et omnibus necessaria, specialis 'vocatio'*). Indeed, the Church as the People of God is also – according to the teaching of St. Paul mentioned above, of which Pius XII reminded us in wonderful terms (*doctrinam mirabiliter a Pio XII expositam*) – "Christ's Mystical Body." Membership in that body has for its source a particular call, united with the saving action of grace (*Ius ad illud Corpus pertinendi pro-*

*cedit ex particulari invitatione, ad quam actio salvifica gra-
tiae accedit*). Therefore, if we wish to keep in mind this
community of the People of God (*Si vere conscii nobis esse
cupimus huius communitatis Populi Dei*) ... we must see
first and foremost Christ saying in a way to each member
of the community: "Follow me" (Jn. 1:23). It is the community of the disciples, each of whom in a different way –
at times very consciously and consistently, at other times
not very consciously and very consistently – is following
Christ. This shows also the deeply "personal" aspect and
dimension (*proprietas*) of this society, which, in spite of all
the deficiencies of its community life – in the human
meaning of this word – is a community precisely because
all its members form it together with Christ Himself, at
least because they bear in their souls the indelible mark of
a Christian (*proprium eius, qui Christianus est*).

– According to this text, the first, indispensable criterion
for membership among the people of God is a "particular
vocation." The reason given is: For the Church as people of
God is also the "Mystical Body of Christ." This is proposed
with a reference to St. Paul and to Pius XII (Encyclical
Mystici Corporis?). But it is precisely the Apostle and Pius
XII who explicitly demand faith, over and above a mere
"particular vocation." Pius XII specifically requires the faith
of the Catholic Church. Appropriately enough, the Encyclical makes no mention of this.

– The second criterion is "the right to membership" in
the Mystical Body on account of a "particular call." In this
text, such a "right" is compared with an "invitation" to a
party or a dinner, which gives the "right" of admission. But
there is no reference to Our Lord's parable of the invitation
to the royal wedding feast (Matt. 22:1ff).

– The third criterion is the grace associated with the
"particular invitation."

– The fourth criterion is that of the "community of the
disciples" who follow Christ.

The Church is thus a kind of "loosely structured

Church[19] which has a special "personal profile" all
the same.

– The fifth criterion is the union of all the baptized
(implied by "*signum indelebile*") with Christ.

Faith is not even mentioned. Thus it forms no decisive
criterion for membership in the Church.

In summary, then, the elements required for membership in the Church, the Body of Christ or the people of
God, are the particular vocation, the particular invitation
and the grace united with it, the personal readiness to
follow Christ, and finally baptism. The Church is the community of all the baptized in Christ.

Faith is not mentioned here as a criterion, but we can
add it to complete the list. For it is obvious that the notion
of "Church" here described fully agrees with that of the
"ecumenical Church," sketched by the Encyclical in Article
11, along with the "ecumenical faith." That becomes abundantly clear later on in the Encyclical text (*RH* 21,3):

> The Second Vatican Council devoted very special at-
> tention to showing how this "ontological" community of
> disciples and confessors (*confessorum*) must increasingly
> become, even from the "human" point of view, a commu-
> nity aware of its own life and activity. The initiatives
> taken by the Council in this field have been followed up
> by the many further initiatives of a synodal, apostolic and
> organizational kind. We must, however, always keep in
> mind the truth that every initiative serves true renewal in
> the Church and helps to bring the authentic light that is
> Christ (*LG* 1), insofar as the initiative is based on ade-
> quate (*consentanea*) awareness of the individual Christian's
> vocation and of responsibility for this singular, unique
> and unrepeatable grace by which each Christian in the
> community of the People of God builds up the Body of
> Christ. This principle, the key rule for the whole of Chris-
> tian practice – apostolic and pastoral practice, practice of

---

19 After the last war, Josef Klein was known for his idea of a "loosely
structured Church" (*Kirche der freien Gefolgschaft*).

interior and of social life – must with due proportion be applied to the whole of humanity and to each human being.

The Encyclical itself gives a clear definition of the "ecumenical Church":

> The whole of Christianity (= each Christian) forms the body of Christ. In face of this "ontological" community of the baptized disciples of Christ in the "imperfect unity" (cf. Art. 11) of the ecumenical Church, the division into countless confessions and denominations is a merely historical "human" question. She should work to establish a "human community" (= "perfect unity"), the goal of all ecumenical endeavors.

At the same time, the Pope formulates in the above quoted text nothing less than a *new, fundamental rule for the whole of Christian practice* (*primaria norma est totius vitae et actionis christianae*). As we have seen (cf. *RH* 11), the principle of this universal Christian norm is the vital principle of the "ecumenical Church."

But the Pope formulates not only this primary, universal norm for all Christianity – that is taken for granted, since he mentions it only in passing. What the text really wants to say is found in the main clause and touches all mankind: The principle (*principium*) which holds for the ecumenical Church holds also for non-Christians, for the whole of humanity and for each human being – of course with due proportion (*iusta proportione servata*). That means, as in Article 11, the application of the double idea of the Church, namely of the visible and the hidden Church, to all mankind. In the Pope's theology, the Mystical Body of Christ comprises all mankind in a wider sense, on various levels.[20] That is surely what he means by the expression "with due proportion."

---

20 Karol Wojtyla, *op. cit.*, pp. 108-118. – Part I, pp. 67-73.

The Encyclical urges all Christians, from the Pope down to the lowest worker, to apply the ecumenical principle to himself and to make it his own, to live by and to act upon this ecumenical awareness (cf. Art. 11). From this premise the Pope infers the office of royal service for the Church and for each Christian. The exact words are (*RH* 21,3):

> It is precisely the principle of the "kingly service" that imposes on each one of us, in imitation of Christ's example, the duty to demand of himself exactly what we have been called to, what we have personally obliged ourselves to by God's grace, in order to respond to our vocation. This fidelity to the vocation received from God through Christ involves the joint responsibility (*commune officium conscientiae*) for the [whole] Church (*totam*) for which the Second Vatican Council wishes to educate all Christians. Indeed (*etenim*), in the Church as the community of the People of God under the guidance of the Holy Spirit's (*a Spiritu Sancto*) working, each member has "his own special gift" (I Cor. 7:7; cf. 12:7,27; Rom. 12:6; Eph. 4:7), as St. Paul teaches. Although this "gift" is a personal vocation and a form of participation in the Church's saving work, it also serves others, builds the Church and the fraternal communities in the various spheres of human life on earth.[21]

On this analysis, the purpose of Vatican II was to educate the whole of Christianity to loyal observance of the office of "kingly service" as a consequence of the ecumenical principle. We can now summarize the Encyclical's doctrine on the Church's kingly office: The "kingly service" of each Christian consists in the imitation of Christ and is a participation in the redemptive work of the *ecumenical Church* led by the Holy Ghost.

After extensive reflections on "kingly service" after the example of Christ, the Encyclical says by way of summary

---

[21] The English translation should here be compared with the official Latin text.

(*RH* 21, 5):

> His Church made up of all of us, is "for men" in the
> sense that, by basing ourselves on Christ's example (cf. *LG*
> 36) and collaborating with the grace that He has gained
> for us, we are able to attain to "being kings," that is to say
> we are able to produce a mature humanity in each one of
> us. Mature humanity means full use of the gift of freedom
> received from the Creator when He called to existence the
> man made "in his image, after his likeness."

After the Encyclical has finished proving that, according
to the doctrine of Christ, "the best use of freedom is charity, which takes concrete form in self-giving and in service,"
the article (*RH* 21,6) closes:

> The full truth about human freedom is indelibly in-
> scribed on the mystery of the Redemption. The Church
> truly serves mankind when she guards this truth with
> untiring attention, fervent love and mature commitment
> and when in the whole of her own community she trans-
> mits it and gives it concrete form in human life through
> each Christian's fidelity to his vocation. This confirms
> what we have already referred to, namely that man is and
> always becomes the "way" for the Church's daily life.

What exactly is meant by man's self-actualization, by the
Church's kingly service to mankind in God-given freedom
after the example of Christ, was already analyzed thoroughly in Articles 12 and 17.

It is evident that the Encyclical hardly reflects pre-Vati-
can II teaching on the kingly office, on the power of jurisdiction belonging to Christ and through Him to the
Church. Christ's kingly office or power of jurisdiction presupposes unredeemed mankind. The purpose of this office
is to deliver mankind from their separation from God,
which is a result of sin, and to set them on the way towards
their supernatural end. And this way is none other than
Christ, not merely as a lofty human example, but as the

Good Shepherd and King, as Legislator and Judge of all mankind, as sovereign Lord and God, who requires faith in Himself. "I am the Way" and "no one comes to the Father except through Me" (Jn. 14:6), *refers primarily to faith in Christ as the foundation of this way.* Secondly, Christ's words: "My kingdom is not of this world" (Jn. 18:36), hold for the kingly office of Christ and the Church. The office is not simply placed at the service of man and of mankind, but is meant to accomplish the purpose of the Redemption. It includes particularly the functions which bring about the establishment, growth and perfection of the supernatural kingdom of God.

Looking back on Chapter 4 as a whole, which relies on the new, deeper insight of Vatican II into the mystery of Christ and into the Church's nature and mission as the basis for Christ's triple office and the exercise of those offices needed in the modern world, there emerges a general outlook of concern for the welfare of man, whereby a central dogmatic theme is derived with astonishing coherence from the principles of "double revelation," hence of universal salvation. But the question remains: how can this conception be reconciled with Holy Scripture and the faith of the Catholic Church?

22. Mary, mother of the Church.*

The last article is dedicated to Mary, "Mother of the Church." During the Council, this was a controversial title. For the sake of dogmatic clarity, the use of the title was avoided in the Chapter: "The Blessed Virgin Mary and the Church" of the Constitution on the Church (*Lumen Gentium* 60-65).[22] But in his closing address at the end of the

---

[22] Otto Semmelroth, Herder Commentary on *Lumen Gentium*, Chapter 8, *LThK* XII, 326.

* Title in the English Translation= "The Mother in Whom We Trust."

third session, Paul VI declared the Mother of God as "Mother of the Church" (Nov. 21, 1964). In the inaugural Encyclical, John Paul II places Mary, the Mother of the Church, at the center of his final meditation on the mystery of the Redemption (cf. *RH* 22,2).

For a correct understanding of this new title of the mother of God, the idea of the Church is of course fundamental. That means that, in the Encyclical, we must also view the title of Mary, mother of the Church, in the framework of John Paul II's idea of the Church.

On the controversy over the new title during the Council, Otto Semmelroth, in his Herder-commentary makes some informative remarks, which go to the dogmatic heart of the matter and could help us towards a deeper understanding of the Pope's remarks in the Encyclical. There it is said:

> As early as St. Augustine, the Church was said to play the role of the mother and the child. Considered as a whole, the Church is said to be the mother; considered in her members, she is said to be the children. The Church, considered as the community of salvation existing prior to the individual members, is the spiritual mother, into whose womb the individual faithful must enter as children, in order to partake of the life of grace given by Christ. From the earliest tradition, they are reborn to the life of grace in the womb of the Church through baptism. In this respect, the Church is herself the spiritual mother of the faithful. And since this very idea corresponds to the Catholic understanding of the Church, namely to see the Church as the community of salvation existing prior to the individual members, whereas the Protestant understanding of the Church during the Reformation saw the Church rather as the sum total of many individuals, one can understand why there are certain misgivings about calling Mary the mother of the Church. ... But if instead one means by "Church" the society of many individuals ... one can also call Mary mother of the Church, in addi-

tion to her undisputed spiritual motherhood.[23]

It is obvious that the Reformation's understanding of the Church represents as it were the vehicle for the Pope's idea of the Church. However, the Pope's "double idea of the Church" has its peculiarities: It is much more broad-minded than that of the Reformers. More specifically, it includes not only all individuals as children of God in the visible, but also in the invisible Church, which comprises all mankind. Moreover, as a consequence of universal salvation, the visible Church is merely a "function" and has only a "sense of identity" concerning her mission. This is precisely the understanding of the Church which lurks beneath the Encyclical's remarks on Mary, the mother of the Church:

The Church, we read, who draws her life from Christ (the Universal Savior) in the mystery of the Redemption, wishes only one thing: that all men have the fullness of life in Christ, and have it more abundantly. The exact words are (*RH* 22,1):

> This fullness of life in Him is at the same time for man. Therefore the Church, uniting herself with all the riches of the mystery of the Redemption, becomes the Church of living people, living because given life from within by the working of "the Spirit of truth" (Jn. 16:13) and visited by the love that the Holy Spirit has poured into our hearts (Rom. 5:5). The aim of any service in the Church ... is to keep up this dynamic link between the mystery of the Redemption and every man.

That brings up the question: Why does the Church become a Church "of living people," given life from within by the Holy Ghost, only by "uniting herself" with all the riches of the Redemption? The Encyclical's only answer can be: Because it was through the "opening made by Vatican

---

[23] *Ibid.*, in a paragraph on that subject, pp. 339ff.

II" that Christianity was first able "to reach a more complete awareness of the mystery of Christ" (cf. *RH* 11,3).

By reason of this more complete awareness, the Encyclical makes bold to keep up the "dynamic link between the mystery of the Redemption and every man" as the "aim of any service in the Church." From the standpoint of universal salvation, this aim in view is fully understandable.

From this all-embracing task of the Church, it becomes increasingly clear why "the Church is a mother" and why Mary is "the mother of the Church" (*RH* 22,2). The Pope's remarks on this subject have an ecumenical purpose. They should uphold tradition and still be recognized as the common patrimony of all Christians, of the ecumenical Church. Thus the Encyclical goes on (*RH* 22,2):

> Accordingly, we who form today's generation of disciples of Christ [= all Christians] all wish to unite ourselves with her [Mary] in a special way. We do so with all our attachment to our ancient tradition and also with full respect and love for the members of all the Christian communities (*et simul plane reverentes et amore complectentes membra omnium Communitatum christianarum*).

After the Pope has turned to Christ, "who is Lord of the Church Lord of man's history on account of the mystery of the Redemption," he now turns to Mary, for nobody else can bring us "into the divine and human dimension of this mystery" better than she, for nobody "has been brought into it by God Himself as Mary has." Furthermore, it is in this "that the exceptional character of the grace of the divine Motherhood consists" (*RH* 22,3).

If nobody else can bring us "into the divine and human dimension of this mystery" (cf. *RH* 9;10) better than Mary the mother of the Church, then she will lead us into the mystery of universal salvation!

The Encyclical describes the nature of this motherhood as follows (*RH* 22,4):

The special characteristic of the motherly love that the Mother of God inserts in the mystery of the Redemption and the life of the Church finds expression in its exceptional closeness to man and all that happens to him. It is in this that the mystery of the Mother consists.

The Church, who "wishes to make this mystery her own in an ever deeper manner," recognizes her own way precisely in this: Man is the way for the Church (*RH* 22,4). That is how the Pope has introduced "the mystery of the Mother" into his conception of man as the way for the Church (cf. *RH* 13;14).

But the connection between the Father's love, which revealed itself in the Son, and the mother of the Son still needs to be specified. That connection is made in the following excerpt (*RH* 22,5):

> The Father's eternal love, which has been manifested in the history of mankind through the Son whom the Father gave, "that whoever believes in him should not perish but have eternal life" (Jn. 3:16), comes close to each of us through this Mother and thus takes on tokens that are of more easy understanding and access by each person (*offertur per hanc Matrem atque hoc modo signa accipit ad intelligendum accommodatiora et faciliora cuique homini*). Consequently, Mary must be on all the ways for the Church's daily life.

As in the first article (*RH* 1,1) so also in the last article we get the quotation from St. John (3,16), which requires faith as a condition for salvation. But everything that lies between the first and last articles eliminates this condition. Just as the Father's love was manifested (*manifestus est*) in the history of mankind through the Son, so also in a motherly way through the mother of the Son. Both must always be present on the Church's way to man.

The Encyclical names yet a final aspect, which assigns Mary her place in the Pope's entire theology of the Redemption (*RH* 22,5):

Through her maternal presence the Church acquires certainty that she is truly living the life of her Master and Lord and that she is living the mystery of the Redemption in all its life-giving profundity and fullness, Likewise the Church, which has struck root in many varied fields of the life of the whole present-day humanity, also acquires the certainty and, one could say, the experience of being close to man, to each person, of being each person's Church, the Church of the People of God.

Since when has the Church struck root in all mankind or (literally) in all men (*universorum hominum*)? Only if all men are united with Christ in the sense of universal salvation. Only if all mankind is the invisible Church. In the Encyclical, the theology of the Redemption rests on this axiom. In this sense the last article is the mariological vision of the mystery of universal salvation, Mary is the "mother of the Church."

The humble call to prayer forms the Encyclical's impressive conclusion. That forms the link between the first and the last article, from the prayer of the Church in the Advent of our era to the prayer of the early Church in the Upper Room after Our Lord's Ascension. The Pope's request for prayer runs (*RH* 22,6):

Above all, I implore Mary, the heavenly Mother of the Church, to be so good as to devote herself to this prayer of humanity's new advent, together with us who make up the Church, that is to say the Mystical Body of her only Son. I hope that through this prayer we shall be able to receive the Holy Spirit coming upon us, and thus become Christ's witnesses "to the end of the earth," like those who went forth from the Upper Room in Jerusalem on the day of Pentecost.

– The Pope's message is a new message, still more universal than that of the Risen One. It is the message of the "full dimension of the whole mystery of the Redemption" (cf.

RH 18,4), of universal salvation. It leads the Church and mankind towards Assisi!